WTO AND INTELLECTUAL PROPERTY RIGHTS

WTO AND INTELLECTUAL PROPERTY RIGHTS

TALWAR SABANNA
Karnatak University, KRC P.G. Centre
Belgaum, Karnataka (India)

SERIALS PUBLICATIONS
NEW DELHI

First Published - 2007

ISBN : 81-8387-067-8

Published by

SERIALS PUBLICATIONS
4830/24, Ansari Road, Darya Ganj
New Delhi-110002
Phone : 23245225
Fax : 91-11-23272135
E-mail: serials@satyam.net.in

CONTENTS

INTRODUCTION

Intellectual property rights (IPRs) are granted by governments to attempt to correct a market failure that produces less than optimal amounts of investments in innovative activity. Patents are used to protect products and processes. It is often less costly to reverse engineer a product than to undertake the research and development (R&D) to create the innovation. In the absence of any laws preventing companies from engaging in reverse engineering or similar activities and then marketing their copies, all firms would wish to be the "copy-cat" firm and soon there would be no innovations to copy. Innovations are viewed as a very important factor in increasing welfare for societies. IPRs grant the owner the exclusive right to prevent a third party from using, reproducing, selling, exporting or importing the product or process that is protected. In exchange, the owner must disclose all information relevant to duplicating the product or process. This provides the firm with a temporary monopoly in which they can potentially earn monopoly rents. In exchange for exclusive marketing rights, their acquired knowledge is made available to the public. The potential profits available to a firm induce it to undertake expensive and risky R & D.

Agricultural biotechnology is one sector that will be significantly affected by the international protection of IP. By undertaking genetic modification of a variety of plants and animal species, scientists are uncovering ways to create nutritionally enriched foods, herbicide, pesticide and disease tolerant crops and increase yields. The potential benefits for developing countries are substantial. Genetically modified cotton in China, for example, has significantly reduced the amount of pesticides used in cotton production leading to less environmental contamination and a reduced incidence of pesticide poisonings for farmers and labourers while at the same time, increasing yields. Blindness caused by Vitamin A deficiency may be significantly reduced with the introduction of "Golden Rice" – a genetically altered rice enriched in Vitamin A. The impact will likely be greatest in very poor regions where rice is consumed as the staple food and other sources of Vitamin A are too expensive. There are many other potential ways to use agricultural biotechnology to help some of the world's poorest. In order for the maximum benefit to be realized, however, additional funds will need to be invested in areas of research of particular importance to developing countries- for example, in tropical plants. If these funds are to come nom private firms, those making investment decisions in research and development activities must be able to foresee a reasonable chance of recouping their investment. Thus, strong IPRs are required.

With this background, an interesting and heartening feature of the Journal of World Intellectual Property Rights is that the contributors come from all parts of India, even outside India, and particularly by young scholars in colleges, universities and research institutes. This fact alone establishes the national and international character of the Journal. Thus, the Journal has great future as a forum for debate and interaction about Globalisation, World Trade Organisation and Intellectual Property Rights.

DR. TALWAR SABANNA

INTELLECTUAL PROPERTY RIGHTS (IPRs): INDIA IS CHASING AND WORLD IS RUNNING– AN UNBRIDLED QUESTION

B.N. Nimbur and G.S. Hiremath***

Introduction

It is an ancient recognition that 'Knowledge is Power'. The accumulation and growth of knowledge can add to the changing materialistic production of goods and thereby help to increase income. Similarly in the past, it was a social stigma in India that the knowledge is the prerogative of the few privileged people in the society. The Kings and Queens or Prince and Princes recognised the special materialistic[1] and mental[2] intellectualism of few well-accomplished people in the society. The Indian ancient philosophy (greatly stressed on knowledge) which attentively known as intelligence from which the term "*intellectualism*" gets originated. The well recognized literature of India, that is, Panchatantra points out that:

For if there be no mind
Debating good and ill,
And if religion send
No challenge to the will,
If only greed be there
For some material feast
How draw a line between
The man-beast and the beast?
Scholarship is less than sense,
Therefore seek intelligence.

* Professor, Department of Economics, Gulbarga University, Gulbarga-6, Karnataka.

** Research Scholar, Department of Economics, University of Hyderabad, Hyderabad.

Indeed, the Indians and for that matter East-Asians with great deeper root in the civilization emphasized more on spiritual aspect of intellectualism. In other words, the intellectualism and spiritualism went almost side by side for guiding the individual and social life of the people. As against this, the western society particularly from fifteenth century started placing greater emphasis on materialism. This led to revolutionary thought by Karl Marx who gave the idea of *dialectical materialism.* Further, the western political consequence on the east started invading the life of people in the east. However, the Indian born writer Rudiyard Kippling may be remembered for his saying that "east is east and west is west and both can never meet". This is what the root problem of intellectual property rights (IPRs) which has been originally possessed by India but is slowly eroded and taken away by the other countries of the world. Therefore, India is chasing and the world is running.

With the above background, this paper attempts to dispel the origin of intellectualism and points out the intellectual properties possessed by people and community or society in India. Then it goes to examine the possibilities of protecting the intellectual properties considered as rights in the wake of liberalisation, privatisation and globalsation, together a situation in which India going to become a full-fledged member of the World Trade Organisation (WTO). The paper also throws light on the highly illiterate background of the society in general and that of the people who possess intellectual properties in many areas who are either indifferent, ignorant and not least to say innocent regarding the legalities of these matters as rights in particular. The intellectual property of the people and the community in various areas have been dealt, though not at length but sweetly and briefly. Lastly, the paper points out the pre-requisites for the successful implementation of the laws relating to the protection of intellectual property rights which would ensure materialistic gains to the traditional Indian knowledge and intelligence-a matter of practice for centuries. The urine of cow is one thing[3] and goal is the other[4], the difference between the two will reflect the status of IPRs in India and the West.

Part I: Intellectual Property as a Factor of Production

This paper, for brevity assumes that there are no problems if knowledge and intellectualism or intellectual properties are used interchangeably. As such, here we deal with knowledge as a factor of production conceived in economics. One of the propositions of technological foundation of the economic theory of production is that output is determined by inputs. In Ricardo's framework of farm analysis, the output of corn depends on inputs of capital, labour and land. This analysis was became more clear and definite in the production function formulation of Wood (1888), Clark (1890). A technological relation between inputs and outputs is an embodiment of knowledge may seems obvious. But the point has more force when productive knowledge changes, that is when it becomes a variable. However, Ricardo's analysis does not explain the technological progress. Adam Smith, the father of economics, had sketched the theory of growth in which he emphasized division of labour which could improve productivity (Smith A. 1776). The one of the reasons for the increase in productivity due to division of labour is increased skill of the labour and innovation.

Schumpeter is the first economist who introduced the concept of innovations into economics more clearly (Schumpeter 1939). He distinguishes between inventions and innovations. According to him, inventions are ideas or concepts; they are conceived as floating about and freely available and they possess intellectual properites. Innovations have to be translated into usable products or process, a costly step that constitutes innovation. The costs are recouped by short-term monopoly profits.

Robert Solow's model of economic growth which is the starting point of literature on economic growth consists four variables viz., output capital, labour, and knowledge (Solow 1956, 1957). Output is produced from capital, labour and knowledge, while knowledge is produced from knowledge alone. Knowledge, as we know, is a public good.

There are different approaches to the study of innovation and growth. For instance, Rosenberg (1982) and Landes (1998) have systematically analysed the development of innovations. Schmooklur (1966) made an attempt to show the extent to which innovation is driven by demand based on data about innovations. In a decentralised economic system, knowledge is localised. An entrepreneur does not know what another entrepreneur knows. Under such conditions, price system arranges for allocative efficiency in the absence of widespread knowledge of the production. Nevertheless, the historical evidence reveals the fact that new technological ideas diffused and gradually absorbed by others. The Griliches's (1957) study shows the spread of corn while the study made by David (1974) empirically shown the diffusion of the reaper. The other studies made by Rashevsky (1947), Coleman and Katz (1966), Mansfield (1961) emphasised concern for economic considerations like profitability. When the knower and unknower of a particular knowledge meets randomly, the non-knower would learn about innovations and this profit would accrue to him.

Production of knowledge is virtually different from production of goods. The production of knowledge, obviously requires not only knowledge but also capital and labour. It should be noted that knowledge is not knowledge in general but highly specific in nature; this is true for knowledge both as an input and as an output. Ideas can be put together to create new ideas (Weitzman 1998). The significant question, which arises at this juncture is that where the knowledge is located? Some knowledge is embodied in individuals, in a tacit and in implicit form. Other knowledge is available in codified form, such as books, patents and databases and can be transmitted and received with low resource cost. This second kind of knowledge gives rise to problems of intellectual property. Tacit knowledge joins in the general market for resource use. The marketable resources have to be invested; this will not happen unless there is some protection for investor's rights to some monopoly use of knowledge. In contrast, it is better to have a free flow of ideas, because everyone will benefit from the ideas of others in arriving at new ideas.

The innovation bestows monopoly power in the market. In many cases, it leads to first mover advantages. A monopolist always realizes surplus from current output. Thus, an innovation by the monopolist that competes with those outputs will destroy an existing profit, at least partly offsetting any gain in new markets (Arrow 1999). Once the product is on the market, its method of production can spread through imitation, public agencies, search by firms and informal communication. The mobility of workers across firms is another important source of diffusion of intellectual property.

Part-II: Properties of Intellectual Property

The intellectual property(s) has different properties, as a result of which it is very difficult to associates it with an individual, a community, a firm or a corporation. However, we have attempted to identify few of the peculiar properties of intellectual property(s).

(a) Take for instance as it is known as intellectual property, it belongs to the mental horizon of an individual or group of individuals or may even be the community at large.

(b) The intellectual property is not transferable as long as its actions or reactions remain intangible (not visibly seen output or gains as the case may be).

(c) It has a very peculiar property in the sense that it is either gained by an individual through the sustained work or by chance factors[5]. The same property holds good even if it is associated with a particular community.

(d) It is also true to say that the intellectual property being individuals are belonging to a family or group is subject to diffusion, if they wish to show. In other words, if they are not interested to disclose then the intellectual property vanishes away.

(e) The intellectual property and its growth in less developed traditional society or economy has some times a general or mass base. It is also a property that is adopted by the society at large. For example, many women in the household are familiar with the various peculiar properties of food articles used in day to day life and knowledge is freely exchanged and passed on generation to generations.

(f) There are many intellectual properties of the rural uneducated people, which aligned to the subject jurisprudence and they themselves do not considered it as a property and they do not bother about it as an enforceable property right.

(g) Intellectual property can be used for philanthropic/ humanitarian considerations or else may be used for making money or profit.[6]

Part-III: Intellectual Properties in India

It is a well recognised fact that India has been a country of many saints and sadhus who had the power of producing miracles. Many of them had bequeathed with intellectual property so as to give attention to the health of the people around. They had the capability to cure not only social but the physical ills associated with an individual or community or the entire society. They always directed people and their attention to not the materialism but the spiritualism. The spiritual way of life was considered as complete and capable of providing salvation to the last or marginal man of the society. Besides, some of the trained disciples to whom they transmitted some of (if not all) intellectual property(s) possessed by over a period of their lifetime. They emphasised more on sanctity, discipline, secrecy and its impact that it would create on the people around.

The intellectual property relating to the plants was another which had grown with individuals who constantly practiced with herbs, leaves and branches of various plants. In the modern days, these are known as medicinal plants. The Sanskrit texts spell out various plants with their names and the use that can be made from them for the good health of the people. There are also cases in which a persistent disease or a horrible disease can be cured from these plants. Unfortunately, the Sanskrit as a language as almost disappeared from its most common use and as a result the medicinal plants have remained unknown to many Indians. Besides, the degradation of forests have resulted in destruction of these precious medicinal plants. The other intellectual properties such as trademarks, patents, copyrights, geographical indications, bio-diversity etc. could only be found in the legal books in India only from 1950s. Indeed, the history of patent goes back to 1856. The barter economy, the objectives of self-sufficiency and simple way of living are the things, which pushed towards spiritualism of the Indian society. The geographical terms, for instance *"Made in India"* has been unknown to most of the people even after Independence. Patents, trade markers, industrial designs, copyrights etc., are completely unknown to Indian people and Indian economy. The Industrial development was very negligible. Therefore, the concept of *"Intellectual Property"* and considering it as an enforceable right has been as good as the accepted old Indian parabola that *agriculture is a way of life* in which no trade marks, patents, copyrights, etc. have hardly any place. If we think of intellectual property and considered them as right to be enforced, this has became subject of recent emergence and has posed a numerable problem for the country and the economy while India has joined WTO.

Part-IV: Intellectual Properties in the West

As against illiterate intellectual society based on the long experience and wisdom of India, the intellectual properties in the West have become very articulated, systematic and authentic. They are bound by legal codes which can be enforced. The multiplication or diffusion of the gains of this property requires a legal sanction. Therefore, the West has given greater importance to materialism in which everything is measured in terms of money. The allopathic or chemical medicines, for example, are patented and produced in large quantity and sold at high profit by a particular company which has its patent. Similarly, the western society has been built upon patents, copyrights, plant varieties, geographical indications, traditional knowledge, industrial designs, integrated circuits, bio-diversity etc.

A patent is a monopoly right granted to a person who has invented a new and useful article or an improvement of an existing article or a new process of making an article. Anybody can use the invention only after expiry of the patent term. The main objective of the patents is to encourage and develop new technology and industry. Patent monopoly stimulates technical progress. Any invention, which satisfies the conditions like novelty, inventive step, utility etc., is considered as patentable invention. Similarly, copyright, is a form of intellectual property law, protecting original works of authorship including literary, dramatic, musical, and artistic works, such as poetry, novels, movies, songs, computer software and architecture. An artistic, literary or musical work is the brainchild of the author, the fruit of his labour and so, considered as his property. Further, trademark is another type of intellectual property right. A trademark is a mark used or proposed to be used in relation to goods for the purpose of indicating or as to indicate a connection in the course of trade between the goods and same person having the right to use the mark. Designs, industrial know-how, geographical indications are the other forms of IPRs which have their origin in the west. It is noteworthy fact that the evolution of the intellectual property rights has ultimately crystalised into Trade Related Intellectual Property Rights (TRIPs) of the WTO.

Part-V: Legal Framework for IPRs in India

Property, in the legal sense, is essentially a bundle of rights flowing from the concept of ownership and possession. However, intellectual property is a non-physical property which stems from, or is identified as, and whose value is based upon some idea or ideas. India like many other countries has provided legal framework to protect the IPRs. The history of patent policy in India began as back as 1856. However, the actual attention of policymakers towards patents began right after Independence. India's Patent Act of 1970 is one of the important milestones in the history of patents in India. The law relating to intellectual property rights in India is undergoing changes in order to conform to stipulations in

TRIPs of the WTO. The government has brought amendment to patent act and enacted Patents (Amendment) Act, 2005. The act defines patent as any invention or technology which has not been anticipated by publication in any document or used in the country or elsewhere in the world before the date of filing of patent application with complete specification. The grants of patents may stimulate technical progress by encouraging research and invention. The government in order to conform stipulation in the TRIPs, introduced the Patent and Seeds Act, 2004. The government has stipulated that seed growers should get their seeds patented. The farmers will not be allowed to exchange their seed without patent. The provisions of the act are really a cause of concern. Because, the illiterate and ignorant farmers of India since many centuries have been exchanging the seeds with neighbor farmers. The act would become bane instead of boon to the farmers of India. "The Seed Act, 2004 has nothing to offer to farmers in India but after a promise of a monopoly to private seed industries" (Shiva Vandana 2005).

A new act known as Plant Varieties and Farmers Rights Act, 2001 was enacted by Government of India with the objectives like establishing an effective system of protection of plant varieties, protection of farmers' and breeders' rights. Broad based definition of breeder, exclusion of varieties containing gene or gene sequence involving any technology which is injurious to the life or health of humans, animals or plants, compulsory license and recognition of rights of communities are some of the important positive features of the act. However, inter alia, the legal and policy framework will determine the shapes of things and its impact in forthcoming days (Ravishankar A. and Sunil A. 2000). Government has enacted Indian Copyright Act as long back as in 1957, which conforms exclusive right to do or authorize others to do certain acts in relation to literary, dramatic, musical and artistic works. Further, cinematograph firm sound recordings also come under the orbit of Indian copyright act 1957. In concomitant to TRIPs, government has implemented new act known as Design Act 2000 with the objective to ensure effective protection to registered designs. Further, under the new act, the Semi Conductor Integrated Circuits Layout Design Act 2000, designs can be registered and rights are available for a period of ten years.

Thus, the ongoing attempt to harmonise and strengthen the intellectual property protection regimes world wide, as part of the TRIPs Agreement, appears to be adversely affecting technological activity in the developing countries like India by choking the knowledge spill over from industrialsed countries to developing countries. Further more, the implementation of the provision of TRIPs Agreement threatens poor people's access to and affordability of life-saving drugs by pushing up their prices. This has been highlighted by the recent controversy regarding the availability of AIDS drugs in South Africa (Kumar 2003). Recent changes in India's patent policy indicate a paradigm shift in seeking greater protection of IPRs. On one hand, this has given rise to fears being expressed over the impending collapse of local firms, on the other there is optimism amidst expectation of a large increase in patent activity of domestic actors (Ramanna 2002).

Part-VI: Problems of Implementation

Indeed, it is very complicated fact that the intellectual property has grown in different areas among different people in India. One may also add that the intellectual property has spread to various aspects of life and cover innumerable, number of activities. Indeed, if one has to say about the human, some people in India have such intellectual property so as to regulate birth as well as death. It would be premature at this stage to say that the people of India who would lucky to have intellectual property in relation to prevention of death will be kind of incredible miracle. Because, we are not aware of whether some people are engaged in finding out bio-diversity and medicinal plants in the Himalayan belt. It has been noted in our religious path finding narration that there is something called sanjeevini plane by[7] which dead man can be made alive. There is also the anecdotal reference in the Indian mythodology that brother of a dead king (Rama's brother Laxman who was shot dead) has been made alive by bringing sanjeevini by Hanuman from the Himalayan mountain to Sri Lanka. If so facto, the sanjeevini may exist either at Himalaya or Sri Lanka is a hypothesis one can construct. It is evident from our persistence discussion that the intellectual property has grown in a traditional way with the people and used it as a way of life. The people's consciousness increases with education. Therefore, without increase in the level of education the intellectual properties will be used as way of life and will never be considered as an enforceable right through the legal system. It may also be remembered that not only intellectual properties the consumer protection, family problems, problems of common property management, problems of environment management, management of water, management of forest etc. To put in a nutshell, everything in India is a way of life which can be changed only through level of education. If this is the case, the implementation of IPRs is a big joke for the people of India and will be putting the development of Indian Economy cart before the horse.

Conclusion

India is a country having large amount of natural resources and many people and community with intellectual property to make use of them. However, people are faraway from formal, scientific and legal practices insofar as using the intellectual properties as a legal right. Further, it is a country with largest democracy in the world. There is open society. The Indian gates are opened to the formal and informal invitation to the people of other countries. After the departure of British particularly in the recent years, people of many countries thronging in India and getting acquainted with the intellectual properties informally mixing with people and community. They have full access to all the natural resources and their best use in various aspects of life and activities. They have attempted and also attempting to acquire IPRs on the use of Indian natural resources. The British alone made political exploitation of the country. Whereas people of other countries including the British have been exploiting Indian intellectual properties and claiming legal rights on them. In the due course, very shortly it may not be surprising that India stands as an exploited country with legal rights by others. It would be made to pay in its own coin for its own resources and in its own geography itself. Alas! Keeping this in mind, the Minister for Commerce and Industry, Government of India has been sensing this fighting jointly with underdeveloped countries at the negotiating table in the WTO meetings. It is appreciable at the movement that he has not been cowed down. The developing countries and its people with Indian IPRs want to exploit India itself. Therefore, we may say that India is chasing and world is running.

NOTES

1. The 'Vaidyas' (greatly practiced doctors not in allopathy but in herbal and plant medicines) were summoned to the courts for curing the ills of members of royal families that existed in India for years to come. Not only Indian Princes or Kings but also the Mughals who ruled for long had also a royal 'hakeem' to treat the health problems of rulers.
2. For example, Birbal was considered as the best Minister for Akbar, the Great. Similarly, the Rajpurohits were consulted for taking up any important and auspicious (including waging and timing of the wars) work by the royal family.
3. It is a well recognised traditional knowledge in India that urine of the cow consists of highly processed chemical components which can be used for curing many ills and hard bound diseases such as diabetes, cancers and others.
4. 'Goal' is a commercially intellectual word coined by a German Wine manufacturer to manufacture a beer with branded name "GOAL" in keeping with the ongoing Football World Cup Championship, which has low alcoholic content and expects a grand sale during the days of the play (June to July 2006) in which people from various parts of the world will coming to Berlin.
5. The curing of snake bite and cavity in the teeth has been discovered by some individuals with the help of the juice of leaves of some plants which they have not and they will not disclosed to others (including their own spouse, kits and kins). The story goes that a man whom the authors know one day early in the

morning could see a fight between snake and mongoose in a green field and was able to see that mongoose after killing the snake which went and bited leaves of a tree which are capable of acting even anti-cobra venom. Unfortunately, he died without passing his knowledge of plants to others.

6. Snake bite can be treated without cost with the help of plant leaves as against the allopathic anti-venom treatment with removal of poisonous and inserting fresh blood which would cost several hundreds of rupees to a patient. The former is done most often in India free of cost. The same may be said about the treatment of various types of frequently occurring disease called as Jaundice.

7. In the West the equivalent term is known as elxiser.

REFERENCES

Arrow J.K. (1999), Knowledge as a Factor of Production. Keynote Address, Annual World Bank Conference on Development Economics, Washington D.C. pp. 15-20.

Clark, John Bate (1890), The Law of Wages and Interest. Annals of the American Academy of Political and Social Science 5. pp. 289-318.

Coleman, J. and E. Katz (1966), Medical Innovation: A Diffusion Study. Babbs Merrill, Indianapolis.

David, P.A. (1974), The Mechanization of Reaping in the Ante-Bellum Midwest. In P.A. David, Ed., Technical Choice, Innovation and Economic Growth, Cambridge University Press, New York.

Griliches, Zvi. (1957), Hybrid Corn. An exploration in the Economics of Technological Change. Econometrica 25: pp. 501-522.

Kumar, Nagesh (2003), Intellectual Property Rights, Technology and Economic Development: Experiences of Asian Countries. Economic and Political Weekly; Jan. 18, 2003, pp. 209-225.

Landes, David (1998), The Wealth and Poverty of Nations. Norton, New York.

Mansfield, Edwin (1961), Technical Change and the Rate of Imitation. Econometrica 29: pp. 741-66.

Ramanna, Anitha (2002), Policy Implications of India's Patent Reforms: Patent Applications in the Post-1995 Era. Economic and Political Weekly; May 25, 2002. pp. 2065-2075.

Ravishankar, A. and Sunil, Archak (2000), Intellectual Property Rights and Agricultural Technology: Interplay and Implications for India. Economic and Political Weekly; July 1, 2000. pp. 2446-2452.

Ricardo, David (1817), Principles of Political Economy and Taxation. Murray, London.

Rosenberg, Nathan (1982), Inside the Black Box. Cambridge University Press, New York.

Schmookler, Jacob (1966), Invention and Economic Growth. Harvard University Press, Harvard.

Schumpeter, Joseph (1939), Business Cycles. McGraws-Hill, New York.

Shiva Vandana (2005), Sowing the Seeds of Dictatorship. Swadeshi Patnika, April 2005.

Smith, Adam (1776), An Inquiry into the Nature and Causes of the Wealth of Nations. Strahan and Cadell, London.

Solow, Robert M. (1956), A Contribution to the Theory of Economic Growth. Quarterly Journal of Economics 65: pp. 65-94.

——— (1957) Technical Change and the Aggregate Production Function. Review of Economic Statistics 39: pp. 312-20.

Weitzman, Martin (1998), Recombinant Growth. Quarterly Journal of Economics 113: pp. 331-60.

Wood, Stuart (1888), A New View of the Theory of Wages. Quarterly Journal of Economics 3: 60-86, pp. 462-80.

INTELLECTUAL PROPERTY RIGHTS IN INDIA UNDER WTO REGIME

*Akash S.B.**

Introduction

Intellectual property rights played significant role in order to earn desire profit by the business communities, because, it is a class of property emanating primarily from the activities of the human intellect. Any property movable or immovable is legally protected to prevent it from being stolen. Similarly, the intellectual property rights also have protection from infringement.

The importance of intellectual property rights in India is well established at all levels like statutory, administrative and judicial and India ratified the agreement establishing the World Trade Organization. This agreement, inter, alias, contains an agreement on trade related aspects of intellectual property rights which, came into force from 1st January 1995[1]. And it lays down minimum standard for protection and enforcement of intellectual property rights in member countries, which are required to promote effectively, and adequate protection of intellectual property rights with view to reducing distortion and impediments to foreign trade. However Indian position in the world in terms of Intellectual properties, during 2004, witnessed filing of the million international patent applications. A recorded number of applications, over 1,20,000,were filed in 2004, using the Patent Co-operative Treaty (PCT) of the World Intellectual Property Organization[2] (WIPO). The USA continued to top the list of the largest users, but biggest rates

* Faculty Department of Studies in Commerce KUPG Centre, Karwar (Karnataka).

of growth came from the Asian continent viz., Japan, Republic of Korea and China[3]. The PCT is the cornerstone of the international patent system and offers a rapid, flexible and cost effective way to obtained patent protection in 126 countries including India that have signed-up to the system[4].

According to WIPO estimates, further growth is expected from Asian continent in the coming years and China will overtake Australia in the year 2005 to become the 12th largest user of the system.[5]

Concept of Intellectual Property Rights

The intellectual property is an ownership rights over their material possession. In other words intellectual property is product of intellect, which is owned in some way an individual, or business enterprise. Black's Law Dictionary[6] defines "intellectual property" as "a category of intangible rights protecting commercially valuable products of the human intellect. The category comprises primarily trademark, copyright, and patent rights, but also includes trade-secret rights, publicity rights, moral rights, and rights against unfair competition." The terminology regarding intellectual property has shifted over time, with the term "industrial property" giving way to the various terms that exist today. According to WTO intellectual property rights are the rights given to person over the creation of their minds. They usually give the creator an exclusive right over the use of his/her creation for a creation period[7].

Features of Intellectual Property Rights

Intellectual property rights are the rights given to persons over the creations of their minds. They usually give the creator an exclusive right over the use of his/her creation for a certain period of time. However the important features of intellectual property rights are Intellectual property is an asset. It can be bought, sold, licensed, exchanged or gratuitously given away like any other form of society. It provides rights to owners to prevent the unauthorized use or sale of property. It is an intangible property, so cannot be define or identify by its own physical parameters. It is a product of intellects. It is related to creation of an aesthetic character (e.g. artistic works and industrial design) as well as information and signs of a purely commercial value (e.g. trade mark) It has protection like physical assets. It is applicable to different field like chemicals, drugs, plastic, electronics, printing, entertainment (audio, video, motion, picture), soft ware, broad costing, agriculture and food industry, clothing, automobiles electronics, wines, spirits, cheese and others. It includes rights like copyrights, patent rights, trademark, industrial design, plant variety, and geographical indication. It has been characterized by as a composition of ' ideas' invention and creative expression plus the public willingness to bestow the status of property.

Reasons Responsible for Protection of Intellectual Property Rights

The protection of intellectual property right is very important for different reasons such as protect right of the copyrights holders, trademark, and patient, to avoid the infringement of intellectual property rights by others, maintain fair competition among business communities, underpinning economic growth and employment, for sustaining innovation and creation, for promoting technological and cultural advances, for enriching the pool of public knowledge, to encourage creative thinking for search something in unknown field, to encourage the production of original artistic, literary and musical creations from books and painting to movies, recording and soft work etc, to encourage and adequate reward to innovation and creative work, to protect the interest of consumer and to facilities the transfer of technology.

Objectives of the Study

1. To study the role of intellectual property rights in economic development of the country.
2. To identify the possible reasons that is responsible for protection of intellectual property rights.
3. To critically analyze the types of intellectual property rights.

4. To analyze the country wise intellectual property application.
5. To analyze the magnitude of intellectual property application from India
6. To examine the role of WTO in intellectual property protection

Sources of Data

The study is based on secondary data. The secondary data collected from different sources like www.indiapatent.org.in, http//www WWW. Indianembassy. Org/ policy/ipr 2000. Ltm,http//WWW.WIPO.Org/eng/implex/index. htm,http/ WWW.wto.org/wto/intellectul/17wipo.htm,WWW. indiannestop. Com/market-intellectual property rights-19k WWW.laws unidia. Com/ipr.aso-5 k etc. In addition to above, the study also used daily paper like Business line and Times of India etc.

WTO and Intellectual Property Rights

The world intellect property organization describes itself as a Geneva based Agency of the United Nations Organization with the main task of helping to guarantee the protection of intellectual property worldwide However, India is a signatory to the WTO agreement and it required to align its law on intellectual property rights in accordance with the obligations under the TRIPS agreement of the WTO agreement[8]. The WTO TRIPS agreement played a significant role to narrow the gaps in the way these rights are protected around the world, and to bring them under common international rules. WTO establishes minimum levels of protection that each government has to give to the intellectual property of fellow. It means, it strikes a balance between the long-term benefits and possible short-term costs to society. Society benefits in the long term when intellectual property protection encourages creation and invention, especially when the period of protection expires and the creations and inventions enter the public domain. Legislative conforming to obligations under the TRIPS agreement, relating to patents, trademarks, geographical indications and industrial designs have been amended/enacted.

These legislations the opportunity was also utilized to modernize the revamp the legislations incorporate provisions for simplifications of procedures and protection of national/ public interest. The agreement provides norms and standards in respects of intellectual property rights. The agreement covers five broad issues[9] such as how basic principles of the trading system and other international intellectual property agreements should be applied, how to give adequate protection to intellectual property rights, how countries should enforce those rights adequately in their own territories, how to settle disputes on intellectual property between members of the WTO and special transitional arrangements during the period when the new system is being introduced.

Types of Intellectual Property Rights

The important types of intellectual property rights like copyrights and related rights, patents rights, trade mark, industrial design etc.

Copyrights and Related Rights

It is owner of the copyright enjoys the rights to grant or with hold the right others to make copy of the work; copyright is often describes as a restrictive rights because it concerned with stopping others doing something with the work. In other words, copyright is an exclusive right to produce an original work of authorship fixed in any tangible medium of expression, to prepare derivative works based upon the original work, and to perform or display the work such as musical, dramatic, choreographic, sculptural, pantomimes, pictorial, graphic, motion pictures and other audiovisual works and sound recording.

The copyright rules 1956, amended, sets out the procedure for the registration of a work. Both published and unpublished works can be registered. Copyright work published before Jan 21, 1958, that is before the copyright act, 1957 came in force, can also be registered, provided the work still enjoy copyright. However the registration of copyright is to be made form IV along with particulars, as prescribed in the first scheduled to the rules and, if work has been registered as a unpublished and subsequent it is required to published, the applicant may apply for changes in particulars entered in the registered of copyright in the form V with prescribed fees.

In India there are three types of remedies against infringement of copyright the first one is civil remedies. It consists of injection damages or account of profit, delivery of infringing copy and damages for conversion. The second type of remedial measures is criminal remedy. Imprisonment of the accused or imposition of fine or both, seizure of infringing copies. The third type of remedial measure is administrative remedy. The administrative measures consist of moving the registered of copy rights to ban the import of infringing copies into India when the infringement is by way of such importation and delivery of the confiscated infirming copies to the owner of the copyright and seeking to delivery.

The TRIPS agreement provides minimum standards for duration of copyright protection. In case of person, the term is the life of the author plus 50 years. In the case of corporate entity, it is 50 years from the end of the calendar year of authorized publication, or, in the absence of publication, from the end of the calendar year of making. The term of protection for live performances that are recorded is 50 years performer and producer and 20 years for the broadcaster of the work.

Trade Mark

The globalization and liberalization has led to the emergence of the highly competitive global market, wherein quality, quantity, price and such other matters play a vital role. This environment needed that suitable trademark to distinguish the goods of an enterprise from the other enterprise. However the trademark refers is a visual symbol or mark, in the form of word or design, sound, colure, or group of latter's etc. The main aim of trademark is distinguished the goods or services of an enterprise to from those of other enterprise. Such distinguishing marks constitutes protect able subject matter under the provision of the TRIPS agreement.

The trademark act 1958 was guiding with regard to trademarks. However, India under TRIPS agreement, the trade and merchandise mark act, 1958 under went wide spread transformation, thus leading to its way for the emergence of the new trademark act, 1999, which sort to be conformity with the TRIPS agreement. The duration of the trade mark for a period of 10 years, and it may be renewed from time to time, under new acts, the term of registration would be extended to 10 years, subject to renewal. But non-users of register trademark for a continuous period of 5 years is a ground for cancellation of registration of such trademark on the behalf of any agreed party and in India, have suitable remedies for infringement of trademark, therefore trade mark play'ed vital role in competitive market to get competitive advantages over competitors.

Patent

Patent is a contract between societies as a whole and an individual inventor. Due to this agreement the inventor is given the exclusive right to prevent others from making, using, and selling a patented inventing for a fixed period of time. In other words patent is an exclusive right to prevent others from making, using, and selling a patented invention for a fixed period of time. The patent is an exclusive monopoly right conferred to the inventors, as per provision of the patent acts, for the purpose of disclosure of use the invention either for himself or by an authorized person and also obtain others from illegal making, using or selling the invention prior to the expire the term of patent rights. The Indian patent act 1970 has been equipped to provide exclusive monopoly rights for three kinds of patents such as ordinary patents conventional patent and product patent. However, the basic obligation in the area of patent is that invention in all branches of technology whether product or process shall be patented if they meet the three tests of being new, involving an inventive step and being capable of industrial application. In addition to general security which applied to the entire agreement, specific exclusions are permissible from the scope of patent -ability of inventions, the prevention of whose commercial exploitation is necessary to protect public order or morality, human animals, plant life or health or to avoid serious prejudice to the environment. The TRIPS agreement provided for a less terms of protection of 20 years counted the date of filling.

In India, in respect of an invention claiming process or method of manufacture of a substance intended for use or capable of being used as food, or as medicines or drug, the patent shall be for a period of 5 years from the date sealing of the patent or 7 years from the date of patent. The proposed patent amendment bill 2005, the patent shall be for uniform period of 20 years and investment of any other invention, 14 years from the date of the patent, which shall be further extended to 20 years.

Industrial Design

Industrial design refers an idea or conception as to the features of shape, configuration, pattern, ornament or composition of lines or colure applied to any article, two or three dimensional or both, by any industrial process or means which in finished article applied to and are judged solely by the eye or product. In other words industrial designs are that independently created design that are new or original shall be protected. Individual government have been given the option to exclude from protection, designs dictated by technical or functional considerations, as against aesthetic consideration which constitutes the cover age of industrial designs. The industrial design right accruing to the right holds is the right to prevent third parties not having his consent from making selling or importing articles being or embodying a design, which is a copy or a substantially a copy of the duration of protection is to be not less than 10 years. A new design, act repelling and replacing the design act 1911.

Table 1 reveals that country wise I P application and represent of inventors and industry from different country. USA represent 41870 during 2004, it increases 1.9% over previous period. Intellectual property right application from Japan amounting 19982, Germany represent during 2004, constituting 14898 and increases percentage over corresponding previous year amounting 1.5%. France, able to increases I P application between, 2000 to 2004, amounting 27.6%. United kingdom and Netherlands, represents intellectual property application during 2004, 5056 and 4458 respectively. Republic of Korea increases their intellectual property application during 2004 as compared to 2003 constituting 19.3%. China represent intellectual property right application during 2004, 1782 constituting 127.2 per cent increases between 2000 to 2004.Switzerland represent, IP, applications 2875, Sweden, 2721, Italy, 2162, Canada, 2111, Australia 1809 and Finland represent 1677 during 2004.

Table 1
Country wise Intellectuals Property Application

Country	*Year*				
	2000	*2001*	*2002*	*2003*	*2004*
USA	38007 (-)	43053 (13.3)	41293 (-4)	41093 (-5)	41870 (1.9)
Japan	9567 (-)	11904 (24.4)	14063 (18.1)	17376 (23.5)	19982 (14.9)
Germany	12582 (-)	14031 (11.5)	14326 (2.1)	14676 (2.4)	14898 (1.5)
France	4138 (-)	4707 (13.7)	5088 (8.09)	5163 (1.5)	5281 (2.3)
United kingdom	4795 (-)	5482 (14.3)	5375 (-1.9)	5208 (-3.1)	5056 (2.9)
Netherlands	2928 (-)	3410 (16.4)	3977 (16.6)	4453 (11.9)	4458 (0.11)
Switzerland	1989 (-)	2349 (18.5)	2756 (17.3)	2866 (3.9)	2875 (0.3)
Republic of Korea	1580 (-)	2324 (47.1)	2520 (8.4)	2951 (17.1)	3521 (19.3)
Sweden	3091 (-)	3421 (10.7)	2990 (-12.6)	2661 (-11)	2721 (2.2)
EPC member states	36003 (-)	40633 (12.9)	42446 (4.5)	43182 (1.7)	44246 (2.5)
Italy	1394 (-)	1623 (16.4)	1982 (22.1)	2157 (8.8)	2162 (.23)
Canada	1801 (-)	2114 (17.3)	2259 (6.8)	2270 (.5)	2111 (-7.0)
Australia	1576 (-)	1664 (5.6)	1760 (5.7)	1684 (1.43)	18o4 (7.12)
China	784 (-)	1731 (120)	1017 (-37)	1293 (271)	1782 (37.8)
Finland	1578 (-)	1696 (7.4)	1762 (4)	1557 (-11.6)	1677 (7.7)
Others	3922 (-)	4807 (22.5)	5029 (4.1)	5293 (5.2)	4784 (-10.6)

*Sources:*1 WWW.indianpatent:org.in

Note: Figures in parentheses indicate percentage increases/decreases over previous period.

Table 2 reveals that classification of international patent. Pharmaceutical consuming and dental technologies patented

Table 2
Classification of International Patents

Nature of Patents	*Year* 2003	2004
Computer data processing	7053	6152 (-5.4)
Pharmaceutical consuming and dental technologies	7099	6715 (-5.4)
Analysis Material by Determining their Chemical or Physical properties	2922	2856 (-2.3)
Diagnosis, surgery	2423	2447 (1.0)
Net working Telecommunication	3011	3254 (8.1)
Micro-organism or Enzymes	2523	2138 (-15.3)
Telecommunication	1573	1522 (-3.3)
Optics	1609	1497 (-7)
Pictorial Communication	2065	1924 (-6.8)
Information Storage Technologies	1228	1528 (24.5)
Filters Implant- able into Blood Vessels; Prostheses	1534	1522 (0.8)
Organic Chemistry- Carbocycilic compounds	1527	1563 (2.3)
Other	1431	1438 (0.5)

*Sources:*1 WWW.indianpatent.org.in

Note: 1. Other includes, Switches relays, selectors; and electronic switches etc.
2. Figures in Parenthesis indicate percentage increases/decreases over previous year.

Table 3
Intellectual Property Application from India

Year	*No. of Application*
1997	25 (-)
1998	26 (4)
1999	85 (226.9)
2000	185 (117.6)
2001	190 (2.7)
2002	500 (1636)
2003	725 (45)
2004	698 (3.7)
2005*	120

*Sources:*1 WWW.indianpatent.org.in

Note: 1. Figures in Parenthesis indicate Percentage increases/decreases over previous year.

* Up to April 2005.

7099 during 2003 and 6715 in 2004. Information Storage Technologies patented 1228 during 2003, 1528 in 2004, it increases over corresponding year amounting 24.5%. Computer data processing decreased by –5.4 per cent in 2004 over corresponding period. Diagnosis surgery patented 2423 in the year 2003 and it increases by 1% over corresponding previous year. Microorganism or Enzymes and Telecommunication, patented during 2004, amounting 2138 and 1522 respectively. Thus it is clear that most of the international patent decreases during 2004 as compared to corresponding previous year. Table 3 reveals that intellectual property application from India. During 1997, India has registered intellectual property rights 25 only and during 1998, has registered 26; it increases 4 percentages over corresponding previous period. In the year 1999 recorded 185 intellectual property rights constituting 226.9 per cent over corresponding Previous period. During 2000, 185, 2001, 190 and in the year 2002, 2003, and 2004 has recorded intellectual property right amounting 500, 725, and 698 respectively. Thus it is clear that the big population of the nation not produce more intellectual property, because India is produces very list intellectual property as compared to other countries.

Conclusion

The possession of land, labour and capital not sufficient for country progress, the true progress of the country fully depends upon the creation and innovation in different field is must for increases standard of living of human beings and increases economic status of country. The policy adopted by country shall determine the national well being of such strategy with knowledge based, innovation, driven economies, the intellectual property is dynamic tool for the wealth creation, providing incentives for enterprises and individuals to create and innovate, a fertile setting for the development of, and trade in, intellectual assets and stable environment for domestic and foreign investment. However, the importance of intellectual property right in India is well established at all levels like statutory, administrative and judicial, although, in India, BPO mindset has percolated deep into the blood and veins of lakhs of Indians. BPO can go only for IPO, but cannot create intellectual property for India. For this reasons Indians should come forward to create enough intellectual properties and go into application of knowledge to agriculture, health, and industry etc.

NOTES AND REFERENCES

1. www.indianembassy.org/policy/ipr 2000. Ltm.
2. Vijaya Times, Sep. 10, 2005, p. 10.
3. Vijaya Times Opcit, p. 10.
4. Business Line, Feb. 2, 2005, p. 5.
5. http//WWW.WIPO.Org/eng/implex/index.htm.
6. Stetanie Weigman: Research on Intellectual Law in an International Context.LLRX.com.
7. http//WWW.wto.org/wto/intellectul/17 wipo.htm.
8. Francis Cherunilm International Trades and Export Management p. 160.
9. http//TRIPS. htm.
10. WWW.indiannestop. Com/market-intellectual property rights-19 k.
11. WWW.laws unidia. Com/ipr.aso-5 k.
12. Muchkund Dubey, ' Implication Issues in WTO" The Hindu, Sept. 10, 2005.
13. www.dipp.nic.in/ipr.htm 13k.
14. www.ifr.org.
15. Mary J. Hildebrand and Jacueline Klosek IPW est., a Thomson Business, Volume, Issues 20, Feb., 4, 2004.

LIKELY IMPACTS OF TRIPS ON INDIAN AGRICULTURE

Chandra Prakash Singh[*] & Ranjan Kumar Sinha[**]

Background

For alleviating the economic problems of rural people in India, technical progress has long been advocated. This approach has indeed brought results; so much so that India became self-sufficient in foodgrains in the seventies from a position of net importer of foodgrains in 1950s and 1960s. The technological change brought about by the scientific and farming communities, is well known and has been rightly labelled as the 'Green Revolution'. Convinced with the efficacy of this approach, the government maintained its thrust on agricultural research and technology transfer from lab to land in its strategy for agricultural development.

In the decade of 1970s when Indian agriculture was moving towards self-sufficiency, many developments took place, which affected world agriculture. These related to consumer preference, vast technological possibilities in agriculture and perceptible rise in land prices and labour wages in the agriculture of the developed countries. Vast technological possibilities were seen through micro-propagation, micro irrigation and molecular genetics. Agricultural wages in the developed countries were on the rise.

Concomitant to the above developments in the world agriculture, agricultural trade between the US and Europe was

* Lecturer, Dept. of Rural Economics & Co-operation, MAM Colege, Naugachia, T.M. Bhagalpur University, Bhgagalpur.

** Research Officer, Agro-Economic Research Centre for Bihar & Jharkhand, T.M. Bhagalpur University, Bhagalpur.

shrinking. European Union (EU) since early 1960s had followed a comprehensive and well concerted policy for European agriculture, popularly known Common Agricultural Policy (CAP). Through this policy alone Western Europe was converted from a position of a net importer of food until 1960s to a net exporter of food in 1970s. The declining exports from the US were major cause of concern for American policy makers. Consequently, agriculture was included for the first time in GATT negotiations of Punta del Este, Urguay in 1986 (Mirha, 1999).

The above developments in world agriculture are of great importance to India's agricultural sector. The competitiveness of Indian agriculture was clearly established. In relative terms, land prices and agricultural wages were low and agriculture was seen as a foreign exchange earner through export of non-traditional items such as fruits, vegetables, flowers, mushroom, shrimps etc.

The above background has been provided to show how the economic conditions have changed for absorption and diffusion of agricultural research and technology. The World Trade Agreement leading to formation of World Trade Organization has opened enormous opportunities for expansion of Indian agriculture but at the same time brought stringent condition through intellectual property protection mechanism. Each invention has to be rewarded. Member countries of the WTO are expected to put legal mechanism in place of protection of IPR. Thus while the technology of Green Revolution was freely accessible to farming community, the technologies of today will involve cost. The conditions have therefore changed significantly.

The WTO – TRIPs Agreement

The 1995 WTO – TRIPs Agreement covers eight areas: copy right and related rights, trademarks, geographical indications, industrial designs, patents (and plant variety protection – PVP), lay out designs (topographies) of integrated circuits, protection of undisclosed information and control of anticompetitive practices in contractual licenses (Tansey, 2005).

This paper is focused on TRIPs Agreement, which was developed in order to lay down the minimum internationally accepted standards for protection of intellectual property rights. The basic thrust of the Agreement is to provide market access and develop greater trading opportunities. The implication of TRIPs on agriculture under WTO regime has become very important. It is usually said that it has become a de facto enforcer of international food standards guidelines in the sphere of foreign trade although it may not have the de jure authority. With its enforcements, Indian agriculturists and processors will have to adopt these guidelines; else they will have to face non-tariff barriers in the export market.

Perspective

A notable feature of agricultural food products is that their consumption gives essential pleasure and they directly contribute to the sustained healthy life as well. However, spoiled, contaminated, adulterated and inferior quality food can be harmful to one's health irrespective of its taste, and, at times fatal. The lethal contamination of edible oils with argemone oil that led to more than fifty dropsy related deaths in August/September 1998 is a case in point (IE, 1998). Similarly, high levels of pesticides residues in agricultural commodities are carcinogenic; therefore, food sector is perhaps the only sector where the age old warning, caveat emptor is just not enough. 'Shabri' might have offered tasted/tested barris to 'Lord Rama' out of sheer devotion, however, sheer market sense should compel agri-business to realize that in modern times, consumer is king and maintaining high food quality becomes a part of their competitive strategy. It must be emphasized that the ultimate winner of quality improvement process will be the Indian farmer who will receive higher and sustained demand for his produce at remunerative prices.

Consumer concerns about food quality worldwide have found expression in the objectives of quite a few international institutions. Food and Agriculture Organization (FAO) and World Health Organization (WHO) jointly established Codex Alimentarious Commission (CAC) in 1962 with the aim to protect consumer health harmonise food standards, and promote international trade (CAC, 1996). Realizing that mere ex-post inspection methods for agricultural commodities do not guarantee safety to consumers, in 1993, CAC recommended adoption of a food safety management system i.e. Hazard Analysis and Critical Control Points (HACCP). But the recommendations of CAC had no legal backing of any international law. Now CAC recommendations have been endorse and made virtually mandatory due to the 1995 agreements on SPS (Sanitary and Phytosanitary Measures) and TBT (Technical Barriers to Trade), reached by the member countries of WTO. It is to be pointed out here that WTO is not a de jure enforcer of these international standards, rather it enforced de facto this is so because it responds to complaints brought by member nations and determines which national standards are or are not in conformity with international standards through dispute settlement (IFAS, 2000).

TRIPs and Indian Agriculture

As discussed, TRIPs covers-copyright, trade marks, trade secrets, geographical indications, industrial designs, integrated circuits and patents. However, the most confronting issue of TRIPs is patent. Besides, the concept of EMRs (exclusive marketing rights) built into the TRIPs was itself highly flawed. The impacts of TPR on agricultural sector are an important dimension of analysis. It is said to be a gateway of entering multinationals like Hindustan Lever, Cargil, ITC, Pepsicola, Moncento, Godrej, Mahindra etc, into agricultural sector. Genetically engineering varieties of seed of food and cash crops owned multinational companies will be sold in India and such seeds will have so far been absent. Obviously, this will enhance the seed price. Further, since the seeds are protected by patent, farmers may not be allowed to save them from their own harvest. In the circumstances, India will unable to increase the yield rate through high quality seeds to make here product competitive in the world market. The monopolization of input, research and gains by multinational will never allow the benefits to be trickled down.

On the other hand, the development of substitutes of chemical fertilizers as bio-fertilizers and chemical pesticides as bio-pesticides has revolutionized agricultural technology. India has yet not developed fully in this direction. The entry of multinationals into agricultural sector armed with IPR would mean a substantial control over entire range of seed, fertilizers, pesticides and research. They but also have a command on investment production, distribution and marketing. The worst sufferers will be small and the marginal farmers. They would have practically no relevance in the high-tech agricultural production era.

In fact, IPR is an open invitation to multinationals to enter into our agricultural sector with enormous investment potentials, high technological level, market experience and command over research, production, distribution and marketing and by this command, they will also command, control and regulate the agro-based industrial sector, agro-trade and agro-services. Trade can never be fair for all. In other words, in the name of trade-liberalization and globalization we are moving towards monopolization. It is because of the fact that in the name of making ourselves more competitive we have withdrawn the protectionist policies. Moreover, we have accepted the protection of multinationals and of other international agencies. Is it not the beginning of an area of humble slavery ? (Ratnesh, 2002).

Challenges Before Farmers

The widening canvas of IPR resulting from the commitments made by the member countries has raised several new challenges before the farmers. Protection of plant varieties would have to be provided by using patents or an effective Sui Generis system for the protection of plant varieties or a combination of both. Even as the Agreement on TRIPs was being negotiated there was another international initiative, which grew out of the realization that the introduction of plant breeders right could introduce an asymetry between the plant breeders' and the farmers. It was felt that while the plant breeders could secure their rights in the new regime of intellectual property protection, the traditional farmers who have conserved and improved the planting material through the centuries and have made these available to the breeders, stand to receive no recognition. This gave rise to the concept of 'Farmers Rights', which has been seen as a mechanism that can counter balance, the breeders rights (Dhar, 2000).

Farmer's rights was first introduced by the FAO in its resolution in 1989 and it was used to mean "rights arising from the past, present and future contributions of the farmers in conserving, improving and making available plant genetic resources, particularly those in the centers of origin/diversity. The issue of farmers' rights has been taken forward by the FAO through the process initiated for the revision of the international undertaking on Plant Genetic Resources. Article 15 of the proposed International Undertaking contains a formulation on the farmers rights, which recognizes the "enormous contribution that the local and indigenous communities and farmers of all regions of the world will continue to make the conservation and development of plant genetics resources, which constitute the basis of food and agriculture production through out the world. Article 15, if adopted, can raise two contentious issues, viz.

(i) The responsibility for realizing farmers' rights rests with the national government, which would provide these rights in accordance with their needs and priorities.

(ii) Whether or not farmers' rights can be considered as a conventional form of IPRs. This pertains to the identification of the title-holder of such rights.

However, to cope these issues, there have been suggestions that farmers' rights should best being treated as collective rights, where the rights belong to communities or groups of farmers. But the concept of collective rights existed in the traditional societies and this has long been abandoned in favour of the western system in which the legal categories are clearly defined. Thus, getting the right structure for implementation of farmers' rights is the real issue that needs to be addressed. The first step in this direction would be the recognition that a new approach to dealing with rights of traditional communities is required and that 'one size does not fit all'.

Opportunities in TRIPs

The contribution of knowledge as a factor of production is beginning to acquire dominant role in future trade, investment and technological change in agricultural sector. The management of knowledge not just in farms but also in non-farm sector will, thus, become crucial. The strategy should be making Indian agriculture not only globally more competitive but also domestically more progressive by using knowledge as a strategic resource so that agriculture sustains livelihoods of millions in an environmentally sustainable manner. The concept of IPR has not yet been exposed to the inventive potential as has been demonstrated by 'Honey Bee' network over last years through its database having about 10,000 entries of innovations and outstanding examples of traditional knowledge, innovations and practices, the immense contribution that grassroots innovators can make towards this cause. Add to this the potential that Indian Scientists have and one would know why TRIPs under WTO can indeed make R&D in formal and informal sector as the pivot of socio-economic transformation of our society. It is true that India must negotiate changes in TRIPs to suit our requirements and for this lobbying is necessary (Gupta, 2001).

Policy Issues

There are some policy issues, which need to be addressed in future planning:

- A registration system of land races will have to be developed to recognize the community rights;
- Monetary as well as non-monetary incentives for individuals as well as communities as advocated by 'Honey Bee' network and SRISTI (NGO) for last ten years are essential if the asymmetry in the rights of institutional and informal breeders has to be reduced and eventually eliminated;
- National database on local varieties with proper

documentation of local knowledge of population is very necessary;

- Creation of a knowledge network is need of the hour. It will connect creative farmers, scientists and policy makers in real time so that macro policy can be responsive to micro level innovations, and other urges; and
- A national technology mission on non-chemical technology development is must to produce quality outputs.

Besides above, there are a large number of issues to be taken into account for policy direction but aforesaid issues are the prime ones.

NOTES AND REFERENCES

1. Mishra, J. P. (1999); Biotechnology and Intellectual Property Rights'; Yojana, May, Issue.
2. Tansey, G. (205); Global Intellectual Property Rights: A New Factor In Farming, Agriculture and WTO, edited by M. D. Ingco & J. D. Nash, Atlantic Publishers & Distributors, New Delhi.
3. As A Results of the Dropsy Cases, fall in Sales of Mustard Oil was of the Magnitude of Several Crores of Rupees.
4. Indian Express (1998); 'H. C. Judge to Probe Dropsy Cases', Dated 10.09.1998.
5. Institute for Food and Agricultural Standards (2000); 'Markets, Rights and Equity': Food and Agricultural Standards in a Shrinking World, Recommendations from an International Workshop.
6. Ratnesh, K. (2002); WTO-Structure, Functions, Task Challenges, Deep & Deep Publications Pvt. Ltd., New Delhi.
7. Dhar, Biswajit (2000); Will Breeders Trip Farmers' Rights ?, The Economic Times, Calcutta ed. Dated 19.1.2000.
8. Gupta, A. K. (2001); Implications of WTO on Indian Agriculture: The Case of Intellectual Property Rights— —"; Implication of WTO Agreements for Indian Agriculture, CMA, IIM, Ahmedabad, India.

GLOBALISATION OF TOURISM TRADE AND BUSINESS TRADE–IMPACT ON INDIAN TOURISM INDUSTRY AND NATIONAL ECONOMY

*Pushpa P.**

World's highest growth sector of the 21st Century are TOURISM & TRAVEL. As per World Tourism Organisation's (WTO) statistics, tourism is the largest global industry today bigger than steel, automobiles and electronics. Its contribution to World's GNP is above 6.5% equivalent to about US$ 3.5 trillion as early as 1998. To attain this supreme position, tourism industry of the world had undergone two major transitions - one in the wake of International Union of Official Tourism Organisation (IUOTO). IUOTO was the I international organization established in 1947 to promote and foster international tourism. The rebirth of the IUOTO's replica - World Tourism organization (WTO) in 1975 also marched past towards the same mission. Realising the 'MAIDAS' touch potential in foreign exchange earning many countries opted as members of IUOTO and WTO voluntarily to reap the multifaceted benefits. 101 countries being members of WTO in 1981 including India, increased to 121 in 1995. These 2 international tourism organizations globalised the tourism trade and changed the economy of these member countries. Since 1947 to 1995 the global tourism industry thus crossed the I transition.

Globalisation of business trade in 1995 with the birth of yet another WTO (World Trade Organisation) and its off-springs

* Lecturer-SL, Department of Nutrition and Dietetics, Seethalakshmi Ramaswami College, Trichy-620 002, Tamil Nadu.

General Agreement on Trade services (GATS) and Trade Related Intellectual Property Rights (TRIPS) are the latest mantra in the global economic trade. It touched almost all industries of the world including tourism industry. Tremendous increase in the movement of people in tune with global business trade did exert an impact upon tourism industry too directly or indirectly. Thus the tourism industry of all world countries passed through 2 major transitions -one in the era of globalisation of tourism trade and the other in the globalisation of business trade era. Tourism transition signifies the probable changes that the industry has undergone over the past 6 decades highlighting how the global tourist traffic and tourism industry of the world countries were, are and going to be in the broader global scenario.

In this context, Indian tourism industry did cross the 2 milestones with other countries from mere aristocratic product since 1960s to industry status in fourth V-year plan (1969-1974) to hospitality cum service industry and finally to the modern concept of INVISIBLE EXPORT INDUSTRY with foreign exchange earning potential in the VII Five year plan. Having crossed these milestones what are the changes felt by Indian tourism industry? Have the 2 major transitions impacted the Indian tourism industry? Where does it stand in the global scenario at present? How does it compare with others especially with our neighbours in tourism related parameters. These questions are of interest to researchers, academicians, professionals, policy makers, hoteliers and bureaucrats alike. Experts in the field of tourism and hotel are of view that our tourism industry's performance is sluggish and not on par with even small neighbouring countries. This paper is a small effort in analyzing Indian tourism industry in these perspective.

Objectives

The broad objectives to give proper directions to the scientific analysis to this topic are:

1. To study the transition of the Indian tourism industry over the past 60 years.

2. To know about the trends and scenario of Global Tourist Traffic (GTT).
3. To compare our position with global trends.
4. To find out the growth pattern trends of Indian Tourism Industry in terms of global tourist arrival and our expenditure pattern to know how far we forein this parameters.
5. To know about the foreign exchange earning of this industry and its role in our Balance of Payment situation and our position in this parameter in comparision with our south-east Asian neighbours.
6. To examine loopholes if our position is not on par with others and suggest remedial measures to revert the scenario and to boost it as "MAIDAS" touch industry.

Limitations

Only secondary data were used owing to time constraint in eliciting first hand data. Information from books, news papers journals, national seminar and Internet were used to give critical analysis. It has 3 parts-one dealing with tourism industry in global scenario, the other with Indian context in comparison with other countries and the third one focuses the much anticipated outcome of tourism industry i.e. its role in national economy fetching precious foreign exchange.

Global Tourism Transtion

Though tourism is as old as civilization, the emergence of global tourism is the result of rapid industrial society development of the west in the second half of the 19th century. The introduction of "HOLIDAY" concept in the west exerted another face lift. Yet it was a product of luxury till 1947 but today it is a common man's product available to every one. The real impetus of globalisation of tourism happened since 1947 with IUOTO and WTO. These enabled tourism product to be liberalized and globalised at affordable cost with voluntary membership of countries in the pursuit of international tourism promotion. With 6 decades of steady transition, it occupies next to oil industry (II) in the world interms of turnover. Global tourism as an industry cum service has had a limitless phenomenon with immense growth and development potential. Worlds' growth once predominant with agriculture sector's contribution shifted to services sector that contributes more today as it evident form the below given table.

Table 1
Contribution of Various Sectors To World Growth

Sector	*Period & Share*		
	1940s	*1970s*	*2000s*
Agriculture	70%	60%	20%
Manufacturing	20%	25%	15%
Services	10%	15%	65%

Source: International Seminar at SRC Trichy, 2006.

It is obvious that the world's growth once predominant with agriculture sector transformed to depend more on services sector today. Of the services sector, global tourism industry's share is phenomenal and tremendous equaling to 6.5% of World's GNP with 3.5 trillion U.S.$ in 1998 itself. This speaks volume about this service sector's niche position in global economy. India is not exceptional in this scenario as per the facts of RBI - the share of services sector's contribution to GDP growth has been more than 50% since 1997-1998 and 57.6% share of it in 2004-05 to our GDP was higher than in other developing countries as a growth. The below given table justifies the transition trends over the years in the GTT world wide since 1980 for select years.

Table 2 illustrates the steady, tremendous growth rate reflecting fluctuations now and then in global tourists volume since 1980s-from meagre 248.8 millions to phenomenal 697 millions in 2000 signifying lout of every 9 global population being turned out as a global tourist with a net value of 350 billion US $ in 1998 (617 millions) to 397 billion US $ in 2000 which accounted for 8% of total global export earning. It is also clear that growth rate at the rate of 5 years interval period for 1985 - 90 and 1995-2000 periods registered peak GTT with 35.97% and 31.63% respectively. With the 2000s trend, it is now hoped that

GTT growth rate would accelerate in the era of globalisation of business trade in the 2010s as many world countries have attached greater importance to tourism. Also more incentives have been extended to tourism sector by many nations. If the 2000 trend continues it is possible to achieve the same. In such a scenario, who are the globally most favoured tourist destinations. Table 3 portrays it.

Table 2
Global Tourist Traffic Since 1980s

Year	*Number of international tourist arrivals (Millions)*	*Growth Rate (At 5 Years Interval) %*
1980	284.6	–
1985	326.4	14.69
1989	435.2	–
1990	443.8	35.97
1993	476.0	–
1995	531.0	19.65
1998	617.0	–
2000	697.0	31. 63

Source: 1. Tourism by Prof M.R. Thangamani, 2002.
2. Tourism towards 21st Century by Gupta, G., 1998.

Table 3
Major Tourist Destinations of the World in Global Tourism

Region	*in Millions*					
	1980	*1985*	*1989*	*1993*	*2000*	*2001*
Europe	196.0	213.8	280.4	287.5	402.5	399.7
America	53.7	58.6	80.4	102.1	128.5	120.8
East Asia & Pacific	19.9	29.4	48.7	58.3	109.2	115.2
Africa	7.0	11.4	14.2	17.4	27.2	28.4
Middle east	5.8	10.7	8.4	7.2	23.2	22.7
South Asia	2.2	2.5	3.1	3.5	6.1	5.8
Total	284.6	326.4	435.2	476.0	696.7	692.6

Source: WTO web www.world-tourism.org.
Tourism towards 21st Century by Gupta, G., 1998.
Tourism by Prof. M.R. Thangamani, 2002.

It is clear that GTT in volume has undergone fluctuation since 1980. Among major destinations, 1980 had been confined to Europe as a tourist destination leader with as high as 69% of the total volume. America stood in second place with 17% while others shared 12% of the GTT volume. But 2 decades of time changed the global tourism scenario totally. That is in 2001 Europe retained its I position volume wise (2 times) but registered growth decline in total percentage share-57.7%. America registered declining trend in 2001 percentage share wise. Africa, Middle -East and South-Asia witnessed slight increase in growth rate from 1980-2001. It is East-Asia and Pacific that witnessed 5.5 times jumb in volume from 19.9 millions in 1980 to 115.2 millions in 2001. Its growth rate is tremendous from 7% in 1980 to 16.6% in 2003. Thus both volume wise and percentage growth rate wise it is East--Asia and Pacific which reaped good harvest from GTT compared to others and the most revealing fact is that East-Asia emerged as most favoured global tourist destinations as early as 1982 and today they are the global tourism hub. (P. No. 41). It is also evident that on the whole there is decline in GTT in 2001 compared to 2000 in spite of greater movement of people in the wake of globalisation of business trade. Table 4 presents South-Asia's Tourist trade as early as 1982 and comparison of India with them for 1982, 1995 and 2003.

Table 4
Global Tourist Arrivals to South-east Asian Countries in Comparison with India-1982

South-east Asian Countires	*Global tourist arrivals (in Millions)*	*No. of global tourists to each country (285 Million as GTT)*
Singapore	2.96	1 in 96
Hong kong	2.61	1 in 109
Thailand	2.12	1 in 134
Malaysia	2.09	1 in 136
Philippines	1.15	1 in 248
Korea	1.15	1 in 248
Japan	1.06	1 in 268
Indonesia	0.59	1 in 483
India (1982)	0.87	1 in 328
India (1995)	2.12 (531 GTT)	1 in 250
India (2003)	2.80 (697 GTT)	1 in 250

Source: WTO report from Panorama of Tourism in India, 1996.

WTO's data for 1982 GTT to South-East Asia is testimony to the fact that since 1980 South Asia started a phenomenal growth rate in global tourist traffic to come to I position in volume growth in 1993. (Table 3). Countries like Singapore, Hongkong, Thailand, Malaysia, Philippines and Japan crossed a million mark as early as 1982. Countries which were far less in terms of tourist attractions to offer than India crossed 2 million mark of global tourists volume in 1982 when India stood at abysmally lower position. Singapore, Hong kong, Thailand and Malaysia received 1 out of 96, 109, 134 and 136 global tourists to their countries while India attracted just I out of 328 global tourists in 1982 out of global volume i.e. they received 3 times grater than India in total.

Another fact is that India touched 2 million mark global tourists arrival only in 1995. Thus we compare unfavourably with them even in 2003 with their 1982 figures signifying we lag behind our small neighbours in tourism promotion activities. It is a serious concern for a perrineal tourist paradise of the west since time immemorial.

Tourism earning of few South Asian countries for the year 1998-99 in comparison with Indian situation is yet another view of looking at our stand in the international arena and is depicted in table 5.

Table 5
Tourism Earning-Select South-east Asian Countries and India 1998-99

Countries	*Tourist Earning (1998-99)*		
	In US $ (Billions)	*In Indian Value (in Crores)*	*Comparision of India with others in Volume*
China	12.1	54,450	4.0
Hong Kong	10.8	48,600	3.6
Thailand	8.7	39,150	2.9
Singapore	7.9	35,550	2.6
India	3.0	13,500	1.0

Source: Prof M.R Thangamani's Tourism, 2002.

India's earning in terms of foreign exchange from international tourism is insignificant compared to neighbouring

South Asian Countries in 1998-99. Our earnings in 1998-99 was 4, 3.6, 2.9 and 2.6 times lower than China, Hong Kong, Thailand and Singapore respectively. That is they are exploiting global tourism to reap maximum out of it. Thailand much far less to offer in terms of tourist attractions reaped almost 3 times higher revenue than India. In the opinion of Aiyar, P. (2006) China's fear turned out to be "China fever" interms of its global high jacking growth- "the Chinese have also emerged as the largest tourist group in the region bringing with them an image of a richer, more confident, and more influential country than just a few years ago" holds apt testimony here. No wonder China is global tourist leader today in this part of the continent. Among the South Asian countries, China is the Tourism Leader with 5 crores global tourist arrival today with whom we cannot compare our share of 3.2 millions in 2004. God's own country has all to satisfy global tourists. Yet why our position is not significant in the global scenario? The need of the hour is an urgent plunge into it to trace out our short comings.

It is all the more explicit from WTO's Asia-Pacific region-2003 global tourist arrivals report of select countries that our share is not satisfactory in this region of the world as seen in Table 6.

Table 6
Global Tourist Arrivals-Asia Pacific Region-2003

Country	*Global Tourist Share %*	*Comparison of India With Others*
Hong Kong	13.0%	5.6
Thailand	8.5%	4.3
Singapore	4.8%	2.1
India	2.3%	1.0

Source: WTO Report.

India's share in international tourist traffic remained unsatisfactory since globalisation of tourism trade to globalisation of business trade in terms of volume growth though there is steady growth in the country's global tourist growth rate (Refer table 10). Our share is 5.6, 4.3 and 2.1 times lower than the above mentioned 3 countries even in 2003 interms of % growth rate. As seen already our share in comparison with our South Asian neighbours has been unsatisfactory since 1982 (Refer Table 5).

Tourism Transition in India Since 1947

India has been a land of Kaleidoscopic, perrenial tourist paradise since ages. "INCREDIBLE", God's own country has something to offer to everyone-beautiful, ancient monuments, historical sites, ages old architectural temples, exotic hill stations, long coastal stretch with exclusive beach resorts, herbal resorts, colourful people, beat and rhythm of its folk, folk arts, colourful dances, grandeur of snow cladded mountain tops, the quiet back waters of Kerala, to top these the world renowned rich cultural heritage . . . . . the list is endless. In toto, India possesses all those to be a perrenial tourist paradise especially to the west. This image has always had the power to lure the prospective tourists to explore our incredible India. In this regard our tourism industry has much to exploit tourist destinations to reap the benefits.

Tourism a post independent industry started its journey of transition since 1947 through many committies, boards, councils, organizations and policies. It had a very long journey through the routes of-Sargent committee of 1946 to the latest Tourism Convention 2000 and from that born New Tourism policy of India-2000 in the pursuit of elevating tourism industry to enjoy, the 'MAIDAS' touch potential of foreign exchange earning. The findings of almost over 100 committies are universal: India's global tourist traffic share is very meagre compared to other developing nations inadequate infrastructure facilities - roads, accommodation, transport; lack of financial support for tourism development activities and inadequate tourism marketing strategies. There are also voices echoying about the step motherly treatment inspite of its niche position in foreign exchange earning and the resultant role in our Balance of Payment (BOP) situation. Experts are of opinion that Indian tourism industry never receives treatment on par with other services industries. The fourth coming part focuses tourism industry of India in global perspective.

Indian Tourism in Global Perspective

Colonial hangover, then the sociolist wave that gripped the action in its post independence era, priority to most vulnerable sector coupled with inadequate policies failed to place India in the high tourism growth trajectory. Notably several ASEAN countries like China, Singapore, Thailand, Hong Kong, Malaysia and Korea that were once at par or below Indian life styles have surpassed India many years ahead in reaping the high growth trajectories of tourism industry. This happened in those countries by brining tourism policies to the forefront of national policies and thus reaped the potentials out of it as is evident from the facts already discussed (Refer Table 5 and 6). On the contrary when the term ASIA is used in terms of tourism related economic circles, our position is unsatisfactory. This industry despite being one of the largest earner of precious foreign exchange not by exporting services unlike others but by bringing global tourists to Indian subcontinent and selling our tourist attractions and hotels, it had been neglected by successive 5 year plans of India in giving it the much needed face lift. Table 7 projects the share of allocation to tourism promotion over the 10 successive 5 year plans.

Table 7
Indian 5 Year Plans and Tourism Allocation

Plan	*Years*	*Allocation for Tourism (in crores)*
I	1951-56	NIL
II	1956-61	3.36
III	1961-66	8.00
IV	1969-74	46.48
	(Industry Status)	
V	1974-79	73.90
VI	1980-85	229.46
VII	1985-90	336.06
	(Invisible Export Industry)	
VIII	1992-97	272.00
IX	1997-2002	472.00
X	2002-07	2500.00

Source: Prof. M.R. Thangamani's Tourism, 2002.

Realising the significance of development of tourism in national economy, especially in earning foreign exchange which increased from Rs. 2100 crores worth in 1988 to Rs. 13,041 crores worth in 1999 to phenomenal Rs. 18,883 crores worth in 2004. Govt. of India increased its allocation for tourism promotion accordingly as is evident from the above table. Tourism allocation touched Rs. 2,500 crores in the 10th 5 year plan period. In addition to that, private sector in hotel, restaurant, entertainment sectors also incurred a huge amount of investment. Yet the investment looks meagre when compared to South Asian countries like Singapore and Thailand as seen in the table 8

Table 8
Tourism Expenditure of India with Select Countries for 1997

Countries	*Tourism Expenditure (1997)*	*Comparison of India with others*
Singapore	88.0 millions US $	3.2
Thailand	51.1 millions US $	1.9
India	27.5 millions US $	1.0

Source: Secondary.

It is obvious from the above table that our tourism expenditure is not on par with our neighbours. Even small Thailand spends DOUBLE our expenditure. This must be the reason for India lagging behind South Asian neighbours in parameters like international tourist traffic share and foreign exchange earning. The below given Table depicts GTT to India.

Table 9 gives trends in foreign tourist arrival to India during globalisation of tourism trade era (1947-1994) and globalisation of business trade era (since 1995). India has registered an erratic trends during both eras. But the notworthy point is that during globalisation of Tourism trade era growth rate touched a peak of 29.03% and 26.16% in 1986 and 1991 respectively with declaine in growth rate during 1984, 1990 and 1993. Yet it registered an aggregate growth rate of 6.7% per annum. On the other side GTT to India after globalisation of business trade regime never crossed a growth rate of 16.67% (2003) with declaining trends in 1998, 2001 and 2002 with an average growth

Table 9
GTT to India -duringglobalisation of Tourism Trade and Globalisation of Business Trade

Year	*Globalisation of Tourism Trade Era*		*Year*	*Globalisation of Business Trade Era*	
	(in Lakhs)	*Growth Rate (%)*		*(in Lakhs)*	*Growth Rate (%)*
1980	8.00	-	1995	21.24	-
1981	8.53	6.62	1996	22.88	7.72
1982	8.60	0.82	1997	23.74	3.76
1983	8.85	2.90	1998	23.59	-0.64
1984	8.36	-5.54	1999	24.72	4.79
1985	8.37	0.12	2000	26.41	6.84
1986	10.80	29.03	2001	25.00	-5.34
1987	11. 64	7.78	2002	24.00	-4.00
1988	12.40	6.53	2003	28.00	16.67
1989	13.37	7.82	2004	32.00	14.29
1990	13.30	-0.55	2005 (P) upto June	18.08	-
1991	16.78	26.16			
1992	18.68	11.32			
1993	17.65	-5.52			
1994	18.86	6.86			
	Average	6.72	Average		4.9

Source: Annual Report, Ministry of Tourism, Govt. of India, 2000.
RBI Bulletin, Sept. 2005, Annual Report - 2004-05.

rate of 4.9% per year only. As per internet the provision figure of GTT for 2005 upto June registered 18.08 millions with an average aggregate of 3.01 millions per month. Had the same trend continued throughout the year of 2005, it must have registered only 36.12 millions with a rough yearly aggregate of 11.25% only. It is clear GTT to India was significant during Tourism trade globalisation era then during the present globalisation regime. Had the scenario of the former era trend continued, India could have been in a better position. It is a worrying fact, for with increased movement of people in the 21st century our trend is not satisfactory in this regard. The fourth coming table 10 depicts India's global tourist arrival at hand and our share in global tourist traffic as well as our

Table 10
Global Tourist Traffic, India's Global Tourist Arrivals, Its Share in Global Tourist Traffic and Comparison with Select South Asian Countries

Year	*Global Tourist Traffic*	*Global Tourist Arrivals India and its Share in GTT*		*Comparison of India with Asian countries (at 285 as GTT-1982)*			*India & Asian countries tourist earning in 1998-99*
	(in millions)	*(in millions)*	*% share*		*in million*	*(% share in GTT)*	
1980	284.6	0.80	0.28	-		-	
				1982:			
				Singapore	2.96	1.04	
				Hongkong	2.61	0.92	
1985	326.4	0.84	0.26	Thailand	2.12	0.74	
				Malaysia	2.09	0.73	
				Korea	1.15	0.40	
				Philipines	1.15	0.40	
				India	0.86	0.30	
1989	435.2	1.74	0.40				
1990	443.8	1.71	0.39	-		-	
1993	476.0	1.76	0.37	-		-	
1995	531.0	2.12	0.40	-		-	
							China-12.1 US $ billion
							Hong Kong-10.8 "
1998	617.0	2.36	0.39	-		-	Thailand-8.7 "
							Singapore-7.9 "
2000	699.0 (1 out of 9 as global tourist)	2.64 (1 out of 265 GT to India	0.38				India 3.0 "

Year	*Global Tourist Traffic*	*Global Tourist to Arrivals India and its Share in GTT*		*Comparison of India with Asian countries (at 285 as GTT-1982)*		*India & Asian countries tourist earning in 1998-99*
	(in millions)	*(in millions)*	*% share*	*in million*	*(% share in GTT)*	
2001	-	2.50	-	-	-	-
2002	-	2.40	-	-	-	-
2003	-	2.80	-	-	-	-
2004	-	3.20	-	-	-	-

Source: Annual Reports, M of T, Govt. of India - 2000.
RBI Bulletin, Sept., 2005.

comparison with select South Asian neighbours in these parameters for select years.

Master table 10 exhibits India's global tourist arrivals since 1980 at one side and its share in GTT and its comparison with select Asian countries in GTT share and tourist earning for select year at the other hand. It is obvious that India registered a steady growth in GTT arrival since 1980 from mere 0.8 to 3.2 millions in 2004. If seen in numeral volume it looks encouraging especially since 1986 with appreciable rise in volume of global tourists by crossing a million. But if analysed critically it took 20 years of period for India to touch 3 million mark.

The data is also an eye opener for Indians to view and think globally and criticaliy. "THINK GLOBALLY-ACT LOCALLY" holds good in this context. Though there is a steady growth rate in volume of global tourists arrival to India, its share in GTT has been of insignificant nature. It never crossed 0.40% (1989 & 1995) with lowest figure of 0.26% (1985). Infact there is dip in our GTT share in the globalisation of business trade era i.e. 0.38% in 2000. It is understood that lout of 9 global population turned out to be global tourist in 2000 and of that global tourists of 699 million, India received lout of 265 global tourists only to India in 2000 speaks volume about our laps in global tourism promotion.

At the other side, we compare poorly with select South-East Asian Countries in both parameters of GTT share and tourism earning. For e.g. In 1982 we were not even on par with Philippines and Korea, the smallest island and country respectively. Tiny neighbours Singapore, Hong Kong, Thailand and Malaysia registered 3.46, 3.1, 2.5 and 42.5 times higher than India in GTT in that year. Our growth rate is negligible and compares more unfavourably with other South-East Asian countries who enjoy 25-30% annual growth rate which are far less in tourist attractions than India.

In terms of foreign exchange earning again we are far behind our South-East Asian neighbours as is evident from the table content. All the South-East Asian Countries depicted in the table earned 2.6 to 4 times higher foreign exchange earning compared to India in 1998-99. It reveals the fact that we lag far behind our South Asian counterparts in all tourism related parameters. This shows our insignificant position in this part of the continent.

These information reveals the hidden fact that neither globalisation of tourism trade over the last 6 decades nor globalisation of business trade over the past 10 years exerted much expected impact upon Indian tourism industry unlike they did in South Asian countries.

It is pertinent to point out here the research findings of World Tourism Council (WTC) and Oxford Economic Research Forum-2000 (OERF) that global tourist traffic to India is not satisfactory. Our share in GTT is just 0.41% only.

India's Outbound Tourism Scenario

A country's In-Bound Tourism (IBT) with Out-Bound Tourism (OBT) is important to strike a BALANCE or at least BREAK-EVEN. This is highly important especially for developing countries with deficit Balance of Payment (BOP), for higher OBT compared to IBT would increase the global tourism payments, than receipts. A comparison of India's both scenario is presented in Table 11 to findout our position in this yard stick.

Table 11
India's Outbound Tourism in Comparison with Inbound Tourism Traffic

Year	*IBTT (Arrival)*		*OBTT (Departure)*		*Comparison of IBTT to OBTT Growth Rate (%)*
	in million	*Growth rate (%)*	*in million*	*Growth Rate (%)*	
1992	1.9	-	2.2	-	-
2001	2.5	-	4.6	-	+84.0
2002	2.4	-4.0	4.9	6.5	+104.2
2003	2.8	16.6	5.4	10.2	+92.9
2004	3.4	14.29	6.2	14.8	+82.4
	Average	8.96		10.5	90.8

Source: RBI Bulletin 8, Sept. 2005.

It is obvious that India's OBTT registered a steady upward growth rate during the 4 years under study with highest volume 6.2 million in 2004. On the other side our IBTT recorded negative growth rate in 2002 (-4.0%) and there is also decline in growth rate in 2004 (14.29%) compared to previous year (16.66%). It is to be noted that our OBTT crossed 6 million mark while our OBTT touched only 3 million mark in 2004. At the otherside if we look at it, India's OBT traffic registered double the rate of growth compared to IBTT in the globalised business trade era-5.4 and 2.8 millions in 2003 respectively. Also globalisation of business trade era's OBT traffic surpassed the era of globalisation of tourism trade over 2.5 times-5.4 and 2.2 millions in 2003 and 1992 respectively. But similar trend was not reflected in the OBTT-2.8 and 1.9 millions in 2003 and 1992 respectively. In other words the average percentage growth rate of IBTT to OBTT is roughly around 50% only for all the years under study.

There are claims that our travel payments acquired a distinct buoyancy during 2003 and 2004 owing to increase in business travel in the globalisation of business trade which accounted for 60% of our travel payments. OBT for leisure accounted for just 21%. If so the corresponding transition should have reflected in our IBT traffic also in tune with the same concept either on par with or above that figure. But it happened the other way.

The findings of WTC and OERF - 2000 hold apt here too! (Refer table 9). It is to be pointed out that among world countries, expenditure on tourism is growing High among Indians. This must be true, for, through domestic tourism India earned Rs. 76,610 crores in 2000 through 172.2 millions domestic tourists. Another noteworthy point as per Aiyar, P. (2006) is that according to the China's National Tourism Administration, in 2004 China had 3.91akh visitors from India, up 44% from 2003 the largest increase from any country. Table 11a depicts average expenditure per visit of in bound tourist and out bound tourist as a comparison.

It is obvious that India's average expenditure per visit through OBTT is less when compared to world average. But if we calculate it interms of number of departure and arrival the payment is 50% greater than receipts i.e. for 6.2 millions of OBTT it works out to be 5336 million US$ while for 3.4 million of IBTT it is just 3036 millions US$. It goes well with the recent RBI's

(2006) official statement that "India maintains the pace of growth in travel earnings but invisible payments reflected more continuing pace to out bound tourist traffic from India. Thus the contents of table 11 and 11a are striking testimony to our hike in OBT traffic. This scenario is of disturbing nature especially for a developing country and it would have deleterious impact on our BOP situation.

Table 11a
Average Expenditure Per Visit–IBTS & OBTS for 2004

Particulars	*Average Expenditure/ Visit (US $)*
India	855.19
World Average	901.66

Source: Internet World Tourism statistics.

Indian Tourism Industry's Foreign Exchange Earning and Role in Balance of Trade and Balance of Payment

Experts world wide including our president Abdul Kalam, A.B.J. have been of opinion that the best way to use modem tourism is to exploit its foreign exchange earning to boost over all national economy of a country. This is especially significant for developing countries. Realising the efficacy of this fact, many developing nations especially South-East Asian countries started aggressively investing in tourism promotion activities and elevated their economy to sky-high. (Refer P. No. 45). India too enjoys it but to what extent? The forthcoming section is an attempt in that direction.

Export-Import Significance

A country's exports to global countries are either VISIBLE EXPORT (VE) of goods or INVISBILE EXPORT (IVE) of services. All services such as TOURISM, transport, banking, insurance, investment income, software services fall under the IVE category and the amount earned are treated as IVE receipts. Same way amount paid for such services are treated as IVI payments. As per IMF's Balance of Payment statistics year book 2002 India enjoyed as the largest services exporter in the world in 2002 led by rapid rise in business and professional services, travel and software services. Of these services export receipt, TOURISM SERVICES' foreign exchange earning is unique and is seen in the forth coming analysis part. The below given table depicts India's total services export position in the globalised era over the years.

Table 12
India's Export Services

Year	*Amount (US $ Millions)*
1970-71	292
1980-81	2804
1990-91	2551
2000-01	16,268
2003-04	24,949
2004-05	51,326

Source: RBI Bulletin, Sept. 2005.

It is obvious that India's services exports receipt is on a steady transition especially in the globalisation of business trade era. Upto 1990-91 it was 2551 US $ million but a figure of 16, 268 US $ million and upward trend since 2000-01. Of the services sector, Hotels and Tourism-TWIN SISTER INDUSTRIES' not only improved due to recovery in tourism but also contributed maximum towards Indian economy interms of foreign exchange earning inspite of our unfavourable and meagre GTT arrivals and our share in GTT as seen in the foregone analysis. (Refer P. No. 50). Yet its role towards Indian economy is significant inspite of step motherly treatment as depicted in the table 13.

Among the services sector, tourism (travel) and hotel industries are in a niche position today especially in the globalisation of business era (to cater to global business traders cum business tourists) in their contribution to Indian economy especially through foreign exchange earning as seen from the above table data. The modem day concept of tourism is confined to foreign exchange earning and its role in Balance of Trade (BOT), Balance of Payment (BOP) and so on. Table: 14 portrays

India's foreign exchange earning through tourism industry over the select years.

Table 13
Sub Sectoral Performance of the Services Sector in the Globalisation Era of India

	Sub Sector	*Growth Rate*		*Share in GDP*	
		2003-04	*20004-05*	*2003-04*	*2004-05*
1.	Trade, Hotels, Transport, and Communication	11. 80%	11.40%	45.00%	46.30%
2.	Financing, Insurance, real estate, Business Services	7.10%	7.10%	22.70%	22.40
3.	Community, Social and Personal Services	5.80%	5.90%	23.00%	22.40%
4.	Construction	7.00%	5.20%	9.20%	8.90%
	Services Total	100.00	100.00	100.00	100.00

Source: RBI Bulletin, Sept. 2005.

Table 14
Foreign Exchange Earning of Indian Tourism Industry

Year	*Globalisation of Tourism Trade Era*		*Year*	*Globalisation of Business Trade Era*	
	(in crores)	*Growth Rate (%)*		*(in crores)*	*Growth Rate (%)*
1988	2100.00	-	1995	8,633.30	-
1989	2298.20	9.44	1996	9,919.96	14.90
1990	2661. 77	15.82.	1997	10,725.64	8.12
1991	4110.50	54.43	1998	11,540.25	7.59
1992	5886.95	43.21	1999	13,041.00	13.00
1993	6,465.72	9.83	2000	-	-
1994	7,281.66	12.62	2001	16,064.00	-
			2002	14,975.00	6.78
			2003	15,991.00	6.78
			2004	18,883.00	18.09
	Average	24.23		Average	8.81

Source: 1. Annual Report, M. of Tourism, Govt. of India, 2000.
2. Tourism by M.R. Thangamani, 2002.

It is obvious and clear that during globalisation of Tourism Trade era our foreign exchange earning from Tourism industry recorded only upward growth rate with highest trend in 1991 (54.43%) and on an average the growth rate stood at 24.23% per annuam which is a satisfactory growth trend. On the other hand during the globalisation of business trade era our foreign exchange earning registered erratic trends with negative trend in 2002 (-6.78%) and also never crossed a growth rate of 18% (2004). The aggregate growth rate per year stood at 8.81%. Thus it is to be pointed out that our foreign exchange earning was significant during tourism globalisation era. Similar trend was also reflected in our GTT scenario (Refer Table 9). Had the former trend continued our position could have been significant today. If we compare this figure with the target goal of Rs. 20,000 crores wroth of foreign exchange to be earned by 2000-02 as fixed by Ministry of Tourism, Govt. of India, one can know our ills in global tourism marketing and promotion. We could not achieve that target even in 2004. It must be due to the fact that though there is steady upward trend in GTT to India and resultant rise in foreign exchange earning, it is very negligible for a big democracy like India. The facts highlighted as per WTC and OERC-2000 findings and our comparison with South Asian neighbours is noteworthy to pointout here too!

If analysed in another way, if 0.40% of share in GTT could fetch us roughly Rs. 20,000 crores worth of foreign exchange, through 3.4 million foreign tourist arrival, what would be our earnings if we boost this 0.40% to atleast 1 to 1.5% if not like China's % ?. As per simple maths one can forecast foreign exchange earning worth of Rs. 60,000 Rs. 70,000 crores through 85 lakhs to 1.3 crores of foreign tourist arrival. If this is achieved as done in South Asian neighbours, India's unfavourable BOP situation, oil pool deficit - all could be managed at ease. We've a WIN-WIN STRATEGY at our disposal as per the forecast of experts in the field of tourism promotion. Why are we loosing our share in the market? Our leaders question ourselves–"Will we be global hub for small cars in the next 3 to 5 years; if so will we emulate this success story in other sectors; if every second toy and third shoe in the world are made in China, Why can't we emulate these examples" and so on. Similarly why can't we emulate the success tourism model of China which receives 1 out of every 14 global tourists in a year, where our stand is lout of every 260 global tourists to India in a year roughly?

Like Sino-Indian collaboration in software sector that is going to happen, a similar tie-up in tourism sector would substantially enhance our tourism capabilities too! It requires the attention of concerned experts to revert/reverse our unfavourable situation to "WIN-WIN OPPORTUNITY".

Role of Tourism Industry's Invisile Foreign Exchange Earning In Balance of Payment Situation

India has been confronted with unfavourable BOP situation since 1950s, for our exports though grew significantly imports has been overriding it since 1950s. Thus our BOT (Export-Import) deficit gap has been mounting till 2004. Our export registered lower % growth rate while our import registered higher % growth rate and thus the resultant deficit Balance of Trade situation upto 2004 as is evident from the below furnished table 15.

Table 15
India's Balance of Trade and Balance of Payment for the 9th & 10th 5 Year Plan Periods

Year	*Trade Balance (BOT) (Export-Import (in crores)*	*Net Invisffiles Including Tourism Earning (in crores)*	*Net Current Account (BOP) (BOT - Net Invisffiles (in crores)*
1995-96	-11,359	5,449	-5,910
1996-97	-14,815	10,196	-4,619
1997-98	-15,507	10,007	-5,500
1998-99	-13 ,246	9,208	-4038
1999-2000	-17,841	13,143	-4698
2000-01	-12,460	9,794	-2666
2001-02	-11,574	14,974	+3400
2002-03	-10,690	17,035	+6,345
2003-04	-15,454	26,015	+10,561

Source: Govt. of India, Economic Survey 2004-05 from Indian Economy By Misra, S.K & Purl, V.K 2006.

It is clear from the above table that under unfavourable BOT situation and the resultant BOP, the crusadar in such a situation is our services sector export to bring in invisible foreign exchange receipts as they are added to foreign exchange earned through exports. It is also clear that the earnings from net invisibles covered a substantial part of the trade deficit with the result that the current account deficit (BOP) was reduced significantly. Invisibles covered 73.7% trade deficit (BOT) in 1999-2000 and 82.0% in 2000-01. Earnings from invisibles exceeded the deficit on trade account (BOT) in 2001-04 resulting in favourable BOP situation in those years, e.g. In 2003-04, BOT was-Rs. 15, 454 crores, Net invisibles Rs. 26,015 crores and thus favourable current account (BOP) of Rs. +10,561 crores.

Other Options for BOP Deficit Management

- Offering incentives to export of goods/services.
- Finding out import substitutes for our people to be self-reliant to reduce imports.
- Reducing our currency's value to compete in the global trade.
- Repaying our foreign debt as foreign exchange or gold. For this we should have enough foreign exchange reserve and gold reserve.

Already export of goods enjoy considerable incentives. Hence the best alternative under these difficult situations is tourism. Experts are of opinion that of the services invisible export, the best option is TOURISM! TOURISM! TOURISM! only. That is more valuable invisible earnings can be had from tourism services by selling our hotels and tourist product services and thus by exploiting these TWIN-SISTER industries we can bring in more global tourists in crores and augment more foreign exchange to significantly improve our BOP. This is the mantra that worked out in South Asian neighbour countries. Let us also emulate that mantra. This requires our tourism policy to be one with national policy.

High Lights

To sum up, it is understood that our tourism industry in a nutshell projects.

- Of the phenomenal growth spurt rate of GTT touching 699 million in 2000, a figure of lout of every 9 world population turned out to be a global tourist, but India's share stood comparatively static with 0.28% in 1980 to 0.38% in 2000 representing lout of 265 global tourist only having visited India in 2000.

- India compares poorly with South-East Asian neighbours in all tourism related parameters. For ego: The GTT of India in 1993 (2.12 million) was the target reach of Singapore (2.96 million), Hong Kong (2.61 million) Thailand (2.12 million) and Malaysia (2.09 million) as early as 1982. We reached Singapore's 2.96 million target reach only in 2003. It depicts that we lag behind our South-East Asian neighbour far below in international tourist traffic promotion.
- India's OBTT's transition was phenomenal with 3 times jumb from 2.2 million in 1992 to 6.4 million in 2004. On the contrary our IBTT registered just 1.75 times jumb from 1.9 million in 1992 to 3.4 million in 2004. On an average for all the five years of study the percentage of IBTT to OBTT was roughly 50% only.
- Our foreign exchange earning from tourism industry though registered upward growth trend, is not satisfactory when compared to tiny South Asian neighbours leave alone bigger China. Our earning was 3 billion US $ in 1998-99 while that of China, Hong Kong, Thailand and Singapore were 12.1, 10.8, 8.7 and 7.9 US $ billion for the same period.
- Our tourism expenditure is also not satisfactory. It touched Rs. 2900 crores in 10th 5 year plan period. Where as Singapore and Thailand spent 88.0 and 51.1 millions US $ respectively in 1997 while our figure was 27.5 million US $ for that year.

What does these perturbing information and facts depict? It reveals that our tourism promotion is not on par with world countries, we lag behind others and our perrenial tourist attractions have not fully reached the world population due to loopholes in our marketing strategies. All these facts and figures highlight the crux of the need of the hour–"We need to have interventions both from "DEMAND SIDE and "SUPPLY SIDE in order to achieve higher level of GTT volume to India" to boost our invisible exchange earning.

What Is the Need of the Hour?

Although India's tourist products are highly competitive in quality, yet the industry's growth is malnourished and stunted and thus failed to achieve the most. It is a multi faceted potential industry and though it makes substantial contribution in the generation of employment to the tune of 21 million persons employed directly and indirectly and foreign exchange earning to the tune of Rs. 20,000 crores, it has not been accorded due priority in our national plan. It never accounted for more than 1% of the total plan outlay. India has to be marketed as an important tourist destination. Therefore the Indian tourism industry needs accelerated growth strategies like.

Allocation of More Investment for Tourism Promotion

This "MAIDAS" touch industry needs to get priority on par with other services sector like communication, software etc.

Inadequate Marketing and Promotion

India does not keep pace with the aggressive promotion strategies of South Asian neighbours. Within Asian region countries like Hong Kong, Singapore, Thailand and Malaysia have achieved continuous, sustainable growth on aggressive research. A study by Batra et a1 (1998) with 200 domestic tourists revealed the fact that only 20% of them got motivated through advertisement, while 58% got motivated through friends and relations who can do the effective role of ambassadors of tourism promotion by targeting the potential tourists. These 2 modes could be exploited to the fullest possible to boost tourist promotion. India a paradise of cultural, heritage monuments lure more foreign tourists. As per Tiwari, A.A. et al's study (1998) on the impact of International Tourism in Buddhist sectors of Bihar revealed the fact that International Tourism is greatly seen in Buddhist sectors of Bihar due to immense attraction as tourist product and has contributed a lot to elevate the social and cultural life of local people in those tourist spots.

Rising Costs of Travel

Rising travel and hotels cost is another reason for our dwindling volume of international tourist traffic. A study by Pathania, K.S. and Thakur, Y.S. (1998) with 50:50 domestic and foreign tourists visited Himachal Pradesh revealed the fact that of the 50 global tourists 48% preferred budget class hotels. Thus we need to build more budget class hotels than star hotels.

Accommodation Incompetencies

Of the 697 million global tourists traffic of 2000, India could lure only 2.64 millions i.e. only lout of 265 global tourists. It is pertinent to point out here that as per the opinion of Indian tourism circle, due to lack of 46,000 hotel rooms in budget class in 2003, global tourists preferred Sri Lanka, Hong Kong, Malaysia, Nepal and Maldeives and not India. India's 2 and 3 star budget hotels have 84,000 rooms only and to meet the demands of 30 lakhs to 32 lakhs global tourists, the requirement is 1.30 lakh hotel rooms. In the opinion of Indian Tourism Travel Agent's Director Mr. Balpin Mayal Indian Government and Indian tourism industry have to join hands to findout amicable solutions for this problem. This opinion goes well with the findings of Pathania's study results. As per Rabindra Seth (2001) China's capital Bejing alone has 60,000 rooms where as India has 68,000 rooms on the whole. He is of concern that this capacity can hardly support 2.5 million foreign tourist annually. To achieve a modest 5 million target we would need to DOUBLE the room structure. This is all the more important to tackle the upmarket travelers would be coming to India in theglobalised scenario of larger inflows of Foreign Direct Investments in the coming years.

Quality Laps In Existing Tourist Destinations to be Averted

A study by Erasi, K. in Bangalore city with 50:50 domestic and international tourists highlighted the facts that 74% of global tourists had problem in communication; 70% were not much satisfied with the services of travel agents; dissatisfied with

Hygiene and Cleanliness in airport (40%), roads (88%), railway station (76%). Yet majority of them expressed unequivocal stand about our warm, and kind hospitality (60% and 40% respectively). On the other hand as per Batra's study (1998) with 200 domestic tourists in Punjab, 46% and 15% were dissatisfied and highly dissatisfied (total 61%) with hotel accommodation. 43% and 73% of them were dissatisfied with the quality of food offered and the quality of room services respectively. 63% opined unhappiness about inadequate entertainment facilities. Almost same opinion was elicited from domestic tourists too! If unsatisfactory for domestic tourists, how can our budget hotels be of quality one for global tourists? These facts speak our quality laps. This requires urgent attention.

Laps in Security and Safety

Erasi's study (1998) also highlighted the fact that in techno city like Bangalore 12% and 36% of global tourists studied (of 50) expressed the fear of pick pocketing and lack of safety to life and belongings. It is clear that we need to enhance quality in all tourism infrastructure facilities to bring in more global tourists. Therefore all our tourism promotion activities need urgent face lift to compete in the global scenario.

Suggestions

1. Guides with foreign language skills to avert the problem of communication for global tourists.
2. Incentives to global tourists as done by other countries to Indian to go as global tourist to other countries. For eg: of late, international travel agents like Cox and King, STOC and Thomas Cook do lot of incentive offer advertisement to trap the potential Indians to visit abroad. Similar strategies can be adopted to lure global tourists by India.
3. Constructing more budget class hotels to cater to the demands of increasing global tourist traffic.
4. Treating global tourists as "GOD SENT GUESTS" so as to make them "AMBASSADOR" of our country in influencing their friends and relatives.

5. In the words of June Prompt and Jeffery Box of UK, a waiting time of 6 years for knee replacement surgery in UK forced them to look up the Net and spotted Apollo Chennai, where a pay of $ 4,000 (Rs. 3,30,000) fetched him knee replacement surgery. With 10 days stay at sterling resort. Such is our potential in attracting global medical tourists. The cost factor in western countries is 4 times greater than Indian cost. For Eg. Heart surgery and knee replacement cost Rs. 11.5-23 lakh and 7.8-13.7 lakhs in Singapore, UK and US, respectively where as they cost simply 2-4.5 lakhs in India. This is becoming a promising field for India in the opinion of global medical tourists like Yonke Stephan of US, Ayam and Syeda Mohammed of Oman, Helen collie of Seychelles, Yan 2 heng of Beijing, Anna Elizabeth of Germany, Chryssa of Dubai, a few to quote. Therefore medical tourism tie-up with world countries would boost our country's economy. In 2004, India received 1,50,000 medical tourists and earned foreign exchange worth of Rs. 20,000 i.e. even greater than leisure and business tourism.
6. Exploiting "Wellness-health"-tourist spa destinations especially of Bangalore, Goa, Kochi, Kozhikode to the maximum which are of affordable cost compared to Western spas.
7. Somatheertham near Thiruvananthapuram gets referral from German hospitals is testimony to our pioneering role in herbal and health tourism especially for rejuvenation therapy. A lot more tie-up can be had with global countries to attract potential tourists especially those who face the heat and beat of today's hectic, tension packed life style. On the whole, India could be a medical tourism hub in 2-3 years of time with potential of attracting millions and millions of global patients. Outsourcing facilities can be included in medical tourism too.
8. Converting Chettinad mansions into Tamilnadu cultural tourism hub to attract foreign tourists. In the opinion of R. Chandramouli of one of the Chettinad mansion turned out heritage resort attracts good number of foreign tourists

especially from France, England, Germany and Italy. If Tamilnadu converts all the heritage palaces and houses into resorts, it could lure more foreign tourists as well as those 100 years old valuable symbols of India would be preserved.

9. India has tie-up with many foreign universities and the movement of international students to learn in India is on the rise of late. Many foreign universities (Eg. Swedish) offer 5 year programmes of which 18 months are allotted for undergoing training. Such students come here and study about our schools, temples, cultural and heritage sites, historical places. This can be further strengthened to bring in more "TOURING TO LEARN" potential group.
10. We could also adopt our president Dr. Abdul Kalam's suggestion in tourism promotion-modem day foreign tourists come to India to learn about our people and places they visit-a type of "CULTURAL" or "KNOWLEDGE" oriented tourism There is plenty of scope to exploit this potential group through the help of Information Technology i.e. multimedia presentations can be made available in all tourist destinations of India before they start their venture in each such Indian Tourist spots or such image glimpses including local maps can be given even as they are planning their trip to India by electronic media.
11. A nation wide survey can be undertaken simultaneously in all states under the leadership of central tourism organization as a universal programme in the interest of the nation to findout our existing loopholes in our tourism promotion efforts so as to revert the situation, for, TOURISM and TRAVEL are the world's highest growth sectors in the 21st Century especially in the wake of globalisation of business era. Let us go at it with full vigour to put INDIA on a high pedestal on the international tourism map.

Let

"Incrediable India"

"The God's Own Country"

"The Land of Variety"
"The Land of Rich Heritage"
"The Land of Unique Hospitality"

be on the top ladder of International Tourism map.

REFERENCES

Abdul Kalam, A.B.J. and Rajan, Y.S. (1998), "INDIA 2020 A Vision for the New Mellennium", Viking, New Delhi.

Aiyar, P. (2006), "China fear" to "China fever", The Hindu, 27th February.

Annual Report (2000), Ministry of Tourism, Govt. of India.

Avasthi, R. (2004), "Lack of Budget Hotels and Problems of Indian Tourism Development", The Economics Time, 8th August.

Badar, A.I. (1998), "Global Tourism: India in global Perspective", in Gupta, S. and Bansal, S.P. (Ed) Book Tourism Towards 21st Century, Deep and Deep Publications, New Delhi.

Batra, G.S. Chawla, A.S., and Mehta, A. (1998), "Perception of Customers Towards Tourism Services-A Study of Punjab Tourism Development Corporation" in Gupta, S. and Bansal, S.P. (ed.) book, Tourism Towards 21st Century, Deep and Deep Publications, New Delhi.

Batra, G.S. (1998), "Tourism Promotion in India", in Gupta, S. and Bansal, S.P. (ed.) Book, Tourism Towards 21st Century, Deep and Deep Publications, New Delhi.

Erasi, K. (1998), "Opportunities and Problems of Tourism Development in the city of Bangalore-A Study", in Gupta, S. and Bansal, S.P. (ed.) Book Tourism Towards 21st Century, Deep and Deep Publications, New Delhi.

Ghosh, B. (2002), "Return to Nature", The New Sunday Express, 26th May.

Internet-India Tourism.statistics and World Tourism.statistics.

Kavitha, B.D. (2004), "Get well soon in India" The week, October.

Pathania, K.S. and Thakur, Y.S. (1998), "Segmentation Analysis of Tourism Market-A Study of Himachal Pradesh," in Gupta, S. and Bansal, S.P. (ed.) Book Tourism Towards 21st Century, Deep and Deep Publications, New Delhi.

Rabindra Seth, (2001), "Room for Expansion", The Hindu Survey of Indian Industry.

RBI Bulletin (2005) Annual Report-2004-05, September.

RBI Bulletin (2005), "India's Invisibles", March.

Sharma, U. (1996), "Panorama of Tourism in India" Print well Jaipur.

Senapathy, S. (2004), "Add Zing to your Holiday", The Hindu, 22nd February.

Thangamani, M.R. (2002), Tourism-An Introduction, Kongu Publications, Karur, Tamil Nadu.

Tiwari, A.A. et al; (2004), "Tourism; Effects of International Tourism in Buddhist Sectors of Bihar", Paper presented at International Seminar at Pondicherry on "Emerging Trends in Global Business", PUTMA, Pondicherry, 4th September, 2004.

UGC sponsored National Seminar (2005), "Impact of Globalisation on Indian Services Industry-Problems and Prospects", S.R College, Trichy, Tamil Nadu.

WTO AGREEMENT ON AGRICULTURE (AoA) AND HORTICULTURE IN INDIA

*Prakash S. Kamble**

Introduction

Agriculture is the backbone of developing economies in general, and Indian economy in particular. As a result, agricultural development has a significant place in overall development of these economies. With regard to India's economy, even though, the contribution of Agriculture in GDP has declined considerably from 34.9% in 1990-91 to 25.9%[1] in 2001-02, the dependence of population, as a means of livelihood is significant one. Of the total Indian working population, about 61%[2] population was engaged in Agriculture in the year 1998. Agriculture is a broader production sector having many sub sectors. Horticulture, comprising of fruits, vegetables, flowers, mushroom, coconut, spices and plantation crops forms the single largest sub sector of the agriculture[3]. WTO is an international organization, which deals with each and every aspects of the global trade, has made some provisions, rules and regulations, terms and conditions regarding trade in Agriculture.

As international trade has severe repercussions on the overall development of the economy, as well as, the productive sectors such as Agriculture. The provisions, rules and regulations of the WTO affect the development of the productive sectors, as well as, trade and thereby development of the economy. The WTO Agreement on Agriculture (AoA) has, no doubt, repercussions on the trade, as well as,

* Reader, Deptt. of Economics, Shivaji University, Kolhapur,
Email: *pskamble@ sancharnet.in*

development of Indian Agriculture along with horticulture, which demands urgent analysis of the relationship between the WTO AoA and Horticulture with reference to Indian economy, which has prominent and important agriculture sector. It is against this overall background, present paper attempts to analyze the impact of the WTO AoA on the development of Agriculture in general, and more importantly Horticulture in particular, in the context of Indian economy. The paper endeavors to examine the effects of the WTO Provisions on Agriculture on the foreign trade. More particularly, Indian Agriculture export, with focus on Horticulture export, which has repercussions on the development of Horticulture, Agriculture and Indian economy.

WTO Agreement on Agriculture (AoA)

The issue of agriculture trade, except a few products, was excluded from the agreement until the Uruguay Round. The main elements of AoA relate to the three areas of policy[4]: Market Access, Domestic support, and Export subsidies. Another agreements negotiated during the Uruguay Round closely linked with the AoA are the Agreement on sanitary and phytosanitary (SPS) measures, and Agreement on Intellectual property Rights (IPRS).

Commitments under market access involves three things, (i) to replace quantitative restrictions like canalization, bans etc. on exports and imports by equivalent tariffs known as tariffication, (ii) application of Bound Tariff rates to give the protection as of the base year (1986-88) (iii) The new tariffs resulting from tariffication and the applied tariffs are committed to brought down starting since 1995. Developed countries are required to reduce tariff by 36% in 6 years, with a minimum of 15% for each commodity. While Developing countries are required to reduce tariff on the average by 24% in 10 years, with a minimum of 10% for each commodity. For products with extremely restricted trade prior to WTO, the countries were required to give minimum access opportunity commitments at lower rates equal to 3% of domestic consumption in the base period (1986-88), and to be raised to

5% by 2001 for developed countries and by 2005 for developing countries. When imports of certain commodities exceed a trigger level, WTO allows its members to apply special safeguards by imposing additional duty in excess of committed on the imports of an agricultural product. The AoA divides domestic support given to agriculture in two broad categories, (i) trade distorting called Amber box (ii) not trade distorting known as green or blue box. The amber box support is classified into two categories (a) product specific subsidies-the difference between domestic price minus international reference price, (b) non-product specific subsidies-provided for water, electricity, credit, fertilizers, pesticides, farm machinery. The Amber box support (AMS), is considered to be trade distorting and come under progressive reduction, base year being 1986-88, effective from 1995 are–Developed countries: 20% over six years, Developing countries: 13.3% over 10 years and least Developed countries: Nil. The agreement permits deminimis support of 5% each of product specific and non product specific of the value of production of individual products and total agricultural production to developed countries and up to 10% of value of produce to provide input subsidies and output price support to developing countries. The subsidies for long-term interest of maintaining natural resources, environmental protection, approving the general resource productivity use efficiency and improving the farmers incomes are included in green box and blue box. Under the AoA , the export subsidies subject to reduction commitments are (i) direct subsidies on export performance (ii) government export sales or stock disposals at prices below domestic market prices (iii) other payment on the export of an agricultural product financed by government action (including levies) (iv) subsidies on agricultural products due to their incorporation in exported markets, (v) subsidies affecting marketing and transport costs of exports. Developed countries are to reduce amount of subsidy by 36% and the quantity of subsidized export by 21% in 10 years i.e. by the year 2005 and developing countries by 24% and 14% respectively.

Sanitary and phytosanitary (SPS) measures deal with food safety, animal and plant health standards[5]. The WTO's SPS Agreement encourages member countries to use standards set by international organizations: FAO WHO for food safety, International office for epizootics for animal health and FAO secretariat of the International plant protection convention for plant health.

Agreement on Agriculture (AoA) in Post WTO Period

The response of the member countries concerning the implementation of AoA provisions helps us in revealing some implications for India. Developing countries expected big gain in terms of growth in agriculture export and access to developed countries markets. There is slight improvement in share of developing countries in total agriculture export (41.2% in 1991, 41.1% in 1995, 43.3% in 1999) in post WTO period, but this is of no real benefit, because value of agriculture export has declined by about 10% (After 1997) in the same period. Similarly, there is almost no improvement in access to developed countries market by developing countries[6].

According to Ramesh Chand, percentage of commitment actually used shows that developed countries could still significantly enhance input subsidies and price support to their Agriculture without violating their obligation to WTO. Canada, USA, Japan have notified very high level of domestic support for the base line period to protect their produce. In the case of wheat, EC has notified domestic support to the tune of Rs. 4.62/ kg. While Canada and USA notified Rs. 2/kg and Rs. 2.82 and Rs. 7 per kg of cotton and sugar. In contrast to this, domestic support for wheat, rice and cotton in India was negative in 1995. Highest green box support to agriculture is provided by USA, which spends more than one third of its GDP. Japan uses one fourth of its GDP agriculture and Canada, European countries around 13% of GDP as green box support. Among the developing countries, Brazil and Thailand provide about 3 and 7 per cent of GDP for green box support. In 1995, India used only 2.34% of GDP agriculture for green box support, most of which on public stock (food grain) holdings. Total domestic support (excluding export subsidy) exceeded 50% of the GDP in EC and Japan, while USA uses about 38% and Canada one fourth of its GDP agriculture. In India total support to Agriculture was 9% during 1995 excluding negative AMS.

Export subsidy is quite common among European countries and in North America, due to higher domestic prices than international prices. Export subsidies provided by EC members constituted over 50% of the export price earned by them for the export price earned by them for butter and butter oil, and over 20% in the case of skimmed milk powder in 1998, and 50% of export price by the USA[7]. Thus, export subsidy provided by developed countries like North America and members of EC are so high, that they cause serious trade distortions. The WTO classification of agriculture support favours developed countries, particularly, EC, USA, Canada and Japan, which are able to maintain very high level of support to agriculture in exempt category. The level of non-exempt subsidies in developed countries remains awfully high even after meeting reduction commitments. Compared to developed countries the level of support in developing countries like India is so low that, level playing field in agriculture trade is a far cry. In recent years (2000-01 budget) the finance minister in a bid to control the fiscal deficit, targeted the budgetary outlays on subsidies, food and fertilizer subsidy, being the most important in India. The expenditure of the central government in India on subsidies declined from 1.88% of GDP in 1991-92 to 1.56% in 2002-03 (1.32% 1991-92 to 2000-01), and state governments remained at 5.7% of GDP on an average during 1990-2000 on social sector, in which subsidies is one of the major items[8].

Post WTO Trends in Agriculture Trade

Trade is an effective means of economic development. As a result, the efforts are being made more or less by each and every country in the world to promote international trade, particularly exports It will be useful to examine the trends in Agriculture trade in the post WTO period and with reference to the world economy in general, and Indian economy in particular, which has implications for development of Horticulture in India.

(a) WTO and Global Trade (Agriculture Export)

The global scenario of agriculture export in the post WTO period is presented in Table 1.

Table 1
WTO And Global Trade (Agri. Export)
Base 1990 = 100

Year	*Agriculture export*			*Manufactured export*		
	Value	*Price*	*Quantity*	*Value*	*Price*	*Quantity*
1	2	3	4	5	6	7
1990	100	100	100	100	100	100
1991	101	98	103	103	100	104
1992	108	99	109	112	103	109
1993	104	94	111	111	99	112
1994	119	99	120	128	102	126
1995	139	111	126	152	111	137
1996	143	109	131	159	109	146
1997	142	103	139	167	102	163
1998	135	97	139	169	99	172
1999	131	92	143	175	96	182
CGR (1991-95) in %	6.61	2.51	4.13	8.09	2.09	5.63
CGR (1995-99) in %	-1.19	-3.70	2.56	2.89	-2.85	5.87

Source: International Trade Statistics 2000, WTO Geneva, 2000.

Table 1 adequately shows that, in the total world export, the growth in manufacture export was significantly higher than the agriculture export. In the pre as well as post WTO period, the growth in manufacture export in terms of value and quantity was positive and significant. But, the agriculture export remained significant in both the terms and also positive in only pre WTO period. Agriculture export growth was negative in value and price terms and only marginal growth in quantity terms in the post WTO period. This reveals that, the WTO AOA has not succeeded in promoting agriculture export of the world economy as a whole.

(b) *WTO and Agriculture Export of India in Comparison With Developed and Developing Countries*

The place of India's agriculture export in the world export, as well as, Agriculture export of developed and developing countries shows capacities and potentialities of Indian agriculture export in comparison with these categories of countries in the world economy. The data in Table 2 show necessary information.

Table 2
WTO and Agriculture Export of Developed & Developing Countries and India (in Billion US $)

Year	*World total*	*Developing countries*	*Developed countries*	*India*	*India's share in world agri. export %*
1	2	3	4	5	6
1991	211	87	124	3.20	1.51
1992	226	89	137	3.03	1.34
1993	224	89	135	4.15	1.85
1994	258	107	151	4.37	1.69
1995	297	122	175	6.32	2.13
1996	324	134	190	6.83	2.11
1997	331	139	192	6.84	2.07
1998	306	133	173	6.21	2.03
1999	289	125	164	5.67	1.96
CGR (1991-95) in %	7.05	7.00	7.15	14.55	7.15
CGR (1995-99) in%	-0.55	0.46	-1.32	-2.14	-1.64

Source: Agricultural Trade performance by Developing Countries 1991-99 Background paper G/AG/NG/S/6/Rev.1, WTO, Geneva.

It is revealed form Table 2, the agriculture export growth of the world economy was considerable in the pre WTO period and negative in the post WTO period. This proves that, the WTO AoA is not so much conducive for the growth of agriculture export. More or less, the in Agriculture of developed and developing countries were same in the pre WTO period. But, in the post WTO period the growth in agriculture export of developing countries was only marginal, and it was negative for the developed countries, which can be considered as the failure of the WTO AoA in promoting agriculture trade with regard to India, even though, the share of India's agriculture export in world agriculture export was remarkably lower, its growth in value as well as relative terms was attractive in the pre WTO period. But, it remained so much gloomy in the post WTO period is an indicator of severe adverse effects of the WTO AoA on Indian Agriculture with reference to exports.

(c) Post WTO Agriculture Trade of India

The composition of India's foreign agriculture trade i.e. export and import may be considered as the potentialities of trade to develop agriculture, and thereby economy as a whole, as well as dependence to meet needs for agriculture commodities. This demands need for examining India's Agriculture export and import in the Pre as well as, Post WTO Period in the context of the WTO AoA.

Table 3

Post WTO Period Agriculture Trade of India (in Million US $)

Year	*Exports*	*Imports*	*Net exports*	*Total agri. trade 95% of GDP*
1	2	3	4	5
1992 - 93	3028 (5.22)	1618 (2.79)	1410	8%
1993 -94	4023 (5.69)	1317 (1.86)	2706	7.55%
1994 -95	4227 (5.20)	2544 (3.13)	1683	8.33%
1995 -96	6120 (7.37)	3001 (3.61)	3119	10 .98%
1996 -97	6868 (7.30)	2303 (2.45)	4565	9.75%
1997 -98	6634 (6.19)	2893 (3.05)	3741	10.04%
1998 -99	6033 (5.92)	4012 (3.94)	2021	9.86%
1999 -00	5615 (5.30)	4402 (4.00)	1213	9.30%
CGR(1992 -93 to1995 –96) in %.	19.19	16.74	21.96	8.20%
CGR (1995 -96 to1999 –00) In %	1.68	7.94	-17.24	-3.26%

Source: Economic survey, Ministry of Finance, GOI, Various Issues.
Note: Figures in parenthesis are percentages to GDP.

It can be said from Table 3 that, even though, the share of agriculture trade in the GDP is considerably smaller; its growth was noteworthy in the Pre WTO Period, and dismal in the Post WTO Period. Likewise, growth in India's Agriculture export was negative and import increased at rapid rate, is a symptom of fall in export competitiveness of agriculture goods, and may be considered as the bad effect of the WTO AoA. It is also proved by the growth in net Agriculture export, in the Pre and Post WTO Period.

(d) State of Horticulture Export in India's Agriculture Export

The main objective of this research paper is to assess the impact of the WTO AoA on the development of India's Agriculture in general, and Horticulture in particular, via export or international trade and thereby the development of the economy as a whole. The state of Horticulture export in India's Agriculture export, gives us an idea regarding export potentialities and competitiveness of Indian Horticulture Products. The necessary information is presented in Table below.

It is revealed from Table 4, the growth in Agriculture export was significant in the Pre WTO Period, and remarkably dismal in the Post WTO Period. But, the relative place of Horticulture export in Indian Agriculture export during the economic reform period, and more particularly in the Pre and Post WTO Period was important one (16% on an average). The Cashew (41% on an average) and spices (9%) were the major contributors in Aggregate Horticulture export. As far as growth is considered, it was positive in respect of Horticulture in the Pre as well as Post WTO Period, and lower in the Post WTO Period, which indicates smaller degree of the adverse effects of the WTO AoA. The commodity wise growth in export reveals that, Horticulture Products have registered rapid growth (37.80%) in export during the Pre WTO Period, followed by Processed Fruit & Vegetable (26.25%), spices (15.01%) and Cashew (9.58%). In the Post WTO Period, commodity wise export growth rates have declined, but more or less the same commodities have shown better performance in export.

(e) Trends in Agriculture and Horticulture Import of India

The export competitiveness and adequacy of supply, has repercussions on the import and thereby development of

Table 4

State of India's Horticulture Export in Agriculture Export (in Million US $)

Items	*1992-93*	*1993-94*	*1994-95*	*1995–96*	*1996–97*	*1997-98*	*1998-99*	*1999-00*	*2000-01*	*CGR in %* 1992–93 1995-96	*CGR in %* 1995-96 2000-01
1	2	3	4	5	6	7	8	9	10	11	
Agri.& Allied Product	3028	4023	4227	6120	6868	6634	6033	5504	6013	19.19	-0.34
Horticulture Product	547 (18.06)	702 (17.44)	792 (18.73)	888 (14.51)	974 (14.18)	1044 (15.74)	1037 (17.19)	279 (23.24)	1162 (19.32)	12.91	4.59
1. Spices	136 (24.86)	182 (25.92)	195 (24.62)	238 (26.80)	339 (34.80)	380 (36.40)	388 (37.12)	393 (30.73)	356 (30.64)	15.01	6.94
2. Cashew	257 (46.98)	333 (47.43)	369 (46.59)	370 (41.67)	362 (37.17)	377 (36.11)	387 (37.32)	566 (44.25)	412 (35.46)	9.58	1.78
3. Floriculture products	5 (0.92)	6 (0.86)	10 (1.27)	18 (2.03)	18 (1.85)	23 (2.20)	25 (2.41)	21 (1.64)	29 (2.50)	37.80	5.51 5.51
4. Fresh Fruits	–	–	60 (7.58)	69 (7.77)	69 (7.08)	75 (7.18)	63 (6.08)	66 (5.16)	84 (7.23)	7.15	3.35
5. Fresh Vegetable	108 (11.74)	132 (18.80)	79 (9.97)	89 (10.02)	94 (9.65)	84 (8.05)	65 (6.27)	82 (6.41)	100 (8.60)	-4.72	1.97
6. Processed Fruit & Vegetable	41 (7.50)	49 (6.99)	79 (9.97)	104 (11.71)	92 (9.45)	105 (10.06)	109 (10.50)	151 (11.81)	181 (15.57)	26.25	9.64

Source: Same as of Table 3.

Notes: (i) Figures in round brackets are percentages to Total Agri. And Allied product exports.

(ii) Figures in square brackets indicate % share in Total Horticulture exports.

Agriculture as well as, of the country like India, in the context of foreign currency reserves and their proper utilization. On this background, it becomes inevitable to examine the trends in Agriculture, as well as, Horticulture import of India, with reference to the Pre and Post WTO Period, so as to catch the impact of the WTO AoA on Horticulture, as well as, Agriculture development.

Table 5
Trends in India's Agriculture & Horticulture Import
(in Million US $)

Year	*Total Agriculture*	*Total Horticulture*	*Cashew Nut*	*Vegetable Oils*	*Fruit & Nut*
1	2	3	4	5	6
1991-92	1256	250 (19.90)	108 (43.20)	101 (40.40)	41 (16.40)
1992-93	1618	253 (15.64)	130 (51.38)	58 (22.92)	65 (25.70)
1993-94	1317	276 (20.95)	154 (55.80)	53 (19.20)	69 (25)
1994-95	2544	519 (20.40)	220 (42.39)	199 (38.34)	100 (19.27)
1995-96	3001	1002 (33.39)	227 (22.65)	676 (67.47)	99 (9.88)
1996-97	2303	1148 (49.85)	194 (16.90)	825 (71.86)	129 (11.24)
1997-98	2893	1107 (38.27)	207 (18.70)	745 (67.30)	155 (14)
1998-99	4012	2192 (54.64)	230 (10.49)	1803 (82.25)	159 (7.26)
1999-00	4402	2256 (51.25)	276 (12.23)	1844 (81.74)	136 (6.03)
2000-01	2738	1688 (61.65)	211 (12.50)	1301 (77.07)	176 (10.43)
CGR in% (1991-92 to 1995-96)	19.06	32.00	16.03	46.21	19.29
CGR in% (1995-96 to 2000-01)	-1.52	9.10	-32.70	11.56	10.07

Source: Same As of Table 3.
Notes: 1. Figures in round brackets shows percentage shares To total Agriculture Imports.
2. Figures in square brackets are percentage to total Horticulture imports.

The data in Table 5 adequately reveals that, the share of Horticulture import in India's Agriculture import was important one (37% on an average). Besides this, the growth in Horticulture import was significantly higher in the Pre WTO Period (32%), and considerably important during the Post WTO Period (9%), should be considered as opportunities available to promote the output of Horticulture, along with due attention towards their export competitiveness. In total Horticulture import, relatively as well as growth wise, vegetable oils, Fruit & Nut, Cashew nuts have achieved important place, which indicates the promotion of their output is so much beneficial for India, on many fronts. The import of Cashew nuts has received considerable setback in the post WTO period, is a thing of welcome, and should be considered as the good efforts of India to exploit potentialities of promoting the output of Cashew nuts.

Implications for Horticulture Development and Future Course of Action.

The foregoing analysis of the WTO AoA reveals that, the various categories of financial support given to Agriculture export is unequal and discriminatory for the developing countries like India. The financial support given by the developed countries, for promoting Agriculture export is remarkably high, which is very difficult to reach for the developing countries in general, and India in particular. In the Post WTO Period, the Developed countries like European countries, USA, Canada, Japan have not implemented the provisions of the WTO AoA whole heartedly, and have created serious distortions in agriculture trade. It is very difficult for the developing countries like India to increase expenditure on agriculture support at commitment levels of the WTO. For example India is required to spend about 14% of GDP (Ramesh Chand) on necessary support to Agriculture, but the central government spends less than 2% of GDP. It is revealed that, the WTO provisions on agriculture are against and exploitative for the developing countries like India, and pro, favorable and beneficial for the developed countries. In this background also, agriculture trade of India particularly export of Horticulture products have shown a ray of optimism, which requires hard and planned efforts to exploit and properly utilise export potentialities of Horticulture products and thereby the development of agriculture as well as the economy. India could not derive the benefits of Agriculture export in the post WTO period, should be considered as an opportunity and should undertake such purposeful efforts, within the framework of the WTO AoA in future. The post WTO period, India's growth in agriculture export was negative, but, import increased at rapid rate, indicates (i) Promote output of importing commodities, and (ii) Increase export competitiveness of agriculture products, whereby, their export can be promoted. Comparatively, Horticulture has made good performance in agriculture export of India, even in the post WTO period. The commodities like cashew, spices, Horticulture products, processed vegetable & fruit have played important role in Horticulture export, which demands due attention towards the exploitation and utilization, to the maximum level possible, their potentialities and capacities would promote Horticulture export of India. The import of Horticulture products, in the pre and post WTO Period was considerable, which should be considered as golden opportunity, and due attempts should be made to achieve expected level of their output in our country, will curtail import and will be beneficial on many grounds.

It can be said that, India has an opportunity to promote Horticulture export, whereby; the development of Agriculture and economy can be achieved via trade. But rather it is difficult task, which invites multidimensional efforts on many fronts. It is the need of hour, along with other developing countries, India should endeavor to modify the provisions in the WTO AoA in favor of the developing countries in general, and India in particular, through their active participation in ministerial conference and general council meetings. The due role of the Central Government as well as State Governments is very much important by introducing and implementing a variety of measures, conducive for Horticulture as well as overall development of agriculture in India. At present, the government helps through liberalized seed and plant material import policy, separate ministry of food processing industries, National Horticulture Board (NHB), Agriculture and Processed food products Export Development Authority (APEDA), New economic policy provisions, Budgetary support for the development of Horticulture, but not sufficient, which requires increased attention. The attempts should be made to increase expenditure on expected Green and Blue box subsidies and other support. Cooperative institutions should play an increased role for the development of Horticulture, as well as, its export of exportable goods. The voluntary organizations, as well as groups, can shoulder the responsibility of increasing export, along with the development of Horticulture. The provisions of expected investment, coupled with update world market information are necessary to make. The facilities of sanitary and phyto sanitary measures, necessary education and training should be extended at grassroot and individual level to facilitate the development of Horticulture as well as promotion of exports.

Conclusion

Horticulture export has played comparatively considerable role in the development of Horticulture as well as agriculture in the post WTO period also. But, we should accept the reality that, the WTO AoA has made export, as well as, the development of Horticulture difficult through its provisions and clauses. The joint efforts on various fronts for the promotion of export can be a proper solution. The attempts on different fronts such as government i.e. central, state & local, media, Coop. Organizations, voluntary groups as well as individual levels are must, and in expected extent. The performance of this teamwork would determine the success of Horticulture, as well as, development of the economy by using the means of foreign trade i.e. export.

NOTES AND REFERENCES

1. RBI (2001-02): 'Annual Report', Reserve Bank of India, Mumbai, p. 254.
2. Misra and Puri (2001): 'Indian Economy', Himalaya Publishing House, Mumbai, p. 402.
3. M. Sudha (2001): 'Policy Reforms and Impact on Horticultural Development with reference to Fruits, Vegetables and Their Processed Products', a research paper presented in National

Seminar on "Economic Reforms and Rural Transformation" Organized by the Deptt. Of Economics, Shivaji University, Kolhapur on 6.7 Dec., 2001.

4. Chand, Ramesh (2002): 'Trade Liberalization, WTO and Indian Agriculture', Mittal Publications, New Delhi, p. 139.
5. Gupta, K.R. (2001): 'A Study of World Trade Organization', Atlantic Publishers and Distributors, New Delhi, p. 206.
6. Chand, Ramesh: above Cited, p. 86.
7. Ibid, p. 94.
8. R.B.I: Above Cited, pp. 279-282.

WORLD TRADE ORGANISATION AND INDIAN ECONOMY

*S.K. Dhage**

Introduction

The establishment of World Trade Organization is trend to towards globalization of world economy. Over the past 57 years ever since the creation of the General Agreement on Tariffs and Trade (GATT) in 1948, trade has been powerful engine for growth. After the eight rounds of trade negotiations and with the GATT Agreement 1994, the WTO was established on January 1st, 1995. By now the WTO has successfully completed its 10 years of establishment. At present 148 countries are the members of the WTO and about 40 more countries are in line for becoming the members. WTO contains various trade procedures acceptable to both developed and developing countries. In the globalised context, WTO also takes note of matters incidental and ancillary to trade and investment such as employment standards, reduction of tariffs rates, investment protection, trade and environment and trade and employment. In order to see that these provisions are effectively implemented, WTO has provisions for sanctions in case of default by members countries.

Objectives of WTO

(i) The primary objective of WTO is to implement the new world trade system as visualised in the Agreement.

(ii) To promote word trade in a manner that benefits every country.

* Reader in Economics Baburaoji Gholap College, Sangvi, Pune-411027.

(iii) To ensure the developing countries secure a better balance in the sharing of the advantages resulting from the expansion of international trade corresponding to their development needs.

(iv) To enhance competitiveness among all trading partners so as to benefit consumers and help in global integration.

(v) To increase the level of production and productivity with a view to ensuring level of employment in the world.

(vi) To expand and utilize world resources to the best.

(vii) To improve the level of living for the global population and Speedup economic development of the member nations.

On the other hand, the WTO is new international organization set up as a permanent body and designed to play the role of a watchdog in the spheres of trade in goods, trade in services, foreign investment, intellectual property rights etc.

WTO Agreement

Depending upon the major areas for negotiation in the Uruguay Round, the main WTO agreement can be divided in to the following categories:

Agreement on Agriculture

This provides a framework for the long-term reform of agricultural trade and domestic policies over the years to come, with the objective of introducing increased market orientation in agricultural trade. It provides for commitments in the area of market access, domestic support and export competition. The members have to transform their non-tariff barriers like quotas into equivalent tariff measures. The tariffs resulting from this transformation, as well as other tariffs on agricultural products are to be reduced on an average by 36 per cent in the case of developed countries and 24 per cent in the case of developing and countries. The reductions are to be undertaken over 6 years in the case of developed countries and 10 years in the case of developing countries. The least developed countries a need not make any commitment for reduction.

Agreement on Trade in Textiles and Clothing (Multi-fibre Arrangement)

This provides for phasing out the import quotas on textiles and clothing in force under the Multi-Fibre Arrangement since 1974, over a span of 10 years, i.e. by the end of the transition period on January 1, 2005.

Agreement on Market Access

The member nations will cut tariffs on industrial and farm goods by an average of 37 per cent. The USA and the European Union will cut tariff between then by one-half.

Agreement on TRIMs

The Agreement on Trade Related investment Measures (TRIMs) calls for introducing national treatment of foreign investments and removal of quantitative restrictions. It identifies 5 investment measures, which are inconsistent with the GATT provisions on according national treatment and on general elimination of qualitative restrictions. "These are measures which impose on the foreign investors the obligation to use local inputs, to produce for exports as a condition to obtain imported goods as inputs, to balance foreign exchange outgo on importing inputs with foreign exchange earnings through export, and not to export more than specified proportion of the local production." All specific measures in the above categories being applied by any member were to be notified within 90 days of the entry into force of the Agreement establishing the WTO, and they are required to be eliminated in a stipulated time period.

Agreement onTRIPs

Agreement on Trade Related Intellectual Property Rights (TRIPs) set out the minimum standards of protection to be adopted by the Parties, in respect of (i) copyrights and related rights; (ii) Trade Marks; (iii) Geographical indications; (iv)

Industrial designs; (v) Patents; (vi) Layout designs of integrated circuits; and (vii) protection of undisclosed information (trade secrets) and the enforcement of these. A transition period of five years is available to all developing countries to give effect to the provisions of the TRIPs Agreement. Countries that do not provide product patent in certain areas can delay the provisions of product patents for another five years. However, they have to provide exclusive marketing rights for products which obtain patents after January 1, 1995.

Agreement on services

For the first time, trade in services like banking, insurance, travel, maritime transportation, mobility of labour etc. has been brought within the ambit of negotiations. The GATS (General Agreement on Trade in Services) provides a multilateral framework of principles and services which should govern trade in services under conditions of transparency and progressive liberalisation. It spells out certain obligations like grant of MFN status to the other member nations a with regard to trade in services, maintenance of transparency and also a commitment for liberalisation in general terms.

Disputes Settlement Body

Settlement of disputes under GATT was a never ending process. There was ample scope for procedural delays, objections could raised at each stage of the dispute settlement process, and penal reports could be rejected by the offending party. The Disputes Settlement Body (DSB) set up under WTO seeks to plug these loopholes and thus provide security and predictability to the multilateral trading system. It has now been made mandatory to settle a dispute within 18 months. The findings of the disputes settlement panels will be final and binding on all parties concerned.

In addition to the above, the Uruguay Round also reached agreements on the understanding the implication of certain articles of GATT 1947, *viz.*, pre-shipment inspection, rules of origin, import licensing anti dumping measures and countervailing duties, safeguards, subsidies etc.

WTO and India

India is one of the founding members of the GATT and WTO. At the eve of independence, India's share in the world trade was 2.2 per cent that had fallen down to 0.6 per cent in the year 1995–another eve when India became the founder member of the WTO. This share rose to 0.9 per cent in the year of 2003, but despite all efforts India could not attain the target of 1 per cent that is sought for. The reasons tagged to this miserable performance are internal such as slow growth rate of agriculture sector. Vis-à-vis industrial sector and external such as slow growth rate of agriculture sector vis-à-vis industrial sector and external such as slack world economy. But the most important reason had been the trade and non-trade barriers levied by the industrialised nations.

India has sufficiently diversified trade relations. India has more than 7500 commodities to almost 190 and imports more than 6000 commodities from nearly 140 countries. The USA is the major trading Although this share has declined to 11.6 per cent in 2003-04 from 13 per cent in 2000-01.

Indian foreign trade has increased after establishment of WTO. The export of the countries was worth Rs.'32553 crore in 2002-03. It was an increase of 7.84 fold. During the same period, the import went up from Rs. 43198 crore to Rs. 229206 crore registering an increase of 6.85 fold. In the year of 1990-91, 5.6 per cent of the total export was made to OPEC nations, which increased to 13.1 per cent in the year 2002-03 similarly 16.10 per cent of the total export was made to the developing countries in the year 1990-91, which rose to 30.8 per cent in the year 2002-03. However, in the year 1990-91, 53.3 per cent of the total export was made to OECD nations, which came down to 50 per cent in the year 2002-03 similarly 17.9 per cent of the total export was made to EEC in 1990-91 which came down to only 1.8 per cent in 2002-03.

India's major import was 54 per cent in the year 1990-91 from OECD nations. It gradually decreased and came down to 37.9 per cent in 2002-03. Similarly the import from OPEC nations came down to 5.6 per cent from the earlier 16.3 per cent and that from the EEC from 7.8 per cent to 1.3 per cent. There is a distinct change in the field of import. It has increased greatly from the developing countries and other nations except the OECD, OPEC and EEC. It was just 3.5 per cent in the year 1990-91 which went up to 35.6 per cent in 2002-03.

India's foreign direct investment as well as foreign portfolio investment has been increase after globalisation. In 1991, foreign direct investment was barely to the tune of Rs. 174 Crore that rose in 2000 Rs. to 9,338 crore. Thus foreign direct investment has witnessed an increase of 60 times. Similarly portfolio investment has also increase very much. In 1991 net portfolio investment was merely Rs. 11 crore which in 1999-2000 increased to Rs. 13,112 crore. Between 1991 and 2000 number of foreign collaboration projects was 14,230 with foreign investment amounting to Rs. 32,710 crore. In 1990-91 total foreign capital authorized was Rs. 8,123 crore of which actual utilisation was Rs. 6,704 crore on the contrary in 2000 total foreign capital authorised was Rs. 20,319 as against actual utilisation of Rs. 14,405 crore in 1991, foreign exchange reserves of India amounted to Rs. 4,822 crore which in 2000 increased to Rs. 152,924 crore. Thus there has been an increase of 26 times in foreign exchange reserves in India

Disadvantages of WTO Against India

Critics are of the opinion that agreements on the provision of GATT or WTO will be beneficial to developed countries alone and under developed countries like India will stand to lose. Entry of foreign companies in India will rob our culture and traditions and the country will be plundered on the pattern of East India Company.

Disadvantage to Agricultural Sector

It is apprehended that by including agriculture in WTO, Indian farmers will become dependant on multinational companies for improved seeds and agricultural technology. The farmers will not be able to save better seeds from their crop and will be compelled to buy at high rates insecticides, fertilizers, agricultural machinery etc. from multinational companies, every time. Big farmers alone will be able to take advantage of improve farm technology. The cumulative effect of all this will be that small farmers, who are large in humber, will be forced to sell their lands. This will further aggravate the problem of unemployment in rural sector. Plants and cattle feeds will come under the ambit of patents and so will be under the control of multinational companies. This will harm the interests of Indian agriculture. Moreover, it will adversely affect the announcement of minimum support price of agricultural products and public distribution system.

Reduction in Subsidy

Critics are of the opinion that after concluding WTO Agreements, subsidy to agricultural sector will be slashed. It will affect adversely the poor farmers.

Import of Food Grains

It is apprehended that by entering into WTO Agreements, surplus food grains of developed countries will be imported on a large scale. It will adversely affect country's balance of payments.

Restrictions on the use of Brand Seeds

Under WTO scientists and farmers will not be able to use brand seeds for commercial purpose. Under the circumstances, big farmers along could buy foreign expensive seeds. It will be difficult for small and marginal farmers to make use of improved variety of seeds. It will widen the gap of economic disparity.

Patent Rights of Natural Products

It foreign MNCs took initiative and secured patent rights over minor natural products of India, it may lead to serious consequences for Indian agriculture. For instance, neem can be used for making soap, tooth-paste, medicines etc. similarly, there is large demand for Psyllium Husk (Isabgol) in foreign countries. Their foreign patent may prove very expensive for India

Plant Breeding Protection

According to WTO protection of breeding has been determined by Sui-Generis system. Indian farmers will have to spend large amount of money to get new and improved variety of plants and their dependence on multi national companies will further increase.

Argument Against TRIMS

In terms of WTO, India could not impose any restriction on foreign investment. Consequently, multi national companies will be free to establish their industries in India. It will harm indigenous industries. Domestic investors will suffer as they have little capacity to compete with multi national companies. As a result, on the one hand, country's production will get discouraged and unemployment situation aggravated and on the other, dominance of multi national companies over country's economy will go on extending and their profits will continue to rise. All this will harm our economy.

Trade Related Intellectual Property Rights

Presently, India does not recognize patents in the field of medicines, food grains and chemical products. Most of the developed countries accord recognition to product patent. With the enforcement of the provisions of the Agreement, all member countries of WTO will be required to accord recognition to product patent. India has been given a period of ten years to make provision for patent. According to critics, with the enforcement of new system, prices of the existing medicines will rise steeply. Multi national companies may file a claim against copying of any patent before world Trade Organization. Indian researchers will have to face avoidable difficulties to prove their non-involvement in imitation case. They will have to waste their time and money. In this context it may be noted that a complaint will be filed by the complainant in his own country. Dispensation of justice is cheap in India and the amount of compensation is also low. But in developed countries like America it is very expensive and Indian producers may have to spend a lot of money in their defense if a prosecution is launched against them in that country. Thus, justice bought in other countries will be relatively dearer than in India. Indian pharmaceutical industry will be hard hit by patent agreements. MNCs will charge exorbitant prices of variety of medicines.

Foreign Ownership of Plants and Animals

Plants and animals have also been included in the preview of WTO and the same can be purchased by foreign companies. It will not be in the interest of Indian economy, as has been apprehended by the president of Madras Development Institute.

Arguments Against TRIPS

It is argued against TRIPS i.e. Trade Related Intellectual Property, that it will discourage the process of research and innovation in the country. Critics are of the opinion that it is unjust to have uniform standards for all member countries, in matters of TRIPS because these standards vary with economic and technical development of each country. The level of technology found in the developed country can never be reached by developing countries. India will therefore stand to lose. Any setback to research and innovation process will accentuate the backwardness of our agriculture and medical services will be beyond the reach of an ordinary man. It is feared that prices of medicines may rise by 10 to 15 times.

Disadvantages to Service Sector

It is feared that WTO will adversely affect our service sector also. Our banking, insurance, transport, education and hotel services will not be able to complete with the similar services offered by MNCs. As a result, indigenous institutes engaged in these service sectors will gradually wind up and our economic freedom will be endangered.

Disadvantage of Patentisation

Maximum apprehensions are being expressed against the provision of patent for the period of 20 years. Such a long period will have an adverse affect on Indian economy, especially on scientific and medical research. Consequently, prices of most of the goods are likely to increase from six to twenty fold.

Advantages of WTO for India

Above arguments have been advanced against WTO, whereas reality is quite different. A minute study reveals that these arguments present only one sided assessment of the proposals. Some of the arguments are totally baseless.

Multilateral Trade Negotiations

India has been in favour of multilateral trade negotiations from the very beginning because as a result of it all member countries will enjoy the benefits of Most Favored Nation clause. As a member of WTO it will be possible for India to enter into multilateral trade agreements with these 124 countries. There will be no need to enter into bilateral agreements with these countries. (ii) Besides, custom tariffs will fall and trade expand with the opening of new markets. It is hoped that as a result of WTO agreements would trade will witness an increase ranging between 2000 and 3000 crore dollars. India can also increase the value of its trade by 150 to 200 crore dollars. This increase is in addition to the general rise in India's foreign trade.

No Reduction in Subsidies

It is wrong to argue that there will be reduction in subsidies to agriculture as a result of WTO proposal. The question of reduction in subsidy arises, only when the said subsidy is more than 10 per cent of the production cost. In India, such subsidies are already much less than 10 per cent. Presently subsidy being given by government of India to agriculture is 3.5 per cent. It is therefore wrong to believe that on account of WTO subsidy to agriculture will be reduced. The fact is that with acceptance of the proposal, chances of rise in the quantum of subsidy become bright. Because of the membership of WTO, no reduction will be effected in the on going assistance being provided to public distribution system or fair price shops selling food grains to the poor at concessional rates.

No Need of Increase in Imports of Food Grains

On account of WTO Agreement will be not necessary for India to increase import of food grains. It is because import of food grains is not necessary for such countries as face balance of payments difficulties and so have already imposed quantitative restrictions on the imports. India has been facing balance of payments difficulties and as such it is not necessary for her to import food grains. Besides, due to balance of payments problem. India will be free to check imports or impose quantitative restrictions thereon. It is also true that India will not have to face balance of payments problem for all times. Agreement related to agriculture is for a period of six years. But, if at all India has to import food grains, then import duty on food grains will be 100 per cent, on processed food items it will be 150 per cent and on edible oils around 300 per cent. Such a high rate of import duty will render the price of imported food grains in domestic markets quite prohibitive. The question of import of food grains in the country does not arise.

Increase in Export of Food Grains

As a result of reduction in government subsidies on agriculture being given by 7 developed countries, demand for special variety of India food grains will rise in international market. It will provide opportunity to India to increase export of agricultural products. WTO has recommended a cut in custom duties and reduction in import restrictions. It will also promote agricultural export from India considerably. As a result of this proposal, it will be possible for countries like India to export rice to Japan and South Korea.

Freedom to use Seeds

Former Director General of WTO has clarified that the farmer will be free to use seeds, saved from his crop, for the next sowing. He will also be free to get his seeds exchanged with the seeds of other farmers. Researchers will be able to prepare another variety from a reserved variety. However, they will have to seek permission from original breeder for it.

Patent and Sui-Generis System

Government has clarified that in India there is no provision of patenting seeds nor is there any intention of changing this provision in future, as well. It has also made it clear that in the matter of seed-patent and sui-generis system it will make its own provisions under which Plant Breeders will be issued certificates. In this system, it has been further clarified, there will be provision for the rights of the farmers as well as that of the researchers. Farmers will be able to get improved and purified seeds in the market through the medium of the protection of rights of plant breeders and it will benefit Agricultural Research Institutes of India to the maximum. As a result of Sui-Generis system, there will be increased investment in Research and Development in agricultural sector. There will also be further development of high yielding variety of seeds.

Dunkel Draft and Agriculture

Dunkel Draft will not adversely hit the interests of our farmers rather it will promote export of agricultural research and development of high yielding variety of crops. All our major projects of agricultural development are outside the purview of the provisions of the agreement. After the enforcement of WTO Agreement, we will not have to reduce the subsidies already being given to the farmers. We will not have to allow access to our market the agricultural products of other countries. Farmers will have full right to make use of their crops in the form of seeds or get the same exchanged with other farmers. No reduction will be made in the procurement of food grains, construction of warehouses for storage of food grains and subsidy to public distribution system. In the words of Dr. Manmohan Singh, "W.T.O. is expected to diversify Indian agriculture, encourage India's multilateral transactions of scientific knowledge and raise productivity standard and output manifold. Government will enhance subsidy and protection to agriculture."

Trade Related Intellectual Property Rights - TRIPS

Before the formation of W.T.O., Dunkel Draft included copyright, trade mark, trade secrets, industrial designs, power supply, geographical indications, and patents under intellectual property rights. The draft is not going to cause any special harm to India, because expect patents, in all other spheres, India's judicial and executive systems are of international level. Patents, especially in the context of those related to medicines, there is difference between the provisions of Indian law and patent provisions of Dunkel Draft. It is therefore possible that prices of medicines may rise a little. However, it is worth nothing that of the total available medicines in India, hardly 10 to 15 per cent medicines figure in the patent list. As such, there is no point to be over apprehensive on this score. World Health Organization has kept most essential and life-saving drugs outside the purview of Dunkel Draft or WTO. Besides, GATT patent drugs are generally available in our country and the same will definitely help check the rising prices of medicines in the patent list. Even otherwise, despite the acceptance of WTO proposal, till 1998 medicines can be imitated. It is only after a period 10 years that patent laws will come into force. During this period, if adequate facilities are provided to Indian, scientists, they may succeed in manufacturing their own brand of new and effective medicines.

Trade Related Investment Measures-TRIMS:

Provisions of WTO under Trade Related Investment Measures are to the advantage of India. TRIMS that give foreign investors the same rights as indigenous investors, also give full right to the government regarding the extent to which it may allow foreign capital investment in trade. It also accords freedom to the government to decide about the type of foreign capital investment in its country. Again it is the concerned government that will decide about the conditions to be fulfilled to meet the compulsions of exports from the view point of balance of payments. Thus, WTO proposals will have no effect on the economic sovereignty of the country.

Services

By including trade in service sector under WTO proposals, developing countries like India will stand to gain. According to WTO, developed countries will establish large number of trade and service establishment like banking, insurance, transport, hotel, etc. In return, developed countries will allow access to their markets to India for the sale of her products. By allowing MNCs to set up their business establishments in the country, on the one hand, trade in service sector will extend and, on the other, millions of unemployed persons in India will get ample employment opportunities. It will check immigration of young men to foreign countries due to lack of proper employment opportunities within the country and also solve the problem of brain drain.

Clothing and Textile Industry

WTO will benefit clothing and textile industry to most. Under Multi-Fibre Arrangements (MFA) our cloth and ready-made garment trade was subject to quota restrictions. As a result of WTO all these restrictions will be removed in the next ten years. Export of Indian clothes and textiles will receive great fillip. Withdrawal of quota fixation process will encourage our exports to America and European countries. It will boost textile industry and new employment opportunities will be created in this sector.

Progress in Fulfillment of India's Commitments to WTO

The progress in fulfillment of India's commitments to World Trade Organization may be summariSed as under:

Quantative Restrictions (QR)

In 1997, India imposed quantative restrictions (QR) on the import of 2,714 goods on the grounds of Balance of Payment. According to agreement with WTO in 1999, quantative restrictions on imports were confined to 1,429 goods. In recent Export Import Policy 2000-2001, quantative restrictions on imports have been restricted to 715 goods. By the end of 2002, all quantatitive restrictions on imports will be abolished.

Trade Related Intellectual Property Rights (TRIPS)

As per our obligations towards WTO, the agreement on TRIPs sets out the minimum standards of protection to be adopted by the parties, in respect of:

(i) Copyrights and related rights
(ii) Trade Marks
(iii) Geographical Indications
(iv) Industrial Designs
(v) Protection of patents and their enforcement.

According to the provisions of the TRIPS agreement, a period of 5 years is available to India to give effect to these standards. Giving effect to her commitments to WTO, India enforced in 1999, patents (Amendment) Act. As per this act, firms getting patents will be given exclusive marketing rights.

Patents

The government has introduced a bill in the parliament to fulfill its obligation regarding patents. The basic obligation in the field of patents is that inventions in all fields of technology, whether products or process shall be patentable provided they meet the three tests of being novel, including their Inventive aspect and capability of commercial use.

According to WTO, regarding plant varieties, there is an obligation on each country to provide for protection by patents or by an effective sui-Generics or by the combination of both. Government of India has decided to enforce sui-generis system, as it perceived to be in our national interest. A legislation of this effect has been tabled in the parliament by the Ministry of Agriculture.

Copyright Trade Marks and Industrial Designs

In 1999, India amended copyright Act 1957. It has also amended in 1999, Trade and Merchandise Marks Act 1958. A new Act is being formulated to protect Industrial Designs.

Geographical Indications

According to WTO Agreements, different governments will formulate laws to prevent the use of name and presentation of a good, if the good is question originates in a geographical area other than its true place of origin. Government of India has passed in 1999 an Act in respect of geographical indications.

Trade Related Investment Measures

Under the TRIMS Agreement, developing countries like India was given a transition period of 5 years, i.e. upto December 31, 1999 during which they continued to stick to the measures inconsistent with the Agreement by giving prior notice to this effect. India has given such notice to W.T.O. with regard to two TRIMS. Of these one relates to requirements of local raw materials for the production of certain pharmaceutical products and the other relates to divided balancing requirements in case of investment in 22 categories of consumer items.

Tariffs

India stands committed to scale down tariffs to the fixed level by March 1, 2000 in respect of non-agricultural and non-textile items. Necessary steps will be taken to discharge this commitment.

Challenges and Perspective

India had to face many challenges in various sectors by signing the WTO agreement, i.e. in the agricultural sector, industrial sector and service sector. In agricultural sector, challenges like subsidies of developed nation, high prices of agricultural products, lack of investment, environmental degradation, population problem, and lack of technical know-how had emerged. In terms of industrial sector Indian faced challenges like better productivity and technological excellence, problems of industrial sickness, human capital management etc. Just like in industry and agricultural sectors, India faced many challenges in service and patent sector, for example, lack of compositeness, inadequate laws, corruption, problems in the government procurement, legal delay system, etc., that are pulling India in world competition.

India had greater perspectives in terms of natural resources and climate condition; it also had comparative advantage in terms of labour. Indian people are extremely hardworking as compared to other nations. India has to strengthen and develop the scientific base of research and development because in the new era of globalization, knowledge and technology have greater advantages. India is emerging as a leading country in the world under developing nations. India ranks fourth in world's largest economics list, so it should play a vital role in framing fare global rules and regulations and safeguards in WTO. The global scenario should compel India to fight the pressures from within and outside the country because the future is not for the meek but the brave.

Conclusion

Above the facts, it can be concluded that WTO will definitely be of advantage to India. All doubts and arguments against WTO are exaggerated and baseless.

WTO is a gateway for the entry of free trade, foreign investment, foreign technology and know-how which can be made available to third world countries and which will be made available. They need it for their development and self-sufficiency. Through its medium, people living there will be familiarized with new concepts and those goods will be available to them easily about which they had never thought of previously. Role of the Trinity–IMF, World Bank and World Trade Organization–will help and protect the interests of the poor nations.

No doubt WTO has come into being pretty late, nevertheless in the building of new international trade order it is a step in the right direction which is needed for the economic development and transparency of under developed countries. WTO should play its role as depository of trade agreements. India that has joined WTO as its founder – member, can ill-afford to opt out of its remain isolated from rest of the world. It would have been suicidal for Indian economy. What is needed is that WTO provisions be used to safeguard the interests of India and government should make constant endeavour in this matter.

REFERENCES

Banik Nilanjan (2001), "An Analysis of India's Export During the 1990s" Economic and Political Weekly, Vol. 36, No. 44, November 3, Mumbai.

Dutt Ruddar, Sundharam K.P.M. (2004), "Indian Economy" S. Chand & Co. Ltd. Ramnagar, New Delhi-110055.

Govt. of India (2001-02, 2002-03, 2003-04, 2004-05) "Economic Survey" New Delhi, Ministry of Finance.

Handbook of Statistics on Indian Economy, 2001.

Misra S.K., Puri V.K. (2005), "Economics of Development and Planning" Himalaya Publishing House, Mumbai.

Panchamukhi V.R. (2001), "World Trade Organisation and India-Challenges and Perspectives" in Chadha, G.K. (ed.) pp. 3 21.

Rao M.B., Guru Manjula (2003), "WTO and International Trade", Vikas Publishing House Pvt. Ltd., New Delhi-14.

Virmani Arvind (2003), "India's External Reforms: Modest Globalisation, Significant Gains" Economic and Political Weekly Vol. 38, No. 32, Aug. 9, Mumbai.

WTO-World Trade Report for the Years 2003, 2004 and Prospects for 2005.

THE IMPACT OF WTO IN INDIAN PATENT REGIME

*V. Neelamegam**

Introduction

The 21st century will be a knowledge based society and India is likely to be one of the leaders of such a society. The foundation of knowledge-based economy will be intellectual property. Inaugurating India's first state of the art integrated Intellectual Property Rights office building at Dwarka in New Delhi recently, the Union Minister of Commerce and Industry, Mr. Kamal Nath said, Intellectual Property, be it in the form of patents, design, trademarks or geographical indications was becoming increasingly important not only for wealth creation but also for providing employment and improved living standards.

The Indian Patents Act 1970 provided patenting of all processes and products in all areas excepting food, drugs and chemicals. Introduction of product patents in these three crucial areas indicates the sign of confidence and maturity of Indian Industry particularly the emerging pharmaceutical industry. In fact, the new patent regime will help Indian pharma industry, which has made large investments in drug research. It gives a chance to drug development by frontline companies with adequate safeguards to protect the interests of society.

The Government has put in place a new patent regime from January of 2005, keeping in line with the WTO commitments. India is among the few developing economics to have brought in amendments to the existing patent law. As Parliament was not in session the new patent regime was first brought through

* Lecturer, P.G. Department of Economics, Dhanraj Baid Jain College, Chennai.

a Presidential Ordinance, which was subsequently replaced by legislation called the Patents (Third Amendment) bill 2005 with substantial improvements. The new bill which was passed by the Lok Sabha on march 22 and by the Rajya Sabha on march 23, allows patenting of products in areas of food, drugs and chemicals which were not covered earlier.

Benefits of Patent

A Patent is an exclusive right for a limited period of time (Term of patent) granted by the Government to the patentee, in lieu of full disclosure (complete specification) of the invention. The invention should be new, non-obvious and capable of industrial application. It includes manufacturing methods, processes, machines, products or their improvements and also inventions.

A patent is not granted if the invention is already available with the public in the form of published literature or prior/ common knowledge. It must not be from the categories specifically declared non-patentable.

The patentee has the exclusive rights for the use of the patent. He can take legal action against any infringement. He can commercially exploit its potential with the confidence that it cannot be copied or imitated without his permission during the period of patent. It can be licensed, assigned or sold for commercial consideration. The consumer will be benefited because better and cheaper products will become available in the market, as more inventions will be encouraged.

Research & Development activities will receive a boost. After the expiry of the patent term, the invention will be fully and freely available to the public, thereby facilitating easier and faster technology transfer.

Impacts of WTO

In 1995 when World Trade Organization came in to being, it was decided that all member countries including India would allow protection of intellectual property rights under an agreement called TRIPs (Trade Related Intellectual Property Rights). This agreement gave ten years time until January one 2005 to the developing countries to bring necessary changes to the patent regime to allow product patents so that intellectual property rights particularly in food, pharmaceuticals and chemicals could be protected. India has an enviable record of fully adhering to its international obligation. It has done so in the midst of even a balance of payment crisis. It never sought rescheduling or waiver and promptly repaid the loans. Adhering to the January one deadline was part of this consistency.

Accordingly, after taking full advantage of the ten-year period, India has allowed product patents particularly with Indian pharmaceutical industry coming of age china allowed product patents in these four areas in 1992. As the issues involved were no doubt complex and of critical importance to both domestic pharmaceutical industry as well as consumers, the changes have been brought after considerable debate for many years. Responsive to concerns expressed in various quarters, the Government had extensive consultations with all stakeholders before formulating the bill. The Commerce Minister Shri Kamal Nath is right in saying that all the concerns have been fully taken on board in the final amendment to the Patent Act.

Apart from meeting the WTO obligations, India has brought in the new regime, as there is an economic rationale. It enables pioneering firms lead-time to recoup sunk cost on research and development. Of the 12,000 applications in the mailbox for product patents, nearly 9000 are from the pharmaceutical industry. Of the 9000 nearly 2000 are from the Indian pharmaceutical industry. This shows most of the product patent applications are from the drug industry.

There are two areas of major concern expressed in various quarter's apprehensions about rise in prices of medicine and the possible impact of the new patent regime on the domestic pharmaceutical industry.

On the issue of prices, The Commerce Minister has assured all stakeholders that there are enough safeguards built into the bill to protect the interests of consumers by ensuring availability of medicines at affordable prices and hence fears about drug prices rising after the introduction of product patent regime was "unfounded", "the prices of medicines will not shoot up due to patents, because of these strong safeguards, checks and balances", he asserts.

The clear provisions in the amended Patents Act to protect the interests of domestic pharmaceuticals and chemical industry state that domestic companies can continue to manufacture patented products even after a patent is granted in respect of mailbox applications on payment of a reasonable royalty to the patent holder, provision for both pre-grant and post-grant opposition avenues as well as reduction in timeframe for grant of patents in a cost -effective manner are also provided, the re-grant opposition to patents has too been strengthened.

Further the Act also provides to prevent "ever-greening" of patents for pharmaceutical substances, provisions listing out exceptions to patent ability have been suitably amended to remove ambiguity, the conditions for obtaining compulsory licence have been clarified to facilitate export of patented pharmaceutical products by Indian companies, a reasonable period for negotiations between the patent holder and companies seeking compulsory licence has been fixed at six months and research and development has been exempted from the ambit of patents.

There are also certain fears that the patent regime does not have adequate safeguards to check spurious drugs from flooding the market. But this is not correct in the sense that it is not the patent law, which checks spurious drugs, but the quality control which is a separate issue.

The apprehension that traditional knowledge would be hit by the new patent regime is also not true. In fact, traditional knowledge, seeds and over a dozen other items do not fall under the purview of patents and the Indian farmers need have no fears on that score.

Yet another offshoot of the new patent regime would be that more and more multinational pharmaceutical companies might shift their research and development activities to India since they know that their intellectual property rights would be protected. As it is several multinational drug companies have started some of their R & D activities in India because of the availability of cheap qualified manpower.

Overall, the New Patent regime will do more good to India than harm. It is a fairly balanced law. It is also a reflection of the confidence of Indian drug companies, which are going global, and in the process of developing new products through their in-house R & D. Indian pharmaceutical industry is among the most globally competitive industries that we have today with over one-third of its output being exported. The turnover of Indian pharmaceutical industry is about Rs. 50, 000 crore, of which Rs. 16,000 crore is exported. It is one of the fastest growing industries in he country. It is in our interest to have a modern patent regime in line with what most countries have already adopted.

WTO AND MARKET ACCESS FOR NON-AGRICULTURE SECTOR

Shamim Akhtar &*
*Khadija Sultana Khan***

Introduction

A major concern of developing countries with the process of trade liberalization for non-agricultural products in the Uruguay Round has been the persistence of high and peak tariffs, tariff escalation and non-tariff barriers in developed countries on goods of export interest. It has also been shown that process of trade liberalization has been asymmetric with developing countries taking deeper commitments compared to developed countries. The Doha Ministerial Conference sought to address this asymmetry by proposing negotiations on the market access for non agricultural goods to be agreed by May 2003 to eliminate barriers to market access in particular on products of export interest to developing countries. Subsequently, a Negotiating Group on Market Access (NGMA) has been set up at the WTO and different countries have presented proposals on modalities for liberalization.

Against that background this Paper reviews the Doha Mandate on Non-Agricultural Market Access (NAMA). It then discusses the priorities for developing countries in NAMA. The different proposals on modalities are summarized. The implications of the Draft Paper on Modalities of Negotiations prepared by Chairman of NGMA in May 2003 on the basis of various proposals is then commented upon from a developing country perspective. Subsequently, a Revised Draft Paper on

* Lecturer in Krishna College, Bijnor.
** Remote Sensing/GIS Specialist Pvt. Ltd., Delhi.

Modalities was issued by the Chairman of NGMA on 19 August, 2003 where a number of provisions of the may Draft were changed. The implications of the changes are also commented upon. Some concluding remarks are made at the end.

The Doha Mandate: A Comment The Doha Ministerial Meeting had agreed to reduce industrial tariffs under the agenda item Market Access for Non-Agriculture Products.

"16 Market Access for Non-agricultural Products: We agree to negotiation which shall aim, by modalities to be agreed, to reduction of eliminate tariffs, including the reduction of elimination of tariff peaks, high tariffs, and tariff escalation, as well as non-tariff barriers, in particular on products of export interest to developing countries. Product coverage shall be comprehensive and without *a priori* exclusions. The negotiations shall take fully into account the special needs and interests of developing and least-developed country participants, including through less than full reciprocity in reduction commitments, in accordance with the relevant provisions of Article *XXVIII* bis of GATT 1994 and the provisions cited in paragraph 50. To this end, the modalities to be agreed will include appropriate studies and capacity- building measures the assist least-developed countries to participate effectively in the negotiations" cf, (WTO, Ministerial Declaration, WT/MIN (01)/ DEC/W/1, Nov. 14, 2001 Doha, 9-14, November 2001).

The Declaration does not make any reference to an increase in transparency and predictability through a significant expansion of the scope of tariff bindings and through simplifying members' tariffs. A large number of developed countries are defining tariffs in the form of specific and compound duties, which have been found to be relatively high. It is very difficult to put them in the negotiations without knowing *ad-valorem* equivalence and the other implications of such duties.

Priorities for Developing Countries

In the pre-Doha era, many developing countries were opposed to comprehensive WTO negotiations on market access for industrial sector. They had taken this stand probably from the consideration that the level of developed countries' average tariff was low, and a further reduction (or even complete elimination) in industrial tariffs of developed countries would not lead to a substantial increase in market access for developing countries. On the contrary, there was a lurking fear that developing countries would have to give in return substantial market access by significantly cutting down their present level of tariff rates and spread of tariff bindings.

Table 1
Taroff Reduction on Industrial Products by Select Developing Countries

Country	*Trade-weighted Tariff average (%)***			*Simple Average*
	*Pre-Uruguay**	*Post-Uruguay* (based on UR commitments)*	*Applied, 1999*	*(%) Applied, 2000*
Argentina	38.2	30.9	15.4	13.4
Brazil	40.6	27.0	16.2	14.78[2]
Chile	34.9	24.9	10.0	8.96
Colombia	44.3	35.1	11.6	10.99
India	71.4	32.4	27.09[4]	30.82[4]
Indonesia	20.4	36.9	10.5	9.68[2]
Korea Rep.	18.0	8.3	7.6	7.62[1]
Malaysia	10.2	9.1	9.0[2]	
Philippines	23.9	22.2	8.0	8.87[1]
Thailand	37.3	28.0		14.61[1]
Venezuela	50.0	30.9	11.9	

Notes: *Pre-and post-Uruguay Round tariff averages are computed as the trade weighted average of tariff rates on bound tines and applied tariff rates on unbound rates. Due to the significance of ceiling bindings in the post-Uruguay Round tariff averages, no reduction are reported. It excludes the Petroleum sector. For the year 1999, for the year 1998, for the year 1997 and for the year 2001-02.

Source: Mehta (2003), Indian Industrial Tariffs: Towards WTO Development Round Negotiations, RIS.

A large number of developing countries, as a part of trade policy reforms, have been unilaterally reducing their custom tariffs on industrial products. Table 1 shows that applied tariffs of a large number of developing countries are significantly lower than the UR commitment level. Nonetheless, the negotiation process is expected to put pressure on developing countries to reduce/eliminate their tariffs. In the light of a number of studies, developing countries should give emphasis on the following aspects:

Elimination of Tariffs: A Symmetric Framework of Elimination of all tariffs completely would not be in developing countries' interest as it will lead to very high reductions by developing countries as compared to those of developed countries. It will not be consistent with the development dimension and with the principle of 'less than full reciprocity'. Elimination of low/nuisance tariff in developed countries also should not be considered as equivalent to high or deeper reduction by developing countries.

Focus of Tariff Reduction: Developing countries should not concentrate on reduction in the average tariff, but their concerns should be on other aspects like peak tariffs, tariff escalation, credit for autonomous liberalization, and non *ad-valorem* duties, etc.

Bringing Greater Transparency in Tariff Rates: A large number of developed countries are used to the practice of imposing specific and complex duties rather than ad valorem duties. The total number of commodities for which custom duties are given in the form of specific duties, is very large for developed countries for instance EU (1780 tariff lines), US (1455 tariff lines). In most cases, non-ad valorem duties consisting of several specific and *ad-valorem* tariffs associated with a condition of relationships between them. There are many variants of specific duties in the schedules of different countries. Some of these variants are very complex.

It has been noticed that the developed countries have imposed specific duties on a larger number of commodities as compared to developing countries. Although most of the countries believe that the specific duties should be replaced by and ad valorem rates, no decision was made in the UR. In fact, a significant number of UR bound rates had been committed in the from of specific duties. It has been noticed that these specific duties conceal the fact that the countries are indirectly mentioning them in different forums[8].

The specific duties are not suitable for analytical and comparative purposes, and require more common *ad-valorem* tariffs. Hence, these specific duties be converted to add valorem equivalence[9] (AVES). A study by UNCTAD (1999-2000) has computed ad valorem equivalence of specific duties for 18,000 commodities (of different countries) for the year 1996. It shows that the *ad-valorem* equivalence of a large number of products with specific duties are much higher than the average ad valorem rates.

The custom Tariff Database of the US for August 2000[10] also corroborates the above observation. In this databases, the US defines specific duties for around 600 industrial commodities (national lines) and provide the corresponding ad valorem equivalent rates of most of specific duties. It shows that the average tariff rate of commodities with non *ad-valorem* duties is almost three times higher than be average tariff of the rate the commodities whose custom duties is defined in from of *ad-valorem* rates. In this context, it is worth highlighting that adverbial equivalence of found rates is still not available in the literature.

Dealing with the Tariff Peaks: Even if the tariff are reduced by developed countries, tariff peaks seem to be the major hurdle in the market access for certain sector where the developing countries have good export potential.

In the literature[11], a cut-off point has generally been specified for the identification of commodities with peak tariffs. The level of cut-off point is generally taken as 12 per cent (and sometimes 10 per cent or 15 per cent). All those commodities, whose tariff rate is more than 12 per cent ad valorem rate, are called commodities with peak tariff. In the existing literature, the selection of a cut off point is arbitrary and has no relationship with average tariff. Further it does not make any distinction in different groups of countries.

Besides$_5$ number of attempts have been made to identify the commodities with peak tariff. Notably, the study by UNCTAD[12] concludes that, "both frequency and levels of tariff peak rates remain a matter of concern. Over 10 per cent of tariff universe of the quad countries, corresponding to an aggregate 4,000-traiff line, will continue to exceed 12 per cent ad valorem. All four countries maintain high variance in tariff rates. One fifth of the peak tariff of the US, one quarter of those in EU and Japan, and about one-tenth of those of Canada exceed 30 per cent. In the four selected developing countries, tariff peaks are more frequent but reach less extreme rates than in the major developed countries" (emphasis added)[13].

Disciplining the Tariff Escalation: Tariff structures of many countries have traditionally displayed significant escalation favoring domestic processors for a large number of commodities. It was expected that tariff commitments in the UR would provide for gradual reduction of escalation by applying relatively higher cuts to finished goods. However, rapidly rising tariff have been notice from low rates for law material to higher rates for intermediate goods and sometime peak tariff for finished products. A number of studies[14] have confirmed that tariff escalation has continued after UR for a large number of sector, particularly, fish & fish products, textile & textile products, leather & rubber products, footwear and to some extent wood & wood products. Basically, the result conform that tariff escalation is still a major constant for export industries of India and developing countries.

Addressing the Non-Tariff Barriers: The developed countries employ an impressive array of new measure of protection and government intervention. These have been imposed through different instruments, including Non-Tariff Barriers (NTBS). The agreement of the UR have changed the intensity of different types of NTBS. As a result, while some measures of NTBS have lot their significance, of NTBS has increased.

The non-tariff barriers continue to affects the growth of world trade and the UR could not tackle these issues successfully. On the one hand, the importing countries generally term them as NTBs, the imposing countries insists that these instruments are policy objectives. Developing countries should look for a coherent approach for dealing with such issues and participate actively in setting up new (and clear) ruler and provision.

In short, the priorities of developing countries should be focused on peak Tariff, Tariff Escalation and NTBs to get market access and to see that it is consistent with development dimension and less than full reciprocatory.

The Present Status of Negotiation on Modalities

To initiate negotiation on market access for non-agriculture products, the Negotiation Group on Market Access (NGMA) has been formed, such negotiations could be concluded by 1 January, 2005. The fifth Ministerial Conference in Cancun will take stock of these negotiations and recommend appropriately. These proposals include those submitted by China, EU, India, Japan, Korea and the US. The different modalities can be categorized into following five board:

1. Request and Offer
2. Formulae
3. Sector by Sector
4. Zero for Zero
5. Mixed

Proposals submitted by these members to NGMA are summarized below:

Proposals

(a) China[16]

The Chinese formula is specified as:

$$t_0 = \frac{(t_a + (B \times P) \times t_0}{(t_a + P^2) + t_0}$$

Where,

t_a is the simple average of the base rates (A in TN/ MA/20).

P is a peak factor defined as the ratio of the tariff rate over the average rate (t_0/t_a)

B is an adjusting coefficient for the year of implementation. B =1 for 2015 of B = 3 for 2010.

The formula is very similar to the Swiss formula but instead of a fixed co-efficient, a variable factor based on the simple average of the base rates t_a, a peak factor and an additional parameter for the year of implementation have been used. The properties of the Chinese formula are similar to what is known about the properties of the Swiss formula discussed in paragraph 16, such as higher cuts for higher rates. Furthermore it can be shown that for B = 1 the formula reduces any initial tariff rate below a maximum level which is the current average of the base rates. This is equivalent to the effect of the standard Swiss formula using the tariff average as coefficient.

The percentage cuts for any given tariff rate will depend on the tariff average of the Member concerned. For the same tariff rate, Member with lower tariff averages will experience relatively higher reduction rates, members with higher tariff averages. Therefore, the overall result of applying this formula will depend on the statistical properties of different members tariff profiles.

(b) European Communities[17]

European Communities' proposal is within the class of linear tariff dependent formulae, however, with an adjustment, which gives it the properties of a step-wise linear function. The formula is applied across a set of tariff intervals and the tariff rate cuts depend upon the upper and lower bound of the applaudable interval.

The formula is specified as:

$$t_1 = B_1^L + (t_0 - B_0^L) \times \left[\frac{B_1^U - B_1^L}{B_0^U - B_0^L}\right]$$

where B^i_j are the upper and lower bounds of the respective tariff intervals. The superscribed letters U and L are, respectively, the upper and lower bounds of the interval. The intervals are defined as follows:

(c) India[18]

India proposes a simple linear cut on the individual bound tariff lines of each Members, with a higher percentage cut for developed countries than for developing countries. In addition to the linear cut, any tariff in excess of three times the national average tariff shall be reduced to no more than three times the

	Base				Final		
	B_0^L		B_0^U	B_1^L		B_1^U
Interval 1	0	to less than	2	0	to	0
Interval 2	2	to	15	1.6	to	7.5
Interval 3	15	to	50	7.5	to	15
Interval 4	50	to more than	50	15	to	15

national average which results after applying the initial linear cut. The formula is specified as:

Step (1) $t_0 = c' \, t_0$

Where $c = (1 - (A'Y/100))$ and

Step (2) $t_1 \leq 3 \, t_a$

Where

A is defined as 'less than full reciprocity' parameter with

A = 1 for developed countries and

A= 0.67 for developing countries,

Y is the reduction percentage (to be negotiated)

t_{al} is the simple average tariff after applying the linear cut.

The following supplementary modalities are proposed for developing country Members: (a) The actual reductions of at least 15 per cent of currently bound rates can differ from the rates calculated under step (1) under condition that the overall percentage reduction still meets the reduction percentage resulting from step (1) and (b) The flexibility in the application of the formula shall also apply for step (2).

(d) Japan[19]

Japan proposes that each Member sets a target level of a trade-weighted tariff average according to a formula and that each Membra reduce its trade-weighted tariff average to that target level. Each Member will retain flexibility on ways to realize the target tariff level. The formula is specified as:

$$t^W_{1a} = \frac{A \times t^W_{0a}}{A \times t^W_{0a}} + \alpha$$

Where, t^w_{0a} is the weighted tariff average prior to the application of the formula and t^w_{0a} is the weighted average after the application of the formula. A is a constant whose values varies as follows:

$t^{W}_{0a} \leq 10\%,$	A = 10
$10\% < t^{W}_{0a} \leq 20\%,$	A = 20
$20\% < t^{W}_{0a} \leq 30\%,$	A = 30
$30\% < t^{W}_{0a},$	A = 30

The term α in this specification has been proposed as a constant equal to 0.3.

The formula applies to the reduction of the trade-weighted tariff average as opposed to a reduction of the tariff rates on a line-by-line basis. This means that the formula is used to determine the end result, or the objective of the tariff negotiations. A lower coefficient will yield a higher cut and a higher co-efficient a lower cut.

(e) Republic of Korea[20]

The objective of this proposal is to lower the weight tariff average of members by 40 per cent, This is achieved by applying a feduction formula that results in a higher reduction formula that result in a higher reduction of tariff peaks. The starting point is a 20 per cent minimum reduction by tariff line, which is followed by a further feduction aimed at harmonising the tariff profile. Two criteria are used to distinguish which tariff rates should be addressed and the applicable methodology. These are twice the national average and 25 per cent.

For the case where tariff rates are above twice the national average but less than 22 per cent, the following formula is applicable which includes the initial 20 per cent reduction:

$$t_1 = (t_0 \times 0.8)) - (0.7 \times (t_0 - 2 \times t_a))$$

If the rariff rate is less than twice the national average, by still above 25 per cent the following formula is applicable which includes the initial 20 per cent reduction:

$$t_1 = (t_0 \times 0.8)) - (0.7 \times (t_0 - 25))$$

In cases, where the rariff rate is above two times, the simple national average and at the same time above 25 per cent, the final rariff rate shall be whichever is lower after the reduction.

The formula reduces higher tariff rates in a way that takes into account individual tariff profiles since the cut is dependent of the tariff average. This means tariff profiles that have duties predominantly below 25 per cent by above twice the national average will still be subject to further tariff reductions. Alternatively, profiles with duties predominantly above 25 per cent, but with high overall averages will still be subject to reductions since the 25 per cent rule will apply.

The overall result of applying theis formula will, therefore, depend on the statistical properties of each Members' tariff profile. It should be noted though that for all tariff profiles with an average of above 12.5 per cent the tariff rate reductions in per cent are idintical for a given tariff tate, because the 25 per cent rule applies in all cases where twice the national average is greater than 25 per cent.

(f) United States[21]

The United States has proposed a modality, which includes the elimination of tariff rates at or below 5 per cent and the application of a Swiss formula on the tarifff proposed coefficient is 8, which converts the general Swiss formula[22] into the following specification:

$$t_1 = \frac{8 \times t_0}{8 + t_0}$$

What is important to note about the US proposal is the value of 8 for the co-efficient. This implies a maximum tariff tate of 8 per cent after tariff reductions for any tariff profile.

Draft Modalities by Chairman, NGMA: Some Comments

Based on different submissions, as summarized avobe, Chairman of NGMA has prepated a document 'Draft Elements of Modalities for Negotiations on Non-Agricultural Products',

WTO, *TN/MA/W/35*, 16 May, 2003. There are four major components of the NGMA Chairman Draft (NGMA-CD).

1. ***Formula (Core modality):*** All non-agricultural tariff shall be reduced on a line-by-line basis using the fomula applied to the base rates;

$$t_1 = \frac{B \times t_a \; X \; t_0}{B \times t_a + t_0}$$

Where,

t_1 is the final rate, to be bound in *as valorem* terms

t_0 is the base rate

t_a is the average of the base rates

2. ***Sector-by-Sector/Zero-by-Zero Approach:*** The NGMA-CD has also proposed a sectoral elimination approach, in addition to the application of formula, for seven sectors: Electronics & Electrical goods; Fish & Fish Products, Footwear; Leather goods; Motor Vehicle parts & components Stones, Gems & Precious Metals; and Textiles & Clothing.
3. ***Supplementary Modalities:*** In addition to the avobe two approaches, the NAGA-CD proposes that member countries should adopt other procedures for additional tariff reduction and elimination.
4. ***Non-Tariff Barriers:*** The Chairman summarizes some elements for deductions of elimination of non-tariff barriers.

The above components do not summarise elements of 'special & differential treatments', 'newly acceded members' and 'appropriate study and capacity-building'.

A comparative summary of the different proposals is provided in Table 2, Table 3 presents simulations of tariff reductions resulting from different proposals to get a comparative perspectives.

Keeping the priorities of developing countries, the following paragraphs give some pointed observations on NGMA-CD modalities:

Table 2
A Summary of Alternative Liberalization Proposals

"EU"	Initial tariffs under 2 per cent are eliminated, tariffs between 2 and 15 per cent are reduced by 55 per cent with final tariffs capped at 15 per cent. No. reductions in agriculture or services or in least developed countries.
"Korea"	For industrials, as specified by formula. No reductions in agriculture or services or in least developed countries.
"India"	50 per cent reduction in bound import tariffs in developed countries and 33.3 per cent reduction in developing countries for industrials. No reductions in agriculture or services or in least developed countries.
"China"	For industrials, as specified with B=1, No reductions in agriculture or services or in least developed countries.
"US"	All tariffs eliminated. No reductions in agriculture or services or in least developed countries.
"WTO"	Tariffs reduced according to a Swiss formula with maximum coefficient equal to country average. Tariffs eliminated for electronics and electric goods, fish and fish products, textiles and clothing, footwear, leather goods, motor vehicle parts and components, stones, gems and precious metals. No reductions in agriculture or services or in least developed countries.

Note: (Based on proposals, modified to take account of undefined LEMENTS) under the "WTO" simulation, the binding of developing country tariffs at double the applied rate follows the WTO proposal except that the WTO proposes to bind 95 per cent of tariff lines and imports. Obviously, it could be very important which lines are excluded.

Source: RIS based on Laird et al. (2003). Market Access proposals for Non-Agricultural Products (Draft). Trade Policy Branch, UNCTAD, Geneva, 16 July, 2003.

Table 3
Bound and Applied Non-agricultural Tariffs before and after Application of Various Proposals

	Developed Countries		*Developed Countries*	
	Bound %	*Applied %*	*Bound %*	*Applied %*
Initial	3.0	2.0	14.6	8.3
Proposal				
EU	1.6	1.5	5.6	4.6
Korea	2.1	1.8	11.5	7.0
India	1.4	1.3	10.8	7.5
China	1.1	1.1	5.7	5.0
WTO NGMA-CD (B=1)	0.7	0.6	5.8	4.1
USA	0.0	0.0	0.0	0.0

The core modality is based on formula. The formula proposed in NGMA-CD is a modified version of Swiss Formula. Swiss formula does not incorporate the structure and average level of tariff rates of individual member Countries, while the NGMA-CD proposed formula takes care fo average tariffs of member countries. However, this formula (like Swiss Formula) also depends upon the (magic) Value of co-efficient B. In the Tokyo Round, the value of B was taken as 14 (and 16 in some cases). In this modified formula of NGMA-CD, we cannot take B=14 or 16; because it will not lead to deeper reduction as per guidelines of the Doha Declaration. The draft proposal is silent on the value of co-efficient B.

To understand the implication the NGMA-CD proposed formula, we have calculated post-development round binding tariff rates under alternate scenarios depending on values of Band average tariff (t_1). Figures 1 to 5 give select broad scenarios based on NGMA-CD proposed formula using alternate values of B = 0.25, 0.5, 1.0, 1.5, and 2.0, respectively; and average tariff rates of t_a = 5,10,15,20,25, and 30 per cent. One can notice from these figures that the post-development round bound rates for countries with average tariff of 5 per cent and B = 1.0 per cent (Figure 4), will be 70 per cent lower than the pre- development round. In case the uppermost tariffs is 50 per cent, the post-development round tariff will be around 4 per cent. This scenario is close to the tariff structure of a large number of developed countries. On the other hand, a scenario with average tariff of 25 per cent and B = 1, will lead to reduction of around 50 per cent. In case peak tariff is 50 per cent in pre-development round, it will be reduced to 17 per cent in post-development round. This scenario is close to the countries whose average tariff is high. Basically it show that the NGMA-CD formula can take care of (i) reduction of tariffs, (ii) peak and high tariff, and (iii) structure of pre-development round binding rates. In other words, if the average tariff of a country is low, the declining rate of peak tariff will be substantial.

The NGMA-CD formula is sensitive to co-efficient value of B. If the value of B is high (say 2), the reduction will not be significant (see figures 1 to 5). This can be illustrated through a

Figure 1
NGMA Chairman Draft Formula for Tariff Reduction Proposed Tariff = (B*a*X)/(B*a+X), where B = 2.0 and a = average tariff

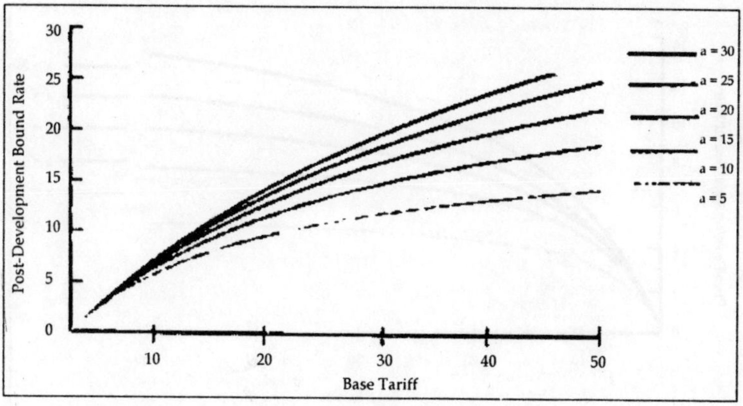

Figure 2
NGMA Chairman Draft Formula for Tariff Reduction Proposed Tariff = (B*a*X)/(B*a+X), where B = 1.5, and a = average tariff

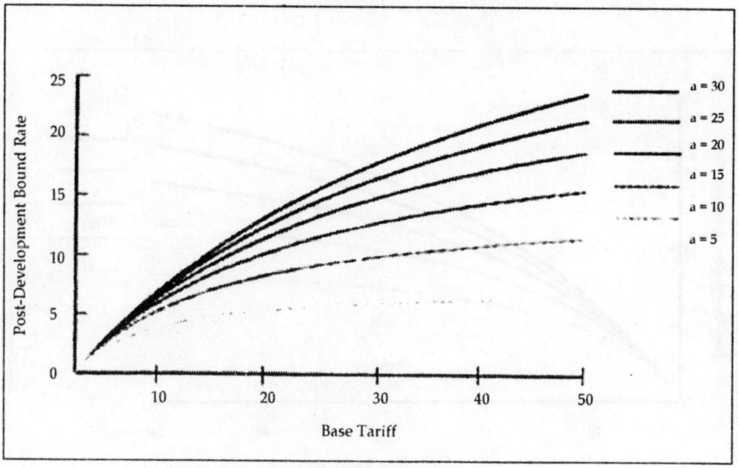

Figure 3
NGMA Chairman Draft Formula for Tariff Reduction
Y = (B*a*X)/(B*a+X), where B = 0.5, and a = average tariff

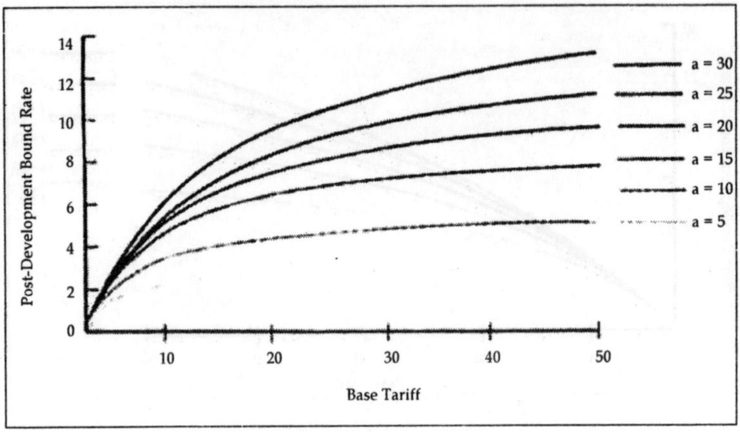

Figure 4
NGMA Chairman Draft Formula for Tariff Reduction Proposed
Tariff = (B*a*X)/(B*a+X), where B = 1 and a = average tariff

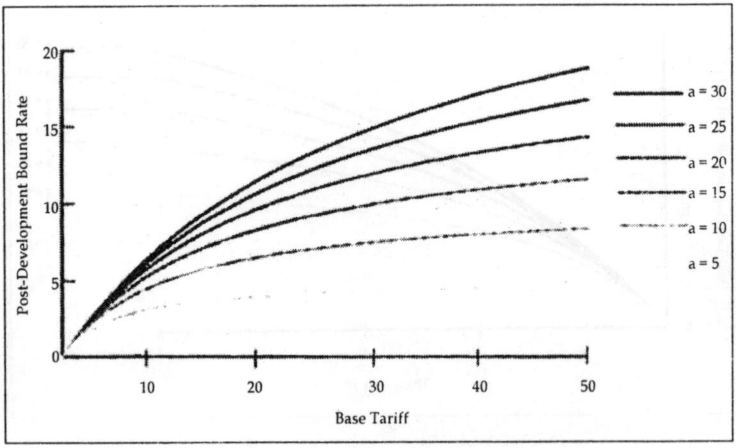

Figure 5
NGMA Chairman Draft Formula for Tariff Reduction Proposed
Tariff = (B*a*X)/(B*a+X), where B = 0.25, and a = average tariff

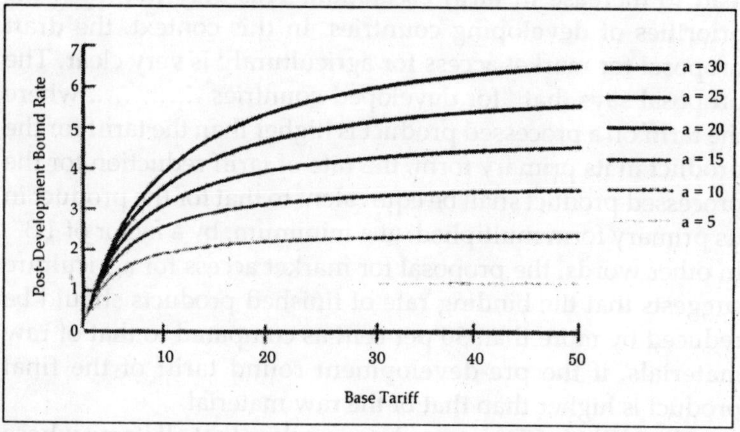

case study. Let us suppose the average tariff of a country is 5 per cent. If we take B = 02, we can expect that it will lead to a decline from 10 per cent level (of a commodity) to 5 per cent level; and a B = 0.25 will lead to a decline from the 10 per cent level to 1 per cent level. Keeping these factors in view, it is clear that the co-efficient value for developed and developing countries should not be unique. In fact, the value of B for developing countries should be higher as compared to that of developed countries.

The zero-by-zero approach for tariff elimination of seven sectors, i.e. Electronics & Electrical goods; Fish & Fish products; Footwear; Leather goods; Motor Vehicle parts & components; Stones, Gems, & Precious Metals; and Textiles & Clothing; is similar to Information Technology Agreement (ITA). Although the NGMA-CD talks about S & D treatment for implementation period in these sectors, it adds, however, very specifically that approach will be applicable to all the products of these sectors, even for developing countries.

The NGMA-CD is completely silent on tariff escalation of non-agricultural products. The formula does indirectly capture it. In case, the NGMA-CD formula is used, the rate of the tariff escalation may decline as compared to as that of Uruguay Round.[23] the 'supplementary modalities' of NGMA-CD may lead to increase in tariff escalation. This may not meet the priorities of developing countries. In this context, the draft proposal for market access for agricultural[24] is very clear. The proposal says that "for developed countries .... where the tariff on a processed product is higher than the tariff for the product in its primary form, the rate of tariff reduction for the processed product shall be equivalent to that for the product in its primary form multiplied, at a minimum, by a factor of 1.3". In other words, the proposal for market access for agriculture suggests that the binding rate of finished products should be reduced by more than 30 per cent as compared to that of raw materials, if the pre-development round tariff of the final product is higher than that of the raw material.

The NGMA-CD proposal is very clear that all items whose duties are difined in the form of specific and complex forms should be included in negotiations. It says " ..... Non *ad-valorem* duties shall be converted to *ad valorem* equivalents (AVE_s) according to the procedures ...." The NGMA-CD proposal also mentions the formula for working out *ad-valorem.*

Equivalence of specific duties are using simple methods. However, it is well-known how some of these specific duties are defined, and it is very difficult to calculate *ad-valorem* equivalence of these duties.[25] The NGMA-CD proposes that in such case of "Non *ad-valorem* tariffs for which AVEs cannot be calculated by the Secretariat because of the technical nature of the duties concerned shall be assumed to have an AVE equivalent to the tariff average (t_a) as used in the formula". India and developing countries should keep a close watch on this, because it has been noticed that the *ad-valorem* equivalence of specific duties, indeed, is relatively very high as compared to those commodities whose duties are defined in the form of *ad-valorem* rates.

NGMA-CD is still not clear about coverage of NTBs to be dealt with. It is probably not very clear about how to deal with non-tariff barriers. It is still talking about (i) identification and examination of various types of NTBs, (ii) categorization,

(iii) collection of information, and (iv) inter-linkage with other bodies of WTO. It says that modalities could include request/offer, horizontal or vertical approaches. Developing countries should ask for clear interpretation of such steps towards, NTBs.

The NGMA-CD proposal says that "for developing countries .... Upto 5 per cent of tariff lines may remain unbound provide that they do not exceed 5 per cent of the total value of a member's imports". Both these conditions of 5 per cent tariff lines and 5 per cent import value are very strict. The developing countries should demand either a 5 per cent tariff line or 5 per cent imports value.

A revised version the May, 2003 Draft Modalities Paper by Chairman, NGMA was issued on 19 August (TN/MA/35/Rev/1). In this revision, a number of provisions were changed. For instance, the flexibility offered to developing and least develop countries to keep up to 5 per cent of tariff lines unbound, provided they do not exceed 5 per cent of the total value of imports. This flexibility has been curbed by amending it to 5 per cent of tariff lines provide that no more than 1 per cent could be taken in one HS Chapter. Another change is the exception allowed to countries having binding coverage of less than 35 per cent from the reduction commitment provided they bind 100 per cent of tariff lines at 27.5 per cent or less.

Concluding Remarks

Market Access for non-agriculture products is one of the principal agenda items in the WTO negotiations. The basic mandate in the Doha Declaration under the category 'tariff and trade of industrial products' is both broad and comprehensive. Developing countries should concentrate on reduction in peak tariffs and tariff escalations. They should also demand that all the countries should define their binding rates in the form of *ad-valorem* rates, because it has been noticed that *ad-valorem* equivalence of non *ad-valorem* duties are very high.

After the adoption of the Doha Agenda, a number of proposals relating to 'modalities' were submitted by member countries to NGMA. The Chairman of NGMA submitted a draft proposal of modalities after a series of formal and informal consultation. The core modality/formula submitted by NGMA-CD does attempt to address: (i) tariff peaks, (ii) tariff escalation, and (iii) *non ad-valorem* duties. However, it also seeks drastic reductions in tariff rates in developing countries. It is not easy for developing countries to completely accept the tariff elimination in seven sectors, even in an extended framework. They should be either made 'zero-for-A, where A is a positive number or alternatively, the coverage of lines in identified seven sectors should be 75 per cent of lines for developing countries. The thrust could be to grade the product tariff according to the developing countries' capabilities.

Keeping in view, the prevailing level of developing and their infrastructure in the developing countries, it needs to be appreciated that tariff is an important instrument for making domestic and trade policies. On the domestic front tariff elimination, it may be recalled, will lead to substantial reduction in customs revenue that is the main form of revenue receipt for the developing countries. The developing countries therefore, should be given full advantage of less than full reciprocity.

NOTES

1. See for example WTO, 2001. *US Trade Policy Review, Geneva.*
2. See, Mehta. 2001, WTO, Liberalization and Industrial Sector: The Case of Market Access, *RIS Occasional Paper No. 63.*
3. See, Mehta, 2003. Indian Industrial Tariffs: Towords, WTO Development Round Negotiations, RIS.
4. UNCTAD, 1999-2000, The Post-UR Rariff Environment for Developing Countries: Tariff Peaks and Tariff Escalation, TD/B/COM/1/14/1,14 September. Mehta (2001), ibid; Mehta (2003), ibid, UNCTAD (2003), Back to Basics: Market Access Issues in the Doha Agenda, UNCTAD/DITC/TAB/Misc,9, and Bacchetta, M. and B. Bora (2003), Industrial Tariff Liberalization and the Doha Development Agenda, WTO Discussion Paper.
5. Amount of Value per unit of imported commodity.
6. See for example, UNCTAD, CDROM TRAINS Winter 1998 and Mehta, R. and S.K. Mohanty (2001), WTO and Industrial Tariff: An Empirical Analysis for India, Reprint, RIS.
7. See Mehta, Rajesh and Mohanty, S.K. 2001, ibid. UNCTAD, ibid.

8. See Mehta, Rajesh and Mohanty, S.K. 2001, ibid. UNCTAD, ibid.
9. See Mehta, Rajesh and Mohanty, S.K. 2001, ibid.
10. Mehta, Rajesh, 2001. ibid.
11. See, UNCTAC, 1999-2000, IBID AND UN, Market Access since UR, Implications, Opportunities and Challenges, Report pepared by UNCTD and WTO, May 1998.
12. See UNCTAD. 1999-2000. ibid for instance.
13. Mehta and Mohanty. 2001. also prove this point using detail data of five developed countries.
14. UNCADL, ibid and Mehta. 2001 ibld in the recent past.
15. A number of proposals have been submitted by different countries. Among these proposals three submissions have been made by India.
16. TN/MA/W/20.
17. TN/MA/W/11/And.1 and Add. 2.
18. TN/MA/W/10/Add. 2; suggestions for the treatment of unbound lines are beyond the scope of this document and have, therefore not been included.
19. TN/MA/W/15.
20. TN/MA/W/6/Add. 1.
21. TN/MA/W/18.
22. For details of Swiss formula, see Hoda, A. 2001. Tariff Negotiations and Renegotiations under the GATT and the WTO, Procedures and Practices, Cambridge University Press, UK and Mehta, R (2003), ibid.
23. Uruguay Round led to increases in tariff escalation particularly for products in which developing countries have export potential. See, Mehta and Mohanty (2001) and UNCTAD (1999/2000), among others.
24. WTO. 2003. Negotiations on Agriculture First Draft of Modalities for the Further Commitments, Committee on Agriculture, TN/AG/W/1/Rev.1, 18 March 2003.
25. See for example UNCTAD, TRAINS, Winte 1998; and Mehta and Mohanty (2001).

WTO AND AGREEMENT ON AGRICULTURE

*Debesh Bhowmik**

Introduction

The WTO is the only one international organization which can function world trade among various nations through multilateral trading rules. The WTO was born from the inception of international trading agreements although the trading agreements and system of GATT in 1948 had incorporated in it. The prime purpose of WTO is to help the flow of international trade as freely as possible so long as there are no undesirable side effects. But, those trading systems must have inclusion of five laws, namely, (i) without discrimination, (ii) tree trade, (iii) predictable, (iv) more competitive, (v) more beneficial to less developed countries.

The structure of WTO is very simple. The topmost body of it is the Ministerial Conference which is composed of (i) General Council, (ii) The Disputes Settlement Body, (iii) The trade policy review body. The General Council have three Functional Councils such as, (a) Council for Trade in Goods, (b) Council for trade in Services, (c) Council for Trade Related Aspects of Intellectual Property Rights (TRIPs).

Under Multilateral Trade Agreements, the Ministerial Conference establishes the following functional Committee e.g, (i) Committee on Trade and Development, (ii) Committee on Balance of Payments Restrictions, (iii) Committee on Budget, Finance and Administration, and Committee on Trade and Environment.

The Council for Trade in Goods have several functions under the bodies of the following: (i) Committee on Agriculture, (ii) Textile Monitoring Body, (iii) Committee on Technical

* International Institute for Development Studies, Kolkata.

Barrier to Trade, (iv) Committee on Trade Related Investment Measures, (v) Committee on Anti--Dumping Measures, (vi) Committee on Customs Valuation, (vii) Committee on Subsidies and Countervailing Measures, (viii) Committee on Rules of Origin, (ix) Committee on Safeguards.

The Agreements on Agriculture among various countries have been edited in the Committee of Agriculture and those are accepted by all under the Ministerial Conference. The committee affords members the opportunity of consulting on any matter relating to implementation of commitments including rule based commitments. For this purpose, the Committee usually meets four times per year. Special meeting can be condneted if necessary.

In this structural framework of WTO, Agreements on Agriculture is to be explained and evaluated in this brief paper.

Agreements on Agriculture

Agreements on Agriculture were effective on 1.1.1995. The preamble of AOA recognizes that agreed long-term objective of the reform process initiated by the Uruguay Round reform programme is to establish a fair and market oriented agricultural trading system. Negotiations on agriculture began in early 2000, under Article 20 of WTO Agreement on Agriculture. By November 2001, governments had submitted a large number of negotiating proposals. The negotiations aimed at, (i) market access (various trade restrictions confronting imports), (ii) export subsidies (methods used to make exports artificially competitive), (iii) domestic support (subsidies and other programme including those that raise on guarantee farm gate prices and farmer's incomes).

Uruguay Round has reduced the extent of uncertainty of tariff rate in agriculture to increase the market access because it has directed to introduce the limit of tariff rate. Yet the percentage rate of tariff limit have been increased in the post Uruguay Round than the pre Uruguay Round due to trade liberalization and free trade. It is shown in the Table 1.

With a view to achieving free trade the developed countries have reduced 36% tariff rate from 1995 to 6 years

Table 1
The Limit of Tariff Rate (%) 1986-94

	Pre Uruguay Round	*Post Uruguay Round*
Developing Countries	21	73
Developed Countries	78	99
Transitional Economies	73	98

and the developing countries reduced 24% tariff rate within 10 years. The underdeveloped countries are exempted from this tariff cut condition. Yet, it is proved from various survey reports that many countries have been lying below this tariff limit rate. There are several reasons behind it, which are given below:

(a) Some countries have been suffering from the defects of the process of research and analysis.

(b) There are innumerable complexities in the ad-valorem and specific tariffs that could not be eliminated even today.

(c) Many countries failed to choose the preferable agreement in the implementation of tariff rate, so that they began to delay through administrative laws.

(d) The trade control index and the trade control index of the merchantilist suffer from internal aggregation problem.

(e) So, it is necessary to impose linear reduction, aggregate reduction and circular stages formula reduction method to cut tariff rate after analyzing the circumstances. Along with the increase in quota, the administrative controls are urgent.

The Domestic Support generally raises agricultural commodity prices and farmer's income. This support has four types, e.g., (i) Green Box or granted policies. It has little impact. (ii) Amber Box where Aggregate Measures Support can be reduced, (iii) Blue Box or Freedom of Agricultural Farm and (iv) De-Minimis where it was stated in 6 (a) and 6 (b) clauses that less than 5% of the value of agricultural production will be reduced from the Aggregate Measures Support of the developed countries. In case of developing countries, less than 10% of the product wise or unproduct wise support of value of production will be reduced from Aggregate Measures Support. Aggregate Measures Support for developed countries will be reduced by 20% within six years and 13.3% within 10 years for developing countries, and there is no limit for the underdeveloped countries. The Blue Box law opened the opportunity of infinite cost for direct transaction of farms of various countries. The users of this law are: EU, Japan, Norway and Switzerland. The transactions of environmental related programme, insecticides and disease control, infrastructure development domestic food aid are included in the Green Box laws.

There are a few industrialized nations where Aggregate Measures Support are above the De-minimis level of 5% whereas India's rate is negative. Because the limited limit of tariff rate of those countries are abnormally high. The progressive reduction of domestic subsidies and limited high tariff rate increased their degree of agricultural protection. So, the urgent need is to establish a relationship between the assurance of market access reduction and the ratio of Aggregate Measures Support and the limited tariff rate. If the Aggregate Measures Support is less than the De-Minimis level then the implementation is not possible in assurance of minimum market access. Yet, to what extent the process of agricultural protection and agricultural support in various countries remain and how much welfare gain can be achieved for, is shown in the Table 2.

Table 2
The Expenditure for Agricultural Protection

	Yearly welfare gain/Gain reducing 50% Ag. Protection (bi$)	*Share of world welfare gain*	*Total Agriculture support measure 1998 (bi $)*
U.S.A. and Canada	6.0	6.7%	101.5
EU	12.7	14.3%	142.2
Japan	43.1	48.4%	56.4%
Underdeveloped countries	10.3	11.6%	n.a.
Other countries	16.9	19.6%	n.a.
World (Total)	89.0	100.0%	362.4

The Table 2 proved that agricultural support increases with the decrease of agricultural tariff rate by which the level of welfare can be increased. So, openness and liberalization in agriculture can stimulate total welfare gain in world trade although there may be inequality in that welfare level. Because the trend of inequality will depend on how much agricultural commodities of developing countries will trade with the developed countries for reduction of tariff and increase in support measures.

Generally, export subsidies are required for increasing export competitiveness in the world market. In this respect, the developed countries will reduce subsidies by 36% within six years and the developing countries will reduce 24% within 10 years. Even the developed countries will cut subsidies exportables by 21% within 6 years and the developing countries will do the same by 14% within 10 years. The underdeveloped countries are exempted from these limits.

There is a list of exportable to be subsidized in the clause 9.1 of agreements on agriculture from where we know the utilization of subsidies in agriculture, which are, (i) the possibilities of direct export subsidies, (ii) the selling price of non-commercial stock of agricultural goods for export will be such that is comparatively less than the domestic market, (iii) the producer expensed for subsidies, e.g., levies are imposed on every commodities for expense of government programme and a part of levies are used for export subsidies, (iv) the export promotion is executed by reducing subsidies to reduce expenditure in which high level implementation cost and international transportation are included with it, (v) to sanction subsidies for agricultural goods such as wheat and biscuit have been treated as exportable.

In agricultural sector, the special and differential treatment is a part and parcel of agriculture and the tropical agricultural commodities is a part of free trade. The most significant element of special and differential treatment is the agreements on agriculture is the exemption from reduction commitments of the following measures required to encourage agricultural and rural development. (i) investment subsidies which are generally available to agriculture, (ii) agricultural input subsidies generally available to low income and resource poor farmers, and (iii) support to producers to encourage diversification from growing illicit narcotics crops.

The special and differential treatment should be included in the green box and amber box but not in the blue box. In green box there were general services, stock for food security, domestic food aid, direct sanction to producer, income support, government participation in income insurance and income security programme, financial assistance for natural calamities and environment and regional support project etc.

In the special and differential treatment, the developing countries committed to reduce at the lowest rate, e.g, 24% of budget expenditure and 14% of exportable and these will effect within 10 years. In the mean time 12 developing countries applied for lowering rate. Five member nations sent notice to WTO for implementation of export subsidies for 1995-98. But the utility of special and differential treatment to developing countries is not so much flexible. In the Uruguay Round, many developing countries, yet, now-a-days the degree of openness has increased to a greater extent. Hence, it is not wise to think, that the item of special and differential treatment is to be eliminated from the charter of WTO. Yet, the amendments would be such that the inequality in agriculture is so high between the developing and the developed nations especially the special and differential treatment may be hampered for the diversion of international trade.

In Doha Round, the developing countries protested that they had no gain from the agreement on agriculture, on the other hand, they got loss. Food and Agriculture Organization stated from a survey of 14 countries that food import induced losses of local farmers so that local economy do not succeed on food security, employment economic growth and poverty eradication. In 1998, it was reported from their observation that net food import prices of developing countries had increased annually by 20% due to decrease in stock of government.

Some Proposals

Recently, in July 2002, USA has submitted some proposals for agreements on agriculture to WTO. The main theme of the proposals are given below:

(a) All the export subsidies must be eliminated within 5 years.

(b) To reduce tariff rate on agricultural commodities within 5years so that no tariff would be greater than 25%.

(c) To reduce trade diversion of domestic support at the rate of 5% of total agricultural produce within 5years.

17 agricultural export countries submitted some proposals on March 2003 for agreements on agriculture. These are given below:

1. The tariff rate for all the developed countries is to be reduced by 25% or more and domestic consumption quota is to be increased by 20%. The special safeguard security is to be eliminated. The tariff cut proposal for developing countries was accepted and the period of effectiveness has extended.
2. The inclusion of dumping in this proposal was agreed upon.
3. The developed countries must eliminate amber box expenditure within 5 years for domestic support and the developing countries must eliminate within 9 years. During the first year the developed countries should reduce amber box expenditure by 50% and by degrees they should completely eliminate to blue box expenditure but it should be remain for the developing countries. This system should be more restricted from the misutilisation of green box.

On the other hand, EU proposed that;

(a) Export subsidies must be reduced by 45%

(b) Aggregate Measure Support level must be reduced by 55%

(c) Tariff rate should reduce 36% from the present level

(d) Exports without tariff and quota will be introduced for the developing countries and full tariff on imports of 55% will be exempted that came from developing countries. Besides, EU proposed to set up a 'Food Security Box'.

(e) Some geographical indicators for foodstuffs should be included.

(f) Strict precautionary measures should be implemented for

maintaining food security laws and rights of monetary incentives of the farmer's for activating the wild animal welfare control laws.

(g) Besides, EU proposed to set up a "Development Box"

Among others Harbinson draft proposal envisaged that;

1. Export subsidies will be completely eliminated within 10 years.
2. Domestic support of the amber box will be reduced by 60% within 5 years.
3. High tariff rate must be cut specially within three stages. 90% tariff rate will be reduced 60% on an average to keep up within 45% tariff rate. From 15% to 90% tariff cut will be available at the minimum rate of 45%. The tariff should be cut down to 45% on an average where the tariff rate is equal to less than 15%.
4. The conditions of green box should be more stricter.
5. The utilization of export credit would be more restricted.
6. The restricted policies are needed in green box if any complex problem emerges.
7. ED approved the environment and wild animal welfare programme of green box.
8. A new "Special Security" that will protect strategic produce will be introduced for low income countries. Its main target will be developing countries' development to maintain the right of high cost level for domestic support.

The proposals of changes in agreements on agriculture should maintain the equal distribution of agricultural food production. It was not mentioned either by the proposal of USA or by EU. The types of agreements on agriculture that were mentioned in the proposals no 1, 2 and 3 of Harbinson which would be accepted in the final stages whose patterns could be recovered in various stages of agreements on agriculture. But, both the proposals of EU and Harbinson were silent on the inequality of developing countries' agriculture. Even, they ignored the large, scale domestic support of developed countries including the export subsidies, so, the developing countries should not open their market for dumped commodities. The concept of forming food security to reduce tariff rate was ignored. So, the interest of poor farmers or the people of below the poverty line may be hampered. The Harbinson proposal desires to cut tariff rate slowly on strategic goods whereas ED is in favour of imposing liberal policies on food security of the developing countries. Yet, both the proposals are in favour of flexible government expenditure for the interest of poor farmers. But, how the developing poor countries protected their markets by imposing tariff policies in the open market in WTO laws, depends on the economic policies taken by them. However, both proposals welcomed the additional uses of developing countries' special safeguard and failed to solve the fundamental problem of internal inequality of agreement on agriculture.

Effects on India and other Developing Countries

As a result of agreement on agriculture, there were mixed results on India and other developing countries. The domestic and export subsidy charters produce complex explanation where some are subsidy exempted and some are reduced rate. These classifications go in favour of developed nations especially for EU, USA, Canada, Japan whose levels of domestic support are very high. In comparison to developed nations the level of domestic support of India is so low that the competition between them in agriculture is baseless. It is not possible to eliminate the disadvantages in agricultural sector in developing countries by increasing the level of domestic support because the developed Countries have to expense 1-2% of GNP if they sanctioned 50% subsidies on agriculture and the developing countries have to expense 14% of GNP (Ramesh Chand and Linu Mathew, 2001). C.H. Hanumantha Rao (2001) thought that India proposed to the agreements on agriculture in WTO that aggregate measures support should be determined by the specific product wise or non specific product wise aggregate support. If the specific product wise support is negative in India, then aggregate measures support will be less than 7.5% of the value of agricultural produce. Naturally, the subsidies of inputs of small farmers transferred to non specific product wise support and reduced to less than half compared to the present rate. Biswajit Dhar (2003) said that the food procurement price in India for food stock is less than the international price in case of aggregate measures support. But, it was proposed that the maximum limit of aggregate measures support of the developing countries will not be greater than 10% of the value of agricultural produce of the developing countries and will not be greater than 5% of the value of agricultural produce of developed nations. If the limits are crossed then the developed nations will reduce 20% and developing nations will reduce 13.3% for implementation.

Another bold argument is that India will be suffered especially on farmers' right and food security by the plant variety protection laws of TRIPs in WTO. Because, farmers cannot procure the seed, exchange their produce or right to sell or even reproduce for commercial purpose under the UPOV laws. The producers' right of the developed countries are protected under the system of Sui-Generis in UPOV-78 and UPOV-91 but the rights of farmers were not protected. Therefore, the emergence of multinational seed corporation is eminent. Then India would lose control of seed production and the food security would be halted. S. Swaminathan and Anklesaria Aiyar (2004) opined that under the free trade doctrine the tariff less developed countries' competitive entry into India has been increasing. This situation is not favourable for India. The only way of escaping from this situation is to replace the multilateral free trade system under WTO. But, as the degree of tariff rate and quota become less under WTO, so that free competitors of tariff less developed countries will be less under free trade agreements. If the agricultural subsidies are exempted in the rich countries, then the international prices of sugar, cotton, rice, wheat etc will rise. Since India has comparative advantage in those commodities, then India will be the chief exporting countries of the world for these goods. This type of explanation is not made by many Indians because they thought that Indian farmers would fall in danger under the liberalization process of agricultural trade in WTO. But it is not always true. If tariff is eliminated throughout the world then the Indian farmers would be high degree competitors and would gain sufficiently in the world trade.

Presently, among the 148 developing nations, 105 countries are net food importers, 63 Countries are net agricu1tural exporters of which 33 countries are net agricu1tural exporters of which 28 countries are the poorest. Moreover, non-homogeneity in geographical distribution were visible in countries area, destination of exports and the source of imports. In case of agricultural exporters, the share of exports of developing countries in comparison with others, their real targets are (1) to reduce competitive cost subsidity, (2) to impose more permanent prices, (3) to introduce protective policy against obstacles and political trade barriers, (4) sanitary and phyto-sanitary laws were not used as obstacles, (5) to introduce protective policies against mis-utilisation of tariff policy on the low priced sell and imports in the foreign markets. In case of agricu1tural imports, they desired confirmation of stairs and comparatively fixed prices. These are possible to realize. The more is the volume of trade the more open the market the more stability of the market. In the low income food deficit country, the short run price stability and the changes of expanded general price level will face difficulties. Historically, the low income food deficit countries cut in food aid which we observed after Uruguay Round Besides, they face several natural disasters like draught, flood, epidemic, earthquake, typhoon etc. Free agricultural trade is harmful to them.

So the requests of developing countries to WTO are, (1) to cut high degree of agricultural tariff rate in the rich countries but most of the nations kept up high rate of tariff following Uruguay Round, (2) agricultural export subsidies should be completely exempted, (3) to reduce domestic support and to suspend the loss system in rich countries due to low prices, (4) sanitary and phyto-sanitary programme and commercial intellectual property right agreements should be utilized and balanced.

Some Observations

In the multilateral trading system under WTO, the transparent trade laws were enacted whereas 800 million people in the developing countries have been fallen into hunger of which 70% are dependent on agriculture. So, the welfare and the interest of the developing countries are desired for agreements on agriculture which was less emphasized in the Cancun agenda so that we can propose five trade policies to all developing countries to maintain transparency in trade laws, e.g., (1) as long as the high subsidy rate of USA and EU occur trade diversion, so the developing countries have the rights to apply to keep up less rate of tariff than the domestic production cost, (2) the developing countries have rights to apply for granting less tariff rate for the principal non-exportable crops, (3) the developing countries should bring flexibility of uses of domestic support cost to raise production for local consumption, (4) the farmers of the developing countries should have option for market structure controlled by the farmers, (5) the developed nations should send food aid to cut food imports of developing and underdeveloped countries if they support agricultural development.

Therefore trade laws should be amended in such a way that, (a) every nation must have right to formulate and to execute its own agricultural and food policies including the rights to manage capital and production, (b) developing countries should have rights to protect agricultural goods of less production cost from dumping, (c) every nation should not given permission for dumping in the international market, (d) farmers should get proper prices of their produce and the buyers should get safe, definite food supply which are environmentally sustainable, (e) markets without competition should be reduced and the market distortion caused by cartels etc should be monitored.

Besides, the developing countries should form a "Food Security Box" to face the unstable food security system. During the experience of effectiveness of agreements on agriculture in last six years, it was proved that high domestic support, high tariff rate, tariffless obstacles of developed countries hampered the developing countries' market access of agricultural exports. Besides, the developing countries could agree upon the systems of direct import control for export subsidies or domestic support for goods of developed countries. It will be wise to eliminate the green box and blue box subsidies of developed countries. The developing countries should make re-agreement for changing the base year of the export subsidies in agreements on agriculture and gave pressure to exempt export subsidies at progressive level. In this respect, the nobel laureate Stiglitz opined that the trade diversion effect would go in favour of agriculture.

In case of intellectual property rights, Swaminathan Foundation of India proposed to set up a Community Gene Fund in the national level after a prolonged research and welcomed for sanctioning in international level. Besides, the policies and laws for geographical indicators in India were forwarded for implementation within 1-1-2000. In the present globalisation era, agreements on agriculture may increase poverty rate in low income countries and food importing countries. The worldwide commercialization in agricultural output can stimulate the number of landless peasants and can increase the intensity of inequality.

Conclusion

The meaning of agreements on agriculture under WTO is to set up the system of free trade era through gradual agricultural trade liberalization. But the reality is that the developed countries forced the developing countries to reduce subsidies whereas they have been raising their subsidies. In this situation the Disputes Settlement Body is not neutral but they opined in favour of the developed countries. Therefore the developing countries should think how much environment protection would be effective through sustainable development process and how much alternative path of economic freedom would be opened to them.

In the agriculture committee a regional representative should be included so that the information system may be developed. The WTO should clear knowledge about the agricultural debt or total external debt of the members because the sustainable debt process may disturb the integrated development structure to execute agreements on agriculture. Therefore WTO must have close connection with other international financial institutions for the interest of development not for the interest of developed countries.

It is true that the harmful sectors of the developing countries were identified after the execution of agreements on agriculture but no socialist integration and not even a progressive forum were formed after the completion of Doha summit in spite of being strong protest against several agenda by member nations. It is necessary to analyse agreements on agriculture properly for developing Countries' interest to frame an integrated policies of forming a bloc. In Seattle and Cancun this possibility was partially seen and the role of China, South Asia, South East Asia were appreciable but not progressive or socialistic.

Last but not the least, the WTO did not include the forestry in agreements on agriculture, so that the effects of international trade in environmental equilibrium and forest goods were unrecognized. But its effects on sustainable agricultural development in present or future generation is being undetermined. It is hoped that future round of WTO will think and discuss the subject carefully and will formulate policies for short run as well as long run.

REFERENCES

Bhowmik D. (2002), Essays on International Money. (Deep and Deep, New Delhi).

—— (2002), Imperialism and WTO: A view from Labour Standard and Environment, Paper Published in 22nd Conference of Bengal Economic Association, Presidency College, Kolkata, pp. 49-60.

Canadian Food Security Policy Group (2003), Fair Trade for Hungry farmers January.

Cato Institute (1999), Seattle and beyond: A WTO Agenda for the new Millennium. Trade Policy Analysis No. 8, November 4.

Chand, Ramesh and Linu Mathew Phillip (2001), Is WTO Providing Level Playing Field? EPW, August 11-17, pp. 3014-3016.

Dhar, Biswajit (1995), The Uruguay Round Agreements: A Critical Appraisal. RIS Occasional Paper No. 48, RIS, New Delhi.

Diao, Xinshen, Eugenio Diaz Bonilla and Sherman Robinson (2003), The Impact of Agricultural Trade Policies on Developing Countries. www.ifpri.org.

Ganesan, A.V. (2003), Seattle Ministerial Conference of WTO: Agenda for India. www.icrier.org.

Green, Duncan (2003), Development and Agriculture in the WTO: A Comparison between Development Box, the ED's Food Security Box and the Harbinson Draft Modalities. www.cafod.org.uk.

Hoda, Anwarul and Ashoke Gulati (2003), Special and Differential Treatment Agricultural Negotiations. Paper presented in International Conference on Agricultural Policy Reform and the WTO Italy June 23-26.

Gulati Ashok and S. Narayan (2003), Price Trade Liberalisation and Poverty. EPW, 4th January, pp. 45-52.

Hansen, Bukh (2002), WTO: Impact of AOA on Developing Countries, in A Collection of Essays on Globalisation in Bengali-Ed by Amiya Kumar Bagchi, Vol. 2, (NBA, Kolkata) pp. 76-83.

Hanumantha Rao, C.H. (2001), WTO and Viability of Indian Agriculture EPW, September 8, pp. 3453-3458.

Hoda, A. and Ashok Gulati (2003), Special and Differential Treatment in Agriculture Negotiations, www.icrier.org.

Institute for Agriculture and Trade Policy (2003), WTO Agreement on Agriculture Basics: Cancun Series Paper No. 2. www.wto.org.

Kumar, Ratnesh (1999), WTO-Structure, Functions, Tasks, Challenges (Deep and Deep, New Delhi).

McCalla, Alex F. (2001), What Developing Countries want from WTO. The Estey Centre Journal of International Law and Trade Policy Vol. 2, No. 1, pp. 165-177.

RIS (2003), Cancun Agenda: TRIPs and Development, PB. No. 6, July.

RIS (2003), World Trade and Development Report: Cancun and beyond. www.ris.org.

Swaminathan, S. and Anklesaria Aiyar (2004), Trade Diversion Down under. ET.18/2/2004.

Watal, Jayashree (1998), Intellectual Property Rights in Indian Agriculture. www.icrier.org.

Watkin, Kelvin and Joachim Von Braun (2002-2003), Trade Policies and food Security. www.ifpri.org.

WTO (2000), WTO Agreement Series (3), Agriculture. www.wto.org.

WTO (2001), Trading into the Future WTO. www.wto.org.

WTO (2005), Doha agenda, Ch. 5, www.wto.org.

WTO (2005), 10 benefits of WTO, www.wto.org.

WTO (2005), The Agreement of Agriculture, ch. 2. www.wto.org.

WTO (2003), The WTO Agreement Series-3 on Agriculture. www.wto.org.

IMPACT OF WTO ON INDIAN PHARMACEUTICAL INDUSTRY

*Tara Kant Jha**

In India, the WTO negotiations have thrown open a debate on the consequences to the health sector in India. The health sector is in the WTO list of services, which will have to be open to trade. Among the issues being discussed is the effect on the quality of health services in India, the prices of drugs, health insurance and the problem of patents. At present, India produces a phenomenal range of drugs. Indian drug prices are among the lowest in the world, approximately five to thirty times lower than in countries with product patents. Production has registered eight fold increase since 1974 with the export of bulk drugs from Indian fetching foreign exchange worth Rs. 1000 crore per year. But situation will be different when the new patent law comes into force as required by the Dunkel proposal. It is expected that patent holders will use their monopoly to effect sharp rise in drug prices. The growth of India's growing indigenous drug industry will be seriously affected (Mishra, 2001, pp. 237-38).

The pharmaceutical industry plays an important role in building a country's human capital. It is among the top-science -based industries with a wide range of capabilities in the complex field of drug technology and manufacture in India.

Life expectancy has improved during the period (1951-2000) from 37 to 65 years. Infant mortality (per 1,000 live births) has come down to 70 from 146. Nevertheless, during the same period, other countries, even in Asia, have made much better progress. Life expectancy has increased in China from 47 to 69

* Reader, University Department of Economics, Lalit Narayan Mithila University, Darbhanga-846004 (Bihar)

years, in Sri Lanka from 62 to 72, in Korea from 54 to 72 and in Indonesia from 41 to 64. Similarly, China has been able to bring down the rate of infant mortality from 150 to 34 (per 1,000 live births), Sri Lanka from 71 to 16, Korea from 85 to 10 and Indonesia from 139 to 51.

One of the reasons for the slow progress in India is the declining expenditure on public health. The investment in health care is only one per cent of the world health investment. Moreover, the allocation for healthcare in India's Five-Year Plans has declined to 1.7 per cent of total plan outlay during the Eighth Plan (1992-97) from 3.3 per cent in the First Five-Year Plan (1951-56). Public health expenditure as a percentage of GDP in India is only 1.3 as against 2.1 in China, 1.8 in Sri Lanka, 2.7 in Korea, 5.2 in the U.K., 5.6 in the U.S., and 5.8 in Germany. (Shahani, 2003, p. 324).

The India pharma industry has shown remarkable growth and maturity during the last four decades, unparalleled in any other industrial segment. Capital investments grew from Rs. 140 crores in 1965-66 to over Rs. 3,000 crores in 2000-01; during the same period, bulk drugs from Rs. 18 crores to over Rs. 4,000 crores, formulations from Rs. 150 crores to Rs. 20,000 crores, exports from Rs. 3 to 4 crore. In spite of such phenomenal growth in value terms, India, which has 16 per cent of the world's population produces only 1.2 per cent of global output of pharmaceuticals and the annual per capita consumption of drugs in India is one of the lowest in the world at $ 3 (Nair, 2003, p. 328).

Indian prices of drugs are some of the lowest in the world and India has one of the largest inventories of highly skilled pharmaceutical professionals. Indian companies have inherent advantages such as:

- Lower input costs owing to indigenously manufactured raw material.
- Low labour costs.
- Lower production cost owing to reverse engineering and minimal expenditure on R & D efforts.
- Inexpensive indigenous machinery.

- Government's policy stipulating promotion of the industry through the small-scale route.

Evidently the potential for growth in the domestic market itself is excessive and considering the rapid strides made in export markets in the last few years, the estimate of $ 25 billion by 2010 seems reasonable. In order to achieve this, large investments are required in a number of areas such as contract production, R & D clinical services and contract research by Indian and international companies operating in India.

Patents, Boon or Bane?

Fears have rightly been expressed that the pharmaceutical industry may force a crisis if the new WTO law is adopted from January 1, 2005. The grant of exclusive marketing rights to multinational drug firms will make drug prices ten times higher.

On May 6, 1981, Indira Gandhi declared India's policy when she said her "idea of a better world is one in which medical discoveries would be free from patent and there will be no profiteering from life and death."

The 1970 Patents Act reflected the experience of the colonial era. The British rulers had used the Indian Patents and Designs Act, 1911, to force products (including drugs) on this country-encouraging import from Britain and discouraging manufacturing in India.

No doubt, the 1970 Act, granting only process patent for drugs, enabled even small and medium Indian companies to produce indigenous versions of drugs developed abroad, especially in the United States and Europe, and even export them.

The power of monopolistic companies is controlled by Governments through anti-trust legislation, price regulation, etc. The limited monopoly that a patent entails is a grant from the state to any innovator-individual or business or institution. The patentee is entitled to compensation from anyone, including a big company or multinational that puts his or her innovation to commercial use. Thus, the patent monopoly granted by the Intellectual Property Rights (IPRs) system is not only different from but also in a sense a counter weight to the power of big firms, especially in a developing country. Also, if, as alleged, the cost of research and development is exaggerated as a ground for product patents, there is no reason for drug companies to rely on copying drugs developed by others. They can as well-develop new drugs at non-exaggerated costs and capture markets. (Gopal Krishnan, 2004, p. 10).

However, one valid objection to the reform of the Indian patent law, already affected, is the introduction of exclusive Marketing Rights (EMRs) in the period of transition (10 years from 1995) to the product patent regime in tune with the TRIPS agreement. The EMR ran counter to the very objective of the transition period. What is more, it linked the grant of EMRs by a member-country of the WTO to grant of a patent to the applicant in any other member country, undermining the philosophy of national sovereignty that to this day covers decisions on the grant of patents (Gopal Krishnan, 2004, p. 10).

When the WTO came into effect, India did not seriously contest America's threats. From 1995 to 2004, a large number of foreign companies filed anticipatory claims under the 'mail box' procedure, which will flower into full-fledged patents on January 1, 2005. The First Patents Amendment Act was passed in 1999, followed by the Second Amendment Act in 2002. A political promise was made that further amendments on social concerns would be incorporated in future. None of the ameliorative amendments was included in the Third Amendment Bill of 2003, which is now being rushed through without change or discussion. The WTO and the U.S. want the law passed before January 1, 2005 under the implicit threat of WTO retaliation for non-compliance.

The proposed Third Patents Amendment should not be rushed through parliament without making a serious effort to deal with issues of health, food and technology thoroughly. The Doha Declaration in 2001 specifically indicated that the WTO and TRIPs agreement "can and should be interpreted and implemented in a manner supportive of WTO members' right to protect public health and, in particular, to promote access to medicines for all and enable access to existing medicines and research and development into new medicines." The HIV-AIDS phenomenon illustrates the problem, which is not limited to it. AIDS has spread to 40 million victims throughout the world. Africa has been hit the hardest. It has spread to all the 31 provinces of China and all over India. It is not just a truckers' disease but has spread to homes. Countries such as Costa Rica and Venezuela have made it the Government's duty to supply medicine for AIDS. In my view, such a duty exists in India too (Dhavan, 2004, p. 10).

Indian drugs service not only the needs of patients, but also those in poor countries across the globe. Little wonder then that there were protests over an Indian legislation in front of Indian embassies in New York and Paris. In a rare gesture, the Director General of WHO has written to our Health Minister requesting that amendments to the Indian law take into account the concerns of millions of poor patients.

It is but natural that the Government has been proactive in marshalling its arguments in support of the ordinance. An oft-repeated argument is that 97% of drugs are off patent and will not be affected by the change. This is, at best, a half-truth. While it is true that most drugs will not be affected, the basis of the 97% figure is a mystery. Independent estimates show that drugs affected in the short-term have a turnover of around Rs. 3,000 crore. This is, however, just the tip of the iceberg. The rate at which old drugs turn obsolete has increased tremendously. So the issue is not just drugs that are off patent today; the more important concern is that new drugs required to replace old ineffective drugs will be patented and unaffordable (Gupta, 2005, p. 12).

January 1, 2005, will also signed the end of the transition period for product patent protection in some areas of technology such as pharmaceuticals. A stronger intellectual property rights regime may have implications for pharmaceutical sectors in these countries and their exports, as well as on prices and access to medicines for their people. At the same time, this may give incentives for innovation and patenting.

The Union Industry Secretary Ashok Jha said, checks and balances and safeguards, such as compulsory licensing would ensure that drugs were available at affordable prices. Indian drug prices were the lowest in the world and studies had shown that-except for normal inflation-the prices had not gone up significantly since the Trade Related Intellectual Property Rights (TRIPs) regime came into being in 1995. Price-rise and patents have no correlation. Any price threat was "imaginary" as several old drugs would go off the patents list while some new drugs were patented. Also, there were only 350 essential drugs and none of them was patented. Several rounds of consultations had taken place before the ordinance was promulgated. About the *Mashelkar Committee* report, it was being "selectively Quoted" to say there were no adequate safeguards in the patent regime to check spurious drugs from flooding the market. It was not the patent law, but the poor quality that threaten those smaller units. Quality was a separate issue, with the Act coming into effect, the process of grant of product patents would start rolling with the opening of the "mail box" where applications had been put in since 1995. There were about 12,000 applications in the mail box and it would take about three to four months to go them.

The Indian Pharmaceutical Alliance has urged the Government to make changes in the proposed Patents Amendment Bill to ensure that the flexibility available in the TRIPs agreement is full utilized to protect the interests of Indian drug companies. It has warned that giant foreign drug companies are trying to keep Indian companies out of the global market for generic drugs so some key modifications are needed in the existing draft of this legislation. The IPA has, therefore proposed that the Patents Act should provide greater clarity to avoid legislation related to patent ability and effectively avoid 'evergreening' or the patenting of new forms of existing products by the drug majors. It feels the current provision in the law is not adequate to prevent such 'evergreening' and if clarity is not brought, it will not only lead to litigation but also delay the entry of generics on the expiry of the main patent (Ramachandran, 2004, p. 11).

According to Indian Drug Manufacturers Association, among the provisions which need to be included in the Final Amendment are stipulations that salts, esters, polymorphs, hydrates, isomers, metabolites or changes- in purity level, particle size and blood levels are not patentable being not substantially different from the original product. This will avoid litigation and prevent evergreening by unscrupulous patent applicants. Besides, it has sought retention of the right of pre-grant opposition as contained in the original patents Act 1970. It has also proposed continued generic production of crucial drugs which are expected to be affected by the mail box patents by allowing statutory royalty payment to the patent holder. Procedures of issuing compulsory licenses will have to be simplified so that such licences needed for urgently required medicines are issued expeditiously to other parties in public interest. This will be subject to payment of reasonable compensation to the patent holder.

In the meeting with the Group of Ministers, the left leaders said that since the Government would be carrying out a Third Amendment to the Patent Act, care should be taken to ensure that the prices of drugs remained in check. The Communist Party of India (Marxist) Polit Bureau member, S. Ramchandran Pillai, said that first there would be a change from process patent to product patent which could result in the possibility of misuse and suggested that the definition of innovation should be as tight as possible. Secondly, the new patent regime could give rise to a monopoly situation that, in turn, could restrict supplies by pushing up prices. In order to check such a tendency, the suggestion was to make use of all measures available under the Trade Related Intellectual Property such as fixing of the quantum of royalty. He said the effort should be to make available patent products to consumers at affordable prices. Another change that was being envisaged was that the right to oppose the grant of patent was being diluted to mere right to represent against such grant. This dilution was more serious since the patent itself was being altered from process to product (Prasad, 2004, p. 11).

According to experts, the Patent Bill in its present form seriously compromises on the "accessibility and availability of medicines," the two important components of the right to health. Public interest groups working on health issues claimed that they were concerned that India, through the Third Patent Amendment Bill, would trade away its rights to protect the public health of people who need access to low-cost and quality-generic medicines. They added that the introduction of a product patent regime would reduce accessibility to new drugs. Till now, India provided for only process patents in the case of medicines. In the case of a process patent, protection is only for the process and method of manufacture and not for the product.

There is an expectation that by legislating a highly protective patent regime such as that of the ordinance-India would attract substantial investment by foreign multinational drug companies and would become an attractive venue for clinical testing of drugs. Such investment, whether greenfield investments, buyouts of, or mergers with, Indian producers could indeed be attractive. However, the downsides are significant. Most likely, prices of medicines in India will go up substantially. It is possible, though not inevitable, that foreign and domestic companies in India will tilt their research towards generating drugs, including the so called lifestyle drugs, for upscale world markets, rather than work on developing drugs for diseases, such as malaria and tuberculosis, afflicting billions of the poor in the developing world. There is a danger that India, instead of promoting a homegrown pharmaceutical revolution, will end up encouraging giant pharmaceutical oligopolies. As the New York Times editorial (March 5, 2005) said: "Seldom has India's Parliament considered anything of such global import. If parliament can preserve India's ability to provide generics it will make the difference between life and death for millions of people at home and abroad." Indian generic manufacturers are too crucial for India, and for the world, to be allowed by a misguided patent law to be wiped out (Abbott, et al, 2005, p. 10).

The Government introduced the Patents Bill in Parliament on March 18, 2005 that will prohibit domestic firms from copying and churning out low-cost generic versions of patented drugs. The legislation, being introduced to ensure that India falls in line with WTO rules, will, however, not prevent drug firms from producing and supplying cheaper anti-AIDS generic drugs to other developing countries. Opposition members in Parliament protested the proposed law, saying that it will raise prices of medicines and put domestic pharmaceutical firms at the mercy of multinational companies.

Parliament approved the Third Patents (Amendment) Bill 2005. Replying to the discussion, the Commerce Minister, Kamal Nath said that the new legislation would not lead to an increase in the prices of essential drugs as there were not covered by the patents regime. He refuted the opposition charge the WTO-mooted law was thrust on India. Rather, India acceded to the changes taking into consideration the national interest. It will be the Indian pharmaceutical industry and not the multinational corporations that will be strengthened by the Bill. Jairam Ramesh (Congress) said that the new regime will not result in shooting up of prices of essential drugs as it is entirely upto the Government to declare a drug as essential and bring it in the drug prices control order. 97 per cent of the drugs were out the patents matrix.

The Government is considering proposals for a new drugs pricing policy based on the draft recommendations of a task force headed by Pronab Sen. The task force has proposed price control of drugs based on the their essentiality, selective de-branding of medicines as well as calculating a ceiling price for drugs based on the basis of weighted average of top three brand of the molecule. It also recommended enactment of a Drugs and Therapeutics (Regulation) Act for price control and establishment of National Authority on Drugs and Therapeutics by merging Drugs Controller General of India and National Pharmaceutical Pricing Authority and Central Drugs Standard Control Organization.

Future Directions

If India is to emerge as the third or fourth largest pharmaceutical force in the world, at least the leading company require to reinforce their commitment to new drug discovery research. The global pharma industry will be driven by R & D and innovation and India has the potential to emerge as a major R

& D and contract manufacturing base for the global pharma companies over the next decade. Indian pharma companies also have significant opportunities in the areas of contract research. There has to be necessarily a restructuring of the industry with the merger of many small and medium companies or their acquisition by larger companies. The opportunity for India to be a major supplier for the global generic markets as well for patented products under license, is well-recognized the world over. Indian players are globally competitive and quality conscious. There will no doubt be a restructuring of the industry driven by branded generics on the one hand and the focus on IPRs on the other.

D.G. Shah, Secretary General, IPA said, the large players in the Indian pharma industry have prepared for the new regime by reducing dependence on the domestic market and venturing overseas, with players such as Ranbaxy having a significant portion of turnover from overseas. These players are striving to create their own Intellectual Property Rights. (IPRs) may be not through New Chemical Entities (NCEs) which have a long gestation period but may be through a Novel Drug Delivery System (NDDS) or a chiral drug. Another strategy is to partner overseas players to introduce products in India. For example, Zydus Cadila, which has two such partnerships. Contract Research, clinical trials and contract manufacturing are also lucrative options chosen by mid-size companies such as Divi's Labs and Matrix Laboratories. Mr. Shah also said that since large players are focused on regulated markets, mid-size players can focus on non-regulated markets such as Russia and Africa. Players such as Ajanta Pharma and Hetro Drugs have reduced domestic focus and are concentrating on these markets (Subbu, 2004, p. 19).

If all these strategies work, then India has the potential to grow three-fold from the current output of Rs. 20,000 crores to Rs. 60,000 crores which in global terms will mean that India will produce 4% of global output of drugs against 1% at present, in the next five years.

The Indian industry, at least the more organized companies, have everything to be globally competitive-low cost of innovation, established prowess in manufacturing, adequate Government support and a highly skilled and scientific workforce. The prescription for seizing this opportunity can be detailed as below:

- Focus on innovation and intellectual property generation.
- Focus on international regulatory compliance, with world class facilities and systems.
- Develop and strengthen the base of drug discovery and pre-clinical evaluation.
- Establish a CRO model in pre-clinical and clinical services for the global industry.
- Broaden the product basket to a wider base of therapeutics, covering both bulk drugs and formulations.
- Last, take the path of collaborative growth through global partnerships and alliances (Rao, 2004, p. 267).

In the early stages, it is advisable for Indian companies to focus on pre-clinical, since they have little exposure to clinical development. After 5-10 years, they would have had significant exposure in all aspects of drug discovery and development and the pool of trained manpower will increase significantly in all areas of drug discovery and development. The dream for any Indian pharmaceutical company will be to move from being a junior partner to being a key driver in collaborative research partnerships. This will take some time, and Indian companies will be well-advised to tread cautiously. Eventually, the drugs to be developed will be decided not just by global life science majors but Indian companies too. Hence, drugs which would address the needs of the third world, not just the denizens of the affluent countries, can also be developed on priority (Jasti, 2005, p. 309).

Medicine without social justice is unacceptable. Patents are not a gift for drug companies to exercise power without responsibility. Nobody ever thought of patenting our age-old wisdom. Globalization has meant adherence to WTO norms and guidelines. WTO helps developed countries by design and developing countries by default.

REFERENCES

Abbott, Frederick M., Amy Kapczynski & T.N. Srinivasan (2005), The Draft patent Law", The Hindu, Delhi, March 12.

Dhavan, Rajeev (2004), "The Patent Controversy", The Hindu, Delhi, December 10.

Gopalakrishnan, R. (2004), "Amending the Patents Act", The Hindu Delhi, December.

Gupta, Amit Sen (2005), "Side Effects: Patents Ordinance to Hitpharma, Software Sectors", The Times of India, Patna, February 17.

Jasti, Venkat (2005), "Drug Discovery: Opportunities in Research", Survey of Indian Industry, The Hindu.

Mishra, Harindra Kishor (2001), "World Trade Organization and India: The Background and Future Tasks", in Jiwitesh Kumar Singh (Editor), International Trade and Business: Emerging Issues and Challenges in the 21st century, Deep & Deep Publications Pvt. Ltd., New Delhi.

Nair, M.D. (2003), "Pharma Industry: Future Growth Route", Survey of Indian Industry, The Hindu.

Prasad, K.V. (2004), "Move to Amend Patents Act Worries Left", The Hindu, Delhi, November 22.

Ramachandran, Sushma (2004), "Drug firms seek changes in Patents Amendment Bill", The Hindu, Delhi, November 28.

Rao, K. Raghavendra (2004), "Pharma Sector: Huge Generic Opportunity", Survey of Indian Industry, The Hindu.

Shahani, Ranjit (2003), "New Patent Regime: Benefits to Consumers", Survey of Indian Industry, The Hindu.

Subbu, Ramnath (2004), "Pharma Sector Confident in New Patent Regime", The Hindu, Delhi, December 30.

INDIA'S CONCERNS TO BIO-TECHNOLOGY AND BIO-SAFETY IN THE WTO

*N. Manonmoney**

Assessment of economic, social and environmental impact of biotechnology is important both for developed and developing countries. These assessments can help policy-makers to identify the most effective strategy to solve the problems in using especially agricultural bio-technology. It is important to evaluate the impact of genetically modified organisms (GMOs) and Non-GMOs biotechnologies. To-day under TRIPS, the global trade regime has to deal with several related issues in regard to bio-safety such as ability of the importing country to assess the risks and deal with them, regulation for labeling, or GMOs products so that the consumers can make informed choice, restrict GMOs which may pose hazard to the viability of the food security.

Biotechnology along with information technology is portrayed as the new technological development that will strongly influence the 21st century. In the beginning, biotechnology's prospects seemed very promising especially in the production of medicinal products and special chemicals. Recently, biotechnology made its introduction in the public debate. In 1996 genetically modified crops were introduced and they were passively accepted in USA as well as in the European Union. Very recently, it is felt that GMOs are not good for human health and potentially hazardous for the environment; therefore European consumers and food industry are actively insisted upon the non-GMOs products. Not only European food industry has switched over to complete non-GMOs products

* Professor and Head, School of Economics, Madurai Kamaraj University, Madurai-625021.

but also countries like Australia, Newzeland, South Korea, Japan and Canada are all developing their own labeling legislation. They also raised doubts about the desirability of genetic engineering of food. Thus in the short run the prospects of agriculture especially in food crops look bleak. In the long run, it is believed that even positive acceptance will be given for GMOs products.

Biotechnology research is giving both the promise of succour from the hunger as well as the threat of loss of bio-diversity and harmful to health of human beings. Biosafety is a tool to ensure that biotechnology benefits mankind has found international acceptance through some protocol resolved through WTO with its strong disputes settlement mechanism. WTO is the inter-governmental organization establishing trades rules has not remained unscathed from these issues.

Assessment of recent developments affecting the adoption and acceptance of agricultural biotechnology on a region by region basis around the world, and the business outlook for GM crops going forward within each regional market lead to raise the following questions to be answered to:

- What is the current situation with respect to the adoption and acceptance of GM crops in countries around the world, especially in developing countries?
- What is the business outlook for GM crops in these countries?
- What is the legislative and regulatory situation in each country?

The Emerging Debate on GMOs Products

On May 2002,the United States, Argentina, Canada and Egypt made a request for the WTO consultations with the EU over its moratorium on approving agricultural biotechnology products. Since 1998, EU has consistently violated WTO rules. EU countries have blocked regulatory approval of new agricultural biotechnology products and without any scientific proof as required under the WTO Sanitary and Phyto-Sanitary (SPS) agreement; they have adopted unnecessary regulatory approval procedure. French Academy of Sciences has pointed out that more than 300 million Americans have been eating bio-engineered corn and soybean for years and no adverse consequences have ever been reported. The supporters of GM corps, have argued that the EU's refusal to meet its WTO obligations is slowing down the adoption of a beneficial technology and developing countries have suffered negative consequences. The poor and undernourished people in developing countries are expected to reap the benefit from agricultural bio-technology. The farmers in the world have recognized the economic, agricultural and environmental benefits of biotech crops. Biotech drought–resistant crops can help to produce more food to feed the growing population in developing countries. Biotech crops can reduce soil erosion and pesticide use. Biotech crops create more hospitable environments for wildlife. The spill over effects of the EU moratorium threatens to negate the benefits of biotechnology to the farmers worldwide. Mr. Richard D. Haynes, the US Consul General in Chennai on June 2003 has stated that US is not trying to force biotech foods on consumers. It is the EU's unilateral, illegal and unjustified action taken without any scientific, health on environmental basis, which constrain choice and opportunity worldwide.

Dr. Richard Fawcett, a consultant and former weed science professor at Iowa state university, studied the benefits of Round up ready soybeans and concluded that the soybeans bring a

- Reduction in farm production costs upto 20 per cent.
- Increased in yield upto 5 per cent
- 20-40 per cent reduction in fuel use and
- 90 per cent reduction in soil-erosion. The progress in genetic engineering will open markets with stronger value-added for the agribusiness firms. Seed industry is at a key position in the area of these new technologies. One who will have the power to produce food products will have an immense economic and political power.

Huge agrochemical firms such as Monsanto, Astrazeneca, Novartis, Dupont are strongly compete each other to buy seed companies. Novartis and Astrazeneca are joined together in the agricultural activity and new firm is called Sygenta, which is number one for agro-chemicals. The acreage of crops with Monsanto bio-technology traits in North American has increased 41 per cent compared with 1998 North American acres. Monsanto invested 8 billion dollars for the plant biotechnology sector during 1994-1999 and the surfaces cultivated in the GMOs increased constantly during the first three years of investment. At present, the agricultural sector, the herbicide, insecticide and fungicide markets and Monsanto economical results are not as good as expected. The present consumers and government disagreements on GMOs; Monsanto is thinking of changing its business activities related to agribusiness sector.

In this situation following questions are raised:

(i) What are the economic consequences for the nations that allow GMO Crops?
(ii) What is the American Strategy?
(iii) What is the EU position?
(iv) Do EU be attached by WTO?
(v) What do the nations that do not allow GMO crops are going to lose?

Concerns of Developing Countries Regarding Biosafety

The developments taken place in genetically modified organisms (GMOs) present both a safeguard and a challenge for developing countries. Developing countries do not become "testing grounds" for new applications of biotechnology. The instruments related to biosafety pose implementation and capacity challenges. These instruments' being the subject of international debate and controversy and it has been suggested that implementation will have to be mediated through further international negotiation. In developed countries GMOs have been the subject of intense policy debate. In developing countries, significant claims have been made about the capacity of modern biotechnology contribute to food security both in terms of increasing agricultural production and enhancing the nutritional value of basic crops.

The next serious concern is about the impact of GM crops on the environment and on human health and their potential socio-economic impacts. There are also concerns about potential distributive impacts of GMOs such as what conditions would GM seeds be made available to farmers, and subject to what restrictions; what impact be on traditional varieties of crops relied upon by farmers in poor countries; and what impact in developed countries have on commodity exports from developing countries. New biotechnology has given rise to concerns about a number of potential rests associated with the release and use of GMOs. Many developing countries have emphasized their lack of capacity to assess and manage human health and environmental risks associated with GMOs.

In discussion in the WTO, developing countries have tended to express concerns about the effect of non-tariff barriers on market access for their goods. They have been concerned not to expand the discussion of trade and environment issues in the WTO. Market access concerns have been at the heart of the position put forward by many developing countries in discussion in the WTO on many technical and agriculture measures. The benefits and risks of new biotechnology remain uncertain. Biotechnology and its application in agriculture will have a drastic impact because it is stated that the future of the application of biotechnology is uncertain. By the introduction of biotechnology only a few companies and a few countries dominate the seed and food industry and for many of the developing countries it would obliviously be unwelcome and these countries have lost by this new technology.

The concerns of developing countries relate to the need to develop capacities to access biotechnology for increasing food production in a cost-efficient manner and to avoid perceived risk of biotechnology both in terms of health concerns as well as bio-diversity concerns. Access to bio-technology is a challenge for developing countries as it offers only the best "tool of choice" for marginal ecological zone-left behind other zones; where more than half of the world's poorest people dependent on agriculture and livestock. Many of biotechnologies inventories are in the hands of MNCs; who may render its access to developing countries is unaffordable. MNCs invest more in research in those crops that are grown by farmers in rich countries and poor farmers in tropical countries are less attractive as commercial customers. The weak IPR policies have also been deployed by developing countries to ensure availability of research results at affordable costs.

A number of developing countries have already invested significant funds in biotechnology like Brazil, India and China. Another issue is the infrastructure needed to support such new technologies. Moreover, the developing countries have poor facilities for risk assessment and risk management. They are important not only from the point of view of safety of products being imported into the country; they are also important in order to ensure that exports meet the requirement of the importing country. It is important for the developing countries to establish "equivalence" agreements with their major trading partners to facilitate exports. Many developing countries have established legislation and rules in regard to "biosafety" but their implementation is tardy. They require technical and financial assistance for institution building, risk assessment and risk-management. Another issue of developing countries is that which of these concerns can be addressed through the WTO. WTO being a trade body; its principle function is facilitating free trade and not development. Controversy exists on whether GM and Non-GM products are "like products" in the context of WTO. Various committees in the WTO provide a possible forum for discussing biotechnology and biosafety issues. Trade in GMOs is not disciplined through WTO rules at present. There are provision in WTO make it possible for members to pursue a policy most suited to their specific circumstances and to defend trade restrictions so long as these are not unjustified or disguised restrictions.

Role of WTO in Bio-safety

The United States has complained to the WTO about several restrictive measures such as European Union's labeling requirements for genetically modified crops, arguing that they lack scientific justification and are a potential barrier to trade. During 1999, 16 new measures concerning new national rules related to biotechnology in food were reported to the previous four-year. WTO is set to re-evaluate the obligation of member states to protect plant materials legally. Patenting life forms has become an internationally contentious issue in the recent decades for cultural, ethical and economic reasons. The interest groups give pressure for set the lines for the new WTO negotiations; where as the biotechnology and seed industry and pressure groups that opposes the patenting of life forms.

The 27.3 (b) of the Agreement on Trade-Related Aspects of Intellectual Property Rights in 1995 (TRIPS) states that the WTO member countries shall provide patent protection for any inventions in all fields of technology. Inventions related to biological materials such as genes and gene sequences are not explicitly excluded, so they are considered to be included in the patent coverage. Member states are allowed to exclude plants and animals from protection. Plant varieties will then be protected by an effective sui generis system, which means an independent legal system specially designed for protecting plant varieties. Growing intellectual property rights on biological materials has proven to be a highly contentious issue. Differences in interest have become most visible in the disputes between countries at various international forums at which negotiations on intellectual property protection took place. Developing countries are certainly attracted to the potential of biotechnology to contribute to food-security. These countries are interested in the debate over the regulation of GMOs and particularly in the protocol negotiations. In discussions on labeling of GM food, India has supported labeling of all foods derived from modern biotechnology in order to ensure consumer information and consumer choice.

The present system of international governance for modern biotechnology does not adequately give answers for these concerns. The various potentials impacts of modern biotechnology to be assessed carefully and mechanisms need to be developed to provide a higher degree of flexibility and autonomy to developing countries in this area. A wide range of justification or trade measures and concerns particularly in relation to food security to be developed. World food production has been outstripping population growth and there has been a long-term trend of declining food prices in real terms. It is estimated that throughout the world more than 800 million people are considered to be "food insecure" and 254 million people are chronically under-nourished in Asia. It is difficult to assume that the food requirements of the people of 2020 will be sustained by the technology of today. Therefore the development in agriculture through biotechnology is expected to play a major role in farm production.

Mr. Atul Kaushik, Deputy Secrertary, Government of India has rightly observed that developing countries as producers of agricultural products have a pressing need to increase production as will as productivity of agriculture, and biotechnology may provide the much-needed remedy. Developing countries have to remain alert of the safety related standards on trade in biotechnology products. They have to build infrastructure to meet legitimate standards for biotechnology products in their markets. They have to participate actively in the work relating to operationalisation of Biosafety protocol.

To day, several new instruments have been developed to biosafety products derived from modern biotechnology are subject to a growing attention of many international institutions. The year 2005 is a momentous one for agricultural biotechnology around the world. The underlying reality is that new legislations, regulations and commercial agreements are coming into place in 2005 in many countries, that will set the framework within which the industry will operate in the coming years. In recent years, many developed countries and MNCs have started major biotechnology research initiative and many developing countries have also invested in this area with a view to find succour from hunger in a cost-effective manner.

REFERENCES

Dowkins Kriston (2000), "Biotechnology and Biosafety: Battle Royal of the 21st Century.

Kaushik Autl (2001), "Advertising Developing Countries Concern Related Biotechnology and Biosafety in the WTO", *TCTSD Workshop on Biotechnology* at Switzerland, 18-20 July.

Lola Nayar (2000), "After IT India Sees Biotech as Next Driver of Growth", *India-Assam News Service.*

Manonmoney, N. (2000), "Impact of Biotechnology for Attaining Sustainable Agricultural Development in India", *Emerging Issues in Indian Agriculture* (ed. book).

Richard D.Haynes (2003), "Biotech Agri Products–Basis for US Review Request", *The Hindu,* June 6.

Sen PhamThi (1999), "Economical Aspects of Plant Biotechnology", Socrates Inter-Science Seminar, University of Wageningen, September.

Wisk, J.Van (1998), "Plant Patenting Provision Reviewed in WTO", *Biotechnology and Development Monitor,* No. 34, p. 6-9.

——*Biotechnology News* (1999-2001), Department of Biotechnology, Government of India.

——"Regional Trends in Adoption and Acceptance", *Agbiotech* (2005).

WTO AND INDIAN DAIRY INDUSTRY: IMPLICATION AND CONSEQUENCES IN THE POST-WTO ERA

*I. Francis Gnanasekar**
*& T. Revathi***

Introduction

In India, dairying has been complementary to agriculture till recent past. Nearly 70 million farm families are dependent on agriculture directly or indirectly for source of income. To uplift their socio-economic standard of living, the Government have taken various strategic efforts under White and Green Revolutions. These programme have enhanced India's production capabilities and made it proud to be the world leader in production of milk, tea and cotton.

Important Factors Influencing Milk Production

India lives in village, 72 per cent of our population is rural and 60 per cent if the population is engaged in agriculture. 70 million farm families, one out of every two rural households, is involved in dairying (Deepak Jain, 2004). The successful implementation of the Operation Flood program has created a vast country wide network of co-operative system. The system is famous as the 'Anand Pattern' essentially structured the farmer into a 2-tier co-operative structure. By the end of phase III of Operation Flood, 9 million farm families were linked to 70000 primary co-operatives and 170 co-operative unions to reach more than

* Reader in Commerce, St. Joseph's College (Autonomous), Tiruchirappalli-620002.

** Lecturer, Department of Management Studies, Christhu Raj College, Panjapur, Tiruchirappalli-620012.

600 cities and towns (Deepak Jain, 2004). They have played a major role in transmitting urban market consumer demand to rural producers, thus enabling them to receive almost 70 per cent of consumer milk price. The income from milk helps them to meet day to day expenses and in reducing rural income disparity.

According to the estimate of central statistical organization, the contribution of livestock and fisheries sector to the agriculture sector was 28.3 per cent of the value of the output. The contribution of these sectors to the total GDP was 7.35 per cent during 2001-2002. The contribution of milk alone (Rs. 103804 crores) was higher than paddy (Rs. 73964 crores). Wheat (Rs. 43815 crores) and sugarcane (28205 crores). This value in terms indicates the significant role of dairying in the socio-economic situation of our country. (R.S. Gandhi, 2005).

The fast changing scenario in dairy industry all over the world due to globalization has thrown new challenges to our dairy industry to compete globally. The world market is protected by the developed countries through domestic and export subsidies and market access. Further, the agreement on Technical barriers to Trade and on Sanitary and Phytosanitary measures were imposed in the form of Non-Tariff barriers, hindered the entrance of developing countries to global trade.

The purpose of this paper is to analyse the impact of WTO agreement on developing countries particularly the Indian Dairy Industry. The paper then suggest policy options for global trade.

Evolution of Dairy Industry

Indian economy is mainly based on agriculture, 70 per cent of the population is engaged in it directly or indirectly. The rearing of cattle and dairying go hand in hand with agriculture and helped to improve the socio-economic conditions of the rural fold.

Historical Background

The importance of animal husbandry is recognized in India since time immemorial. The cow gained prominence with the advent of the Aryans who workshipped it. In olden times, the richness of a household was measured on the cattle strength it possessed. In this period, the cattle were also used as a medium of exchange.

Over the ages, the cattle and buffalo rearing has been neglected due to multiplication of various other trades occupations and commerce.

Dairy Development under British Rule

In British period, dairying, animal husbandry and crop husbandry were all clubbed together under the term 'agriculture' and their development is not considered with much importance.

For the first time in India, in 1886, on the recommendations of the Board of Agriculture, the Department of Defence established a few dairy farms, to supply milk and milk products to the British troops (Agriculture Commission Report, 1976).

In 1914, the Department of Defence on the advice of Board of Agriculture assessed the milk producing capacity of Indian cattle and advised the Government in 1916, to appoint an Imperial Dairy Expert. In 1920, William Smith, the Imperial Dairy Expert recommended the Government to organize training center for Defence Dairy farms to establish it on scientific lines. Thus for the sake of British troops, the Dairy Sector was organized and developed in these periods.

Development of Dairy Co-operatives

In 1937, the first "Lucknow Milk producers Co-operative Union Limited" was established, paving the way for organization of such union in other districts and states.

In 1945, the Aarey milk colony was set up by the Bombay Government Under the Greater Bombay Milk Scheme. In 1947, in Bengal, the Greater Calcutta Milk Scheme was initiated. In 1946, the first Farmer's Integrated Dairy Co-operative Unit (Amul) was established at Anand in Kaira district, Gujarat. Amul and the Greater Bombay scheme helped the dairy industry in India to develop at a faster rate emphaising development of the techniques of Processing and Marketing under Indian conditions.

Dairy Development In India - Under Five-Year Plans

The Government of India did not take up schemes, for development of dairying in India in the initial stages. Dairying was treated only as a part of animal husbandry. In the post-independence era, the dairying is recognized as a source of additional income to the landless labourers and small and marginal farmers.

First Five-Year Plan (1951-56)

In the first five-year plan, the dairy development programme was emphasized in a small way, related to the supply of milk under hygienic conditions to big cities.

Second Five-Year Plan (1956-1961)

In the second plan, the importance is given to quality control, paying remunerative price to milk producer and a reasonable price to the consumer and favoured the organization of village level milk producers' cooperatives to supply milk to the city dairies, creameries and milk drying plants. During this period, the milk and milk products sold is worth about Rs. 11.32 crores. (Planning Commission, 1956).

Third Five-Year Plan (1961-66)

The plan emphasized the need to collect milk by a network of producers cooperatives in villages and to organize the distribution of milk and manufacture of milk products on cooperative lines. The working group organized by the Government of India to review the working dairy industry. It suggested the organization of state level federations of dairy cooperatives and a national level federation to conduct the works of the state level federations. In 1965, as per the recommendation , the National Dairy Development Board (NDDB) is established at Anand (Gujarat). NDDB is a programme launching body and provide technical service on a non-profit basis. (Planning Commission, 1961).

Fourth Five-Year Plan (1969-74)

The Government of India and the NDDB organized the XIX International Dairy Congress first of its kind in Delhi (1974). It aimed at the development of dairy as an instrument of socio-economic change. This was in conformity with the Interim report of the Agriculture Commission (1971).

Operation Flood was started in this plan with the aim to provide a reliable source of income to millions of rural people-dependent on dairying.

Fifth Five-Year Plan (1974-78)

The fifth plan emphasized the need for diversifying agriculture evolving better land-use pattern and assisting the weaker sections of the community, the programmes of animal husbandry and dairying received considerable attention.

In pursuance of recommendations of the National Commission on Agriculture (1976) for assisting the rural poor, 96 projects for rearing of cross-breed heifers were taken up.

Sixth Five-Year Plan (1980-85)

The plan intended to lay special emphasize on project for cattle development through genetic improvement and better health care. And the organization of producer oriented cooperative marketing system. (Mohan, 1989).

Seventh Five-Year Plan (1985-1990)

The plan aim was to provide infrastructure accelerated growth in livestock production and to improve the socio-economic status of the rural population including the small and marginal farmers, labourers, tribals and weaker sections. The country has launched a technology mission for dairy cattle improvement through embryo transfer technology. (Dairy India, 1987).

Eigth Five-Year Plan (1990-97)

As a result of liberalized industrial policy announced by the Government of India during the year 1991, import of technology and machinery has become easier. This has resulted in the industry taking up manufacturer of new products and other high value-added products, which are export oriented and import substitute items. (Source : Website).

Nineth Five-Year Plan (1997-2002)

The realities of the post-GATT world are reflected in the report of the working group on animal husbandry and dairying for the formulation of the plan. Further, the focus of dairy development was shifted from its role as a source of supplementary income to that of an viable enterprise to improve the quality of life of some 70 million farm households, with no land or little land. The plan had also stressed the need to provide credit access to the farmers. Simultaneously, steps have been taken for upgrading and conserving proven breeds of cattle and buffalo. The plan was also proposed to extend the benefit of Operation Flood to the non-operational flood areas through the integrated dairy development project and to popularized the Good Manufacturing Practices(GMP) in dairy plants was also proposed for quality upgradation. (Dairy India, 1997).

Tenth Five-Year Plan (2002-07)

The plan document had given importance to establishment of milk chilling centres in rural areas to connect the disposable milk processing and urban consumption. Further, the Government of India and the State Government have initiated various schemes to provide livestock health services and disease control. (Source : Website).

Operation Flood Programme

Apart from implementing five-year plan, the Government of India implemented Operation Flood programme for the development of dairying in three phase (1970-96).

Operation Flood-I (1970-81)

It was launched in 1970 following an agreement with the World Food Programme (WFP). The overall objective of Operation Flood-I was to lay the foundation of a modern dairy industry in India. Funds for Operation Flood-I were generated by the sale of Skim Milk Powder (SMP) and Butter Oil (BO). It achieved a peak milk procurement of 34 lakh litres per day (LLPD) and marketing of 28 LLPD.

Operation Flood-II (1981-85)

The background of the institutional framework of it essentially comprised the successful replication of the Anand Pattern a three-tier cooperative structure of societies unions and federations. Operation Flood-II helped to market milk in about 148 cities and towns, with a total population of 15 million, through a national milk grid. The peak milk procurement increased to a level of 79 LLPD and milk marketing to 50 LLPD.

Operation Flood-III (1985-96)

The third phase focused on strengthening the institutional management aspect of dairy cooperatives and for productivity-enhancement inputs. Efforts were made to expand infrasturture in all major markets, linking them to milk shields through the National Milk Grid (NMG) to ensure year-round stable milk supply.

The NMG ensured the availability of milk to consumer and a remunerative price to milk producers by leveling out regional and seasonal imbalances in supply and demand further the marketing of indigenous milk product will form an important part of the overall marketing strategy. Marketing facilities for milk and milk products has been expanded to 100 LLPD by the end of third phase.

Globalisation Policy

As a part of the globalisation process, India joined the World Trade Organization on 1 January, 1995. This required a realignment of India's Trade policies with positions that were agreed to under the Uruguay round of GATT. Following the WTO agreement, India had to open its economy. It had lead to hectic competition in the dairy sector.

World Trade Organization (WTO)

The Global trade follows the guidelines set by the World Trade Organization. It is considered as the most significant single package of changes to the International Trading Regime. Agriculture was included as an important issue and this has led to the creation of a completely new framework of rules by World Trade Organization–an institution that has replaced the General Agreement on Tariffs and Trade (GATT) on January 1, 1995.

WTO agreement concerning agriculture including dairy products are Agreement on Agriculture (AoA), Agreement on Application of Sanitary and Phyto-Sanitary (SPS) Measures and Agreement on Technical Barrier to Trade (TBT).

A number of meetings including five Ministerial Conferences have been held, the important ones being Cancun Ministerial Conference, Doha Round Trade negotiations and Geneva negotiations where the framework for future negotiations in agriculture was adopted.

The agricultural declarations aimed at (i) Substantial improvement in market access, (ii) reduction of with a view to phasing out all forms of export subsidies, (iii) Substantial reduction in trade distorting domestic support, and (iv) more effective special and differential treatment for developing countries by taking into account their developmental needs including food security and rural development, [N.R. Bhasin, 2006].

The Hong Kong Ministerial Conference have been addressed based on the issues relating to Agriculture Trade. And on the long-term objectives of the Agreeement on Agriculture.

Agreement on Agriculture (AoA)

The main provisions of the World Trade Organization AOA fall under three main categories: Market Access, Domestic Support and Export Subsides. These are commonly referred to be the three pillars. The objective of this agreement is to establish a more fair and market oriented agricultural trading system. It also aims to strengthen rules and specific commitments on domestic support, export subsidies and protection in order to correct and prevent restrictions and distortions in world agricultural market. The commitment for reduction by the member countries was based on agreed rates of reduction in each area from a base period.

The implementation period for reduction commitment in domestic support and protection provided for developed countries was six years (1995-2000) except for the article on "Due Restraint", which had an implementation period of nine years.

For developing countries, the implementation for reduction in commitment was 10 years. Least Developed Countries (LDCs) had no reduction commitment.

A large number of countries provide subsidies in different forms to assist in the production of agricultural produce. To reduce the distortion effect, the developed countries were required to reduce the domestic support by 20 per cent and export subsidy by 36 per cent in terms of outlay and 21 per cent in quantities in a period of six years. They were also required to affect an average reduction in tariff for all the products by 36 per cent and a minimum reduction per product by 15 per cent in the corresponding period. The developing countries were to achieve reduction commitments of lower dimension in a period of 10 years (1995-2004). [N.R.Bhasin, 2006].

Market Access

The market access provision of the AoA required that non-tariff measures be replaced by tariffs. To have all market access, any exporters should readily measure, understand and predict barriers on common standard-tariff.

The developed countries are against, this view and also they resist to provide access to agricultural exports of the developing world. Further, they have not gone for full tariffication. Instead, they have opted for Tariff Rate Quota (TRQ) system for several commodities, which is restricting the potential gains to the developing world. Tariff quotas are where a country will allow import of certain commodities from some countries only. [N.R. Bhasin 2004].

The tariff binding on livestock products hinder market access, as the average tariff for dairy (about 85%) products exceeded the average for all agricultural products (62%). In

OECD countries, the average tariff is very high in many sectors including dairy (116%). [V.P. Sharma, 2003].

The level of tariff bound in the WTO schedule and that actually impose on the imports exist a vast difference. And this has been called "Watery Tariff Policies".

The Special Safeguards (SSG) provision allows the country to impose additional tariff when certain criteria are met-either an increase in import volume. (Volume Trigger) and fall in import price below specified reference price (Price trigger).

The other constraint restricting market access is the coverage of products in each country. It is found that U.S. gives importance to dairy products. Further U.S. has used price trigger to place additional duties on dairy products.

They are all acting as barriers for the developing countries to have market access of developed countries.

The Market Access to LDCs

Another major achievement of Hong Kong Conference being projected is the provision of duty free and quota free market access for most products from the 32 least developed countries by 2008.

In fact, the LDC group had asked for bound duty and quota free market access to rich country's market for all products produced by LDC. But the developed countries could not agree to that and provided access for 97 per cent of products only from LDC. This would allow developed countries to continue to protect "Sensitive Products" that are of export advantage to LDCs. In other words, the LDCs can have market access for products they do not produce at all (or) do not produce competitively, but access can be blocked for those products in which they are competing. They are only given rights in areas where they cannot realize these rights.

Domestic Support

Government provides internal support to the dairy milk producers, particularly in the form of Green box and Blue box, which is found to be high in developed countries. Domestic support considered as minimally trade distorting (Green Box) is not included in the AMS. Direct payment for production limiting programmes (Blue Box) is not included in AMS reduction under certain condition [IATRC, (2000); WTO 2002]. And in Ambar policies, countries are not able to exceed the level of support to which they have agreed as measured by their AMS (Aggregate Measure of Support).

The estimated producer support for milk in some of the developed countries continues to be quite high being on an average 42 per cent in OECD and EU, 40 per cent in USA, 58 per cent in Canada and 73 per cent in Japan and Switzerland. [N.R. Bhasin, 2006].

Declaration on Domestic Support

The domestic support issue remains as complicated as it was earlier. On domestic support, Hong Kong Declaration say that there will be three bands for reductions in Final Bound total AMS and in the overall cut in trade distorting domestic support, with higher linear cuts in higher bands. In both cases, the Member with the highest level of permitted support will be in the top band, the two members with the second and third highest levels of support will be in the middle band and all other members, including all developing country members, will be in the bottom band. In addition, developed country members in the lower bands with high relative levels of final Bound Total AMS will make an additional effort in AMS reduction. [Vijay Sardana, 2006]. But the tariff sets no level or target for their reduction. The declaration does not make any commitment on domestic support.

Export Subsides

Export subsidy provided by the Government is distorting trade, because they allow subsidizing countries to displace competitive producers in world level.

The root cause of all distortions in the world agriculture is due to the support provided by OECD countries to their agriculture. (OECD, 2001). On the export subsidy, the Hong Kong Declaration says that the developed countries will eliminate it by the year 2013.

The export subsidy, though important are now minor in nature compared to production support. Unless domestic subsidies are cut, export subsidies will continue even after the elimination of export subsidies in 2013.

The Hong Kong Conference would have been more meaningful if there had been a decision leading to substantial cuts in total trade distorting domestic subsidies, so that overall domestic support is really decreased.

It was expected that the implementation of AoA would substantially reform the trade of agricultural products. But this has not happened. High level of subsidies are still being given by developed countries both for production and export, distorting the global market.

Non-Tariff Barriers (NTB)

Non-Tariff Barriers encompass all trade barriers other than tariffs. Tariffs essentially act as a tax on imposed items. It is used as a tool to protect domestic product manufacturers against world price movements and trends, and in minimizing competition from foreign products.

In the case of agriculture, NTBs were required to be converted to tariff equivalents subject to reduction requirements and some were to be completely eliminated (Tariffs Only Rule)

The countries can decide their tariff equivalent for exciting NTB of their own. But it is seen that many countries exaggerated the base level of tariffs. And this newly calculated base-level tariff provided even higher production than NTB that replaced in the base period. [N.R. Bhasin, 2004].

The dirty tariffication have appeared in U.S. tariff and in E.U. tariff that to in the sensitive commodities such as dairy, agricultural and fisheries products [N.R. Bhasin, 2004].

The other NTBs of particular importance to agriculture are sanitary and phytosanitary measures and technical barriers to trade. These are not part of AoA, but covered under separate agreement.

Agreement on Sanitary and Phytosanitary Measures (SPS)

This introduces discipline in International Food Trade and checks the application and use of unjustified sanitary or phytosanitary measures for the purpose of trade protection. If a measure is governed by SPS, then it is excluded from coverage under WTO agreement on TBT.

The agreement recognize the standards, quidelines and recommendations determined by the Codex Alimentarias Commission (CAC) and International Office of Epizootics (IOE) as the minimum basis for international trade in livestock sector. It permits the members to introduce a level of protection higher than that is recommended by the relevant International Agreement, even if scientific evidence is insufficient.

Thus taking advantage of SPS provisions, some countries have adopted regulacions that include unjustified, stringent SPS measures which are difficult for most of the developing countries to comply with.

Technical Barriers to Trade (TBT)

TBT is a specific type of NTB that inhibits or prevents trade through the use of regulations (or) standards. The Codex Alimentarias Guidelines for the Design, Operation, Assessment and Accreditation of Food Import and Export Inspection systems provide a basic framework for creating Mutual Recognition Agreements (MRAs) between countries. [Kalpana Sastry, 2003].

The objective of TBT are very positive for the consumers, the environment, the animals and the plants of an importing country. At the same time it cannot be denied that many TBTs result in a net welfare loss by posing significant and often unnecessary costs to both the exporters of the goods and the consumers of the importing country.

Impact of Hong Kong Negotiation on Indian Diary Industry

India is a minor player in the world trade of dairy products. The removal of export subsidy is not going to improve India's export prospects. Although cost competitive, India has limitations on account of infrastructural inadequacies and lack of a policy support to promote the export.

India has recently entered into SAFTA (South Asia Free Trade Agreement) with its neighbouring countries. To prevent import of dairy commodities from third country to the detriment of domestic market, the agreements provides for a mechanism which requires application of twin conditions of (a) 40 per cent value addition (in case of LDCs 30% value addition) and (b) change in the code classification at four-digit level. The LDCs in the region are seeking disclaimer in regard to change in the code classification at six or eight-digits instead of four-digit level. In case their demand is accepted, it will permit them to import commodities from countries like Australia and New Zealand and re-export to Indian market. The Hong Kong Declaration, providing free access to LDCs is also likely to go against the interest of Indian dairy industry. This would also lead to conflict and tension amongst SAARC nations. India would be required to take adequate precautions not allow such an eventuality to develop. [N.R. Bhasin, 2006].

The WTO's sixth Ministerial Conferences at Hong Kong concluded on December 18, 2005. It is increasingly felt that the Conference has resulted in a imbalanced outcome to the disadvantage of developing countries.

Milk Production Scenario in the Country

The credit for the milk growth in India goes to the Government of India's five-year plan and to the Operation Flood programme implemented in three phase, all had made India to stand ahead in the world milk production.

India has the highest milk production i.e. 84.5 million tonnes in 2001-2002 (Agricultural statistics at a glance 2002) in the world. It is also the largest consumer of milk. Neither position is likely to change in the foreseeable future. India accounts for 15 per cent of world's milk production and its production is growing at the rate of 4 per cent per year as against world milk growth rate of 1.1 per cent per year. (Deepak Jain, 2004).

The number of milk plants in co-operative and private sectors registered under Milk and Milk Product Order (MMPO) have increased from 509 in 1996 to 628 in 2002. Similarly the total milk handling capacity has increased from 55909 thousand litres per day(LPD) to 72979 thousand LPD during the corresponding period [Chauhan, 2005].

Market Share
Milk Flow-2001: Table 1

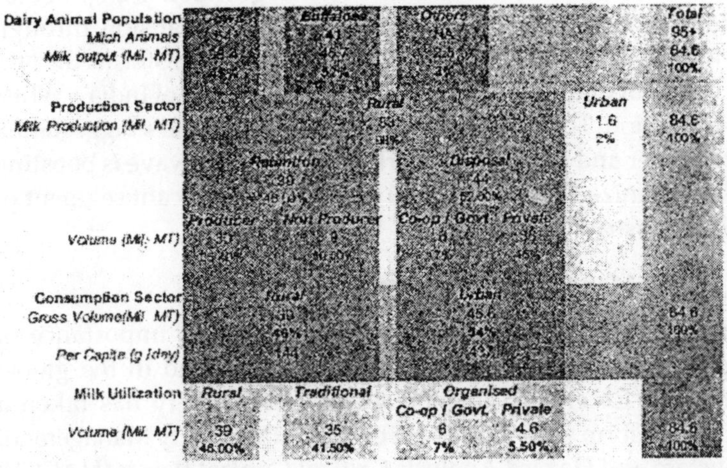

Source: Dairy India Yearbook.

Presently, the organized dairy sector process milk about 10-12 per cent of the total milk production of the country. The percentage handling capacity have to be increased and to meet the growing concern of the quality and safety of milk and milk products.

Indian Ethnic Dairy Products

A GCMMF-TCF survey report has given projected demand of Ghee, Paneer, Shrikhand, Rasogolla and Gulabjamun to be 200,16,5.7,6 and 5.9 thousand metric tones by the year 2009 [Misra, 2000].

Large-scale manufacturing of these products in a hygienically safe manner with assured quality control and proper packaging will certainly do wonder for this sector not only in India but also in abroad.

Sugam, Amul, Dynamix dairy, Saber and Rajkot dairies in Gujarat, Warna dairy, Maharashtra, etc., are all setting standards in dairy production. The modernization trend of organized dairy sector to traditional dairy product manufacturing will aid them to stand-up in the globalized competition and can bring eithnic dairy products into the mainstream of dairy foods. The organized dairy sector development towards product portfolio expansion through value-added indigenous dairy products will transforms the face of the dairy industry. It will be the second wave of India's White Revolution. The first wave made India the world's biggest milk producer and the biggest market. The second wave is boosting the organized sector and will make it a significant segment of the industry.

Quality Management System

Indian Dairy Industries have recognized the importance of quality as an sustaining strategy to withstand in the global market. Excellence in food quality and safety has taken a tangible form with the advent of ISO 9000 Quality Management System and Hazard Analysis Critical Control Points (HACCP) standard.

These standards have assumed importance world wide both as an essential requirement to tap the market potential and as a marketable feature of the company.

Sanitary and Phytosanitary measures is particularly applicable to food industry and adoption of HACCP standard under this agreement makes it mandatory for International Trade.

In 2002, over 30 dairy plants have been awarded the ISO: 9000 and HACCP certification and their number is increasing. It shows a positive sign of growth of the organized dairies in India. [Aneja, 2002]. Indian dairy exports is only 8 per cent as compared to EU (38%) and New Zealand (13%) [S.K. Anand, 2005]. The trend will change in course of time. The opportunity for Indian ethnic dairy product demand is high and this will change the Indian dairy scenario in the world market.

Certification Scheme for Dairy Products Export

To ensure a strong presence in global market, the Government of India had setup the Export Inspection Council of India (EIC) in India as the official certification body. Another step taken towards meeting quality assurance is that it has made mandatory the pre-shipment export certification for dairy products.

Export Prospects

The geographical setup of India itself an advantage as it is located admist major milk deficit country in Asia and Africa. And the world focus India for trade as it has low-cost economy, liberalization process, inexpensive labour, the presence of the world's third largest pool of technical man power and for reason that it stands among the lowest cost milk producers. Almost 70% of the world's milk is more expensive than India [Source: World Dairy Situation 2003, Bulletin of the International Dairy Federation and personal Estimates, 2002]. But the prices of dairy product are amongst the highest in the world.

All these offers Indian Dairy Industry a tremendous scope for growth. Also it has well-developed research facilities in dairy production and project development. Besides National Dairy Research Institute, Karnal along with its regional stations, and the large number of agricultural universities, engaged in research in various aspects of dairy science.

It is projected that India has a significant role to play in the global dairy scene, especially in the region of South Asia comprising of India, Pakistan, Bangladesh, Bhutan, Nepal, Sri Lanka and Maldives account for 20% of world milk production. As the countries have tradition of consuming milk as a part of normal diet. Country-wise figure on production, imports and exports of milk are presented in Table 1.

Table 1
Dairy Situation in South Asia (2001) ('000 tonnes')

Country	*Milk Production*	*Imports*	*Exports*
Bangladesh	2,112.01	254.91	0.167
Bhutan	31.96	5.11	-
India	83,970.00	61.02	136.87
Maldives	-	16.82	-
Nepal	1,197.91	2.42	0.16
Pakistan	26,284.00	81.43	0.81
Sri Lanka	297.56	457.64	0.91
Total	113,890.44	879.33	138.92

Source: Indian Dairy man, 55.3.2003 Page 140.

From the table it is observed that Bangladesh, Sri Lanka are major importers of dairy products. Pakistan also imports considerable quantities of milk products. The requirements of these countries can be met by developing a common milk grid.

Regional Co-operation

It is the time to learn some political lessons from the countries of Greater Mekong Subregion (GMS), the Six South-East Asian nations. The GMS grouping is setting an example for its regional co-operation and economic benefits, by building cross-border connectivity. Whether it is customs integration, the freer movement of people and goods, or even the purchase and sale of electricity, regional co-operation is in the interests of China, Myanmar, Thailand, Vietnam, Laos and Cambodia.

Setting aside their many political differences, GMS nations have locked the region into a co-operative endeavour, which have set the stages for the transformation of their economics. These regional co-operation will boost export and import and in overcoming the restriction of Technical Barrier to Trade (TBT) and Sanitary and Phytosanitary measures (SPS) of developed countries. By this integration they can lift all trade barriers to each other and can have a uniform duty structure in the region. [Source: The Hindu, 2005]

South Asian Free Trade Agreement will be operationalised from July 1, 2006. The question of extend of participation and success in achieving common milk grid depends on the co-operation extended between these countries. Can the South Asian region do it to gain global trade ?

Suggestion

To overcome the challenge of globalization, the Indian dairy sector has to adopt a different marketing approach and it should be:

- New product development and improvement in the quality of existing products to satisfy 'variety seeking' and health and nutritional needs of the consumers.
- Overcome 'affordability' constraints to the extend possible through 'value for money' pricing.

- Effectively promoting consumption of milk and milk products through attitudinal shift and linking it with fun, energy, health, nutrition etc.
- Encourage strategic alliance with some of the leading dairy companies in the world for technical collaboration and marketing tie-ups.
- India is regarded as one of the world's largest consumer market. Indian dairy sector can make avail of this opportunity.
- Indian dairy industry can tap the growing demand of indigenous milk-based sweets produced in modern dairy plants. As the scope for their exports is promising with 20 million NRI overseas.

All these provides an opportunity for India to emerge as an competitive player in the global market.

BIBLIOGRAPHY

Agriculture Commission Report, No. VII, Ministry of Agriculture and Irrigation, GOI, New Delhi, 1976, p. 121.

Second Five-Year Plan (1980-85) Planning Commission, GOI, New Delhi, 1981, p. 125.

Third Five-Year Plan, Planning Commission, New Delhi, 1961, p. 355.

C.M. Mohan (1989), "Dairy Management in India ", Eds (1989), Mittal Publications, Delhi, p. 44. 9, 38-52.

Dairy India a Profile, Dairy India (1987), p. 4.

http://www.faa.org/waiRdocs/LEAD/X6170e2z/htm.

Nineth Plan Proposals, Dairy India 1997, p. 11.

Operation Flood: The Third phase, Dairy India (1997), pp. 147-151.

A. Khattar, Gill J.P.S. and Sharma, J.K. (2005), "A Brief Scenario on Dairy Farmer Verses Dairy Co-operatives" Dairy Planner, Year 2, Vol. 4 November p. 10.

N.R. Bhasin (2006), "WTO Hong Kong Ministerial Conference–A Much Ado about Nothing", Indian Dairyman, Vol. 58, No. 1, January, p. 23-26.

N.R. Bhasin (2004), "Emerging Non-Tariff Barriers", Indian Dairyman, Vol. 56, No. 8, August, p. 37-41.

V.P. Sharma (2003), "Policy Initiatives for Countering Imbalance in Diary Sector in the Post-WTO ERA", Indian Dairyman, Vol. 55, No. 3, March, p. 148-152.

WTO (2002), "Members Usage of Domestic Support Categories, Export Subsides and Export Credits", Committee on Special Session(TN/AG/S/1), March 5, 2002.

World Trade Organization(WTO,2002), "WTO News from http://www.wto.org", Accessed in December 2002.

Vijay Sardana (2006), "WTO Hong Kong Ministerial Declaration and It's Implications for Indian Agriculture", Indian Diaryman, Vol. 58, No. 1, January, p. 29-34.

OECD (2001), "Agriculture Policies in OECD Countries: Monitoring and Evaluation, 2001" Organization for Economic Co-operation and Development, Paris, France.

OECD (2001), "The Uruguay Round Agreement on Agriculture: An Evaluation of its Implementation in OECD Countries", Organization for Economic Co-operation and Development, Paris, France.

R. Kalpana Sastry and B.N. Mathur (2003), "Implications of the WTO Agreements for Indian Dairy Industry", Indian Dairyman, Vol. 55, No. 9, September, p. 61-69.

International Agricultural Trade Research Consortium [IATRC, 2001], "Export Competition: Issues and options in the Agricultural Negotiations", Commissioned Paper No. 15, International Agricultural Trade Research Consortium, St.Paul Minnesota, November 2001.

International Agricultural Trade Research Consortium [IATRC, 2001], "The Current WTO Agricultural Negiotiations: Options for Progress", Commissioned Paper 18, International Agricultural Trade Research Consortium, St. Paul, Mimmesota.

Amit Baruah (2005), 'Can South Asian Region do it too?', The Hindu, November 23, Page 11.

OECD (2004), Agricultural Policies in OECD Countries : At a Glance 2004, Organization for Economic Co-operation and Development (OECD), Paris. Sharma, Vijay Paul (2000), "Assessing the Effect of the WTO Agreement on Indian Dairy Industry: What can we learn from past five years?", Indian Dairyman, Vol. 52, No. 11, November, p. 7-26.

Sharma, Vijay Paul and Ashok Gulati (2003), "Trade Liberalization, Market Reforms and Competitiveness of the Indian Dairy Sector",

MTID Discussion Paper No. 61, Markets, Trade and Institutions Division, International Food Policy Research Institute, Washington, D.C. April 2003.

Vijay Paul Sharma (2004), "From Doha to Cancun to Geneva", Indian Dairyman, Vol. 56, No. 8, August, p. 33-36.

Vijay Sardana (2004), "New Framework for WTO Negotiations and its implications, for Indian Food and Agriculture Sector", Indian Dairyman, Vol. 56, No. 8, August, p. 43-47.

S.K. Anand, A.K. Dang, Mahendra Singh, Rattan Chand, P.K. Aggarwal, R.C. Chopra and N. Balaraman (2005), "HACCP Principles for Tropical Dairy Farming, Indian Dairyman, Vol. 57, No. 2, February, p. 31-41.

A.K. Chauhan, K.K. Kalra, Raj Vir Singh, B.B. Raina (2005), "Profitability in Milk Products Manufacturing in a Dairy Plant", Vol. 57, No. 11, November, p. 25-31.

Agricultural Statistics at a Glance 2002 and Animal Report 2001-2002, Department of Animal Husbandry and Dairying, Ministry of Agriculture, Govt. of India.

Deepak Jain (2004), "Emerging Dairy Countries: The Indian Perspective," Indian Dairyman, Vol. 56, No. 12, December, p. 37-42.

R.P. Aneja, B.N. Mathu, R.C. Chandran, A.K. Banerjee, "Technology of Indian Milk Products," Dairy India Year Book (2002), Dairy India Publication, Delhi-India, p. 32,344.

Misra A.K. (2000), "Think Globally, Act Locally" Indian Dairyman, Vol. 52, p. 141-142.

G.R. Patil (2002), "Present Status of Traditional Dairy Products," Indian Dairyman, Vol. 54, No. 10, October, p. 35-45.

R.S. Gandhi (2005), "Sustainability of India Cattle: Present Scenario and Future Prospects", Indian Dairyman, Vol. 57, No. 11, November, p. 36.

ISSUE OF LABOUR STANDARDS IN WTO REGIME: THE CASE OF NEPAL

*Shyam Bahadur Katuwal**

Introduction

As the culmination of various General Agreements on Tariffs and Trade (GATT) negotiations, World Trade Organisation (WTO) has been established as the international institution with the basic aim of promoting international trade by the means of open, rule-based and non-discriminatory multilateral trading system. Though it is transformation of the GATT, the basis of establishing WTO was to improve living standards, income levels, ensure full employment along with the expansion in production and trade and ensure optimal use of the world's resources (Chakraborthy, 2001: 159).

Formally, WTO is established in January 1, 1995 when the recommendations of the eighth round of GATT, which was started at Putna del Este, Uruguay in September 1986 and concluded at Geneva on December 15,1993 (after seven years of its discussions and deliberations), were approved by the ministerial meeting held at Marrakesh of Morocco in April 1994. The ministerial meeting also agreed upon to upgrade the GATT to the position of WTO effective from January 1, 1995. Thus, the eighth round of multilateral trade negotiations of GATT is important in the history of WTO. This round is also called 'Uruguay Round' or 'Dunkel Round' or 'Draft Final Act Round', which recommended various proposals for agriculture, textiles and clothing, technology, trade related intellectual property

* Lecturer, Faculty of Management, TU Post Graduate Campus, Biratnagar, Nepal. Email: skatuwal@bcn.com.np.

The author is grateful to Prof. (Dr.) Ramesh Chandra Dahal, Department of Economics, TU, Post Graduate Campus, Biratnagar, Nepal for his suggestions.

rights (TRIPs), trade related investment measures (TRIMs), tariff and non-tariff measures, general agreement of trade in services (GATS) etc, along with the recommendation for the transformation of GATT to WTO. The WTO included in its scope of liberalization "non-tariff barriers (NTBs) along with tariffs, and conceived many new norms and disciplines such as sanitary and phytosanitary measures, anti-dumping measures, dispute settlement procedures, safeguard measures etc., with a view to ensuring liberalized effective market access and rule-based trade" (Panchmukhi, 2001:3).

In many aspects, WTO also follows the operational principles of GATT like non-discrimination and progressive liberalization of world trade by the means of elimination of quotas, non-tariff barriers (NTBs), and reduction and binding of tariffs. However, WTO is committed to establish 'market-based trade system and rule-based trading environment' in the world by exercising its power to enforce the commitments, rules and norms of discipline in international trade agreed in the regime of WTO. Under this provision of enforcement, each member nation is expected to follow these provisions so as to be part and parcel of international trade and obtain substantial gain from it.

In the globalised context, WTO also takes note of matters incidental and ancillary to trade and investment such as *trade and labour standards*, reduction of tariff rates, investment protection, trade and environment, trade and employment, trade and competition policy, transparency in government procurement policies etc. In order to see that these provisions are effectively implemented, WTO has provisions for international sanctions upon the defaulter member nations. Thus, WTO is an institutional basis for the application and enforcement of multilaterally agreed trade rules on goods and services and on the protection of intellectual property rights (Dev Raj, 2005:22).

The issue of the insertion of labour standards into trade agreements is much discussed and controversial issue in the field of international trade under WTO regime. It is still undecided issue in WTO because of the strong division and arguments between developed and developing countries regarding the consequences of the insertion of the labour standard issue into WTO regime. This paper attempts to focus the issue of labour standard in WTO regime along with the situation of Nepal.

Labour Standard on the World Trade Regime: A Historical Overview

Primarily, ILO is the only international agency to deal with the protection of labour rights all over the world. However, because of lacking of strong enforcement power of ILO to establish labour rights in the member nation, the search for alternative way is natural phenomenon in the present context of human rights violations. WTO would be the alternative agency to protect the rights of labour all over the world in the absence of other powerful international agency (This part of this article is heavily drawn from the papers of Turnell, 2001 and Stern, 2003, so it is the responsibility of the writer to acknowledge them).

Historically, as noted by Charnovotiz (1986: 566-67), the attempt of inserting labour standards in the trade was started from the Havana Charter of the International Trade Organisation (ITO) but the attempt failed due to the still birth of ITO and with emergence of GATT instead of ITO. As of narrow mandate as compared to the ITO, the GATT could not conceive the issue of labour standards, except of the provision of the prohibition of goods made with prison labour. The next unsuccessful attempt was made by United States in 1953 to include a labour standards article to GATT. The United States again unsuccessfully attempted to cover the issue of labour standards as the Article of GATT in the Tokyo and Uruguay Rounds of the Multilateral Trade Negotiations in 1970s and 1980s.

The international community was put on notice in April 1994 at the Murrakesh singing of Uruguay Round accords that the United States intended to pursue issues of labour standards in future multinational negotiations (Stern, 2003:12). An effort of drafting a 'Social Clause' dealing with core labour standard including trade sanctions for noncompliance with this clause was made to incorporate in the WTO. As a result, in the inaugural ministerial Meeting of the WTO at Singapore in December 9-13, 1996, the United States with the support from European Union, Canada and Japan attempted to establish "Social Clause" in the multilateral trade agreements.

The clause covers a group of labour rights derived from the Article 23 of the 'Universal Declaration of Human Rights', and other human rights covenants (Economic, Cultural, Social, Civil, Political and Rights of Child), which are identical to the categories of 'Core' established by the ILO in 1998. Because of the resist from the developing countries (specially Malaysia and Egypt) and certain developed countries, i.e. United Kingdom and Australia, the Social Clause was defeated in Singapore. The opponents believed the 'Social Clause' as nothing other than an attempt to usher in protection by the back door and to negate developing countries' comparative advantage in low-cost labour (Turnell, 2001:5). Although the Singapore Declaration acknowledged the importance of international labour standards, there was an apparent understanding among members that labour standards would remain the responsibility of the ILO (Williams, 1996: 4).

There was also an understanding in the Singapore declaration that trade liberalization fostered economic growth and development and that labour standards should not be used for protectionist purpose. It also affirmed that developing countries' comparative advantage in low cost labour should not be threatened, but urged that 'the WTO and the ILO Secretariats... continue their existing collaboration (see www.wto.org/english/the wto_e/min96_e).

The ILO, on the other hand, began a study about the integration of social welfares and trade policy (Agrawal, 1995:38). Consequently, with a view to develop a strong enforcement mechanism for the implementation of core labour standards, the ILO Secretariat suggested to work the ILO and WTO jointly, with the concentration of the ILO on monitoring and WTO for the enforcement through trade sanctions. However, in early 1995, the discussion on the trade sanction for alleged non-compliance with labour standards suspended due to the disagreements among representatives of ILO Working Party on Social Dimensions of the Liberalization of International Trade. Instead, the ILO initiated a research program on the effects of trade liberalization on core standard and a review of ILO means of action for the promotion of standards (OECD, 1996:7).

Because of the dissatisfaction from the understanding in the Singapore meeting, United States again raised the issue of labour standards in the successive second Ministerial Conferences of the WTO held at Geneva in May 18 –19, 1998 and in the third Ministerial Conference of Seattle in November 30 to December 3, 1999. These meetings were also terminated without any agreement regarding the inclusion of labour standards into WTO regime because of the disagreement from developing countries. In the Seattle Meeting US presented with clear vision that WTO was the appropriate institution to investigate the effects of the multilateral trading system on the living standards and the employment opportunities of workingmen and women around the world. European Union proposed a joint ILO/WTO Standing Working Forum on 'globalisation and trade'. The proposal of Canada was to form WTO working group to examine the link between trade, development and social and environment policies (Turnei, 2001:6-7). President Clinton gave a speech and press interview during the Seattle Conference calling for WTO trade sanction in case of violation of core labour standards. In spite of the effort of the President Clinton and other developed countries, developing countries denied to include labour standards in the WTO regime. The meeting had also widened the gap between developing and developed countries regarding the issues of agricultural protection and subsidies and antidumping policies.

Similarly, the fourth WTO Ministerial Conference held in Doha (Qatar) in November 9-14, 2001 received a setback when consensus evaded. However, the issue of labor standards acknowledged in the Doha Declaration in spite of the opposition of developing countries against the inclusion of labour standards as the part of the negotiation agenda (Stern, 2003:13). The meeting was concluded with the agreement to launch the next meeting in January 2002 and decide over the issue of labour standards by the end of 2004.

Although the Fifth Ministerial Conference held at Cancun in September 10-14, 2003 could not reach in the unanimous conclusion about the future of WTO, the issue of labour standards is a matter of highly relevant as the U.S. government is taking unilateral initiatives to enforce this agenda in regional and bilateral treaties with individual developing countries (Palley, 2003 and Elliot and Freeman, 2003). The Cancun conference got a boost with the Members adopting a Framework Agreement on August 1, 2004 outlining the elements and principles, which will guide the further negotiations including commitments of each member in respect of agriculture and Non-Agriculture Market Access (NAMA). The framework is the interim arrangement before the Sixth Ministerial Conference of WTO scheduled to be held at Hong Kong on December 13-18,2005 (Dev Raj, 2005:24). The issue of labour standards again remained unsure issue for the WTO even in the Sixth WTO Ministerial Conference.

International labour Standard to Core Labour Standards

International labour standards (ILS) indicate a set of principles for the protection of labour from all forms of exploitation from employers and oppression from the state. It covers divers areas of labour protection. It is very difficult to specify the labour standards because of the multifaceted nature. The scope of international labour standards may vary according to the socio—economic, cultural and political conditions and institutions available in the nation and stage of development of the country. However, Fields (1995:13) defines ILS as "... a set of basic labour rights for workers throughout the world". The International labour standards constitute the conventions adopted by the International Labour Organisation (ILO) for the worldwide maintenance of certain basic minimum standards. Thus, ILO is the primary organisation for the issuance of labour standards, worldwide.

"The ILO is the international forum for dialogue between government, employers and unions to achieve the fundamental objective of raising labour and social standards as integral elements of national economic development" (Commonwealth of Australia, 1991:1). ILO works for the protection of labour rights through it conventions passed by the representatives of the government, unions and employers of the member countries in different ILO conferences. International Labour Conference is a legislative organ of ILO, which is guided by the principle of tripartism. It is an obligation of the government of the member countries of ILO to put forward the convention to the "competent authority"- usually the national parliament for ratification.

Ratification of the ILO conventions is the voluntary obligation of member countries. However, once the member country has ratified the ILO convention, it becomes their responsibility to incorporate them into national policies, legislations and practices and report to the ILO on its application. The ILO conventions are, therefore, reference point in formulating national policies, legislations and practices on areas concerned. Nevertheless, the failure of implementation and enforcement of labour standards by any country is monitored and published by the ILO to put moral pressure on the country, due to lack of power for the enforcement of these standards at global level. Because of which, the implementation of these ratified labour standards become the mercy of the national government.

Since the creation of ILO in 1919 to March 2005, International Labour Conference has passed all together 185 conventions (www.ilo.org / ilolex/ conventions). Among them, member nations at the 86th Session of the General Conference of ILO in June 1998 have agreed to codify the following conventions as the *Core Labour Standards (CLS)* as its 'Declaration of Fundamental Principles and Rights at Work' with a view to protect rights of the working class in the world (ILO, 1999):

(i) Freedom of Association (Conv. 87)

(ii) Right to collective bargaining (Conv. 98)

(iii) Abolition of forced labour (Conv. 29/ 105)

(iv) Prohibition of discrimination in employment and occupation (Conv. 100/111).

(v) Elimination of child labour and worst forms of child labour (Conv. 138/182).

These standards are social minimum standards which are defined at the international level with the objective that they should be guaranteed by the national laws and regulations but not be regulated by the rules of market and expected to be observed by all member nations.

As in other conventions, ILO does not have power to enforce the implementation of these standards at global level. Thus, a worldwide action is highly required to make the implementation of these labour standards effective. Consequently, formal ratification of the ILO Conventions on the core labour standards differ considerably among ILO members, apparently because particular Conventions may be at variance with national laws and institutional practices (Stern, 2003:12). For example, America has ratified only two standards, one abolishing forced labour and the other eliminating the worst forms of child labour. Of the eight core labour standards Convention, China has ratified three CLS Conventions (i.e. equal remuneration, minimum age convention and worst form of child labour), Turkey and Peru have ratified all eight core conventions whereas many other countries have ratified a significantly more conventions (please refer to OECD, 2000: 21-30; Kayser, 2004: 22-23 and Burtless, 2001: 10-13). In fact, it is clear from these studies that ILO Conventions have not formally became recognized as standard for national regulations governing labour standards, and there are many cases in which ratified conventions are not enforced in the member countries.

The CLS appear to be global basic standards for the protection of labour rights only in 1990s, after a long advocacy of ILO, since 1920s (Verma and Gunderson, 2001). The CLS ensures the rights of working group regarding freedom of association, formation of unions and the rights to collective bargaining. It also attempts to abolish the practices of forced labour, discrimination in employment and occupation and child labour. All member countries of the ILO will be required to submit a report on the progress made in implementing the principles enshrined in the above conventions. However, these conventions do not favour linking ILS with trade (Venkata Ratam, 1998:995).

Insertion of Labour Standards into International Trade: A Debate

As the core labour standards are the fundamental rights of working class, the question is whether the violation of these rights should be punished through linkage with trade. The insertion of core labour standards into trade agreement, indeed any thing smacking of a 'social clause', is opposed from various sectors (Turnell, 2001). There is a clear difference between developing and developed countries regarding the issue of linking labour standards and trade. Most of the governments and trade unions from developed countries favour the linkage between core labour standards and international trade whereas employers of some developed countries and the unions, governments and employers in many developing countries have been resisting the linkage. In favour they argue that the countries and companies, which continue to pursue competitive advantage in international trade through the violation of fundamental rights, should be punished through sanction on international trade. The argument from the side of resistant is that it is their rights to enjoy the benefit of trade liberalization on the basis of comparatively low labour costs. They consider the linkage as a non-tariff barrier on international trade and it is the tactics made for neutralizing the comparative cost advantage enjoyed by them. Singh and Zammit (2004:1) state, "the subject is also deeply divisive as it pits workers of the North (the rich countries) against those of the South (the poor countries)".

However, improved working conditions are the matter of interests for both including international communities like WTO and ILO. It is challenge, on the other hand, to find out appropriate solution suitable to all parties because of the differences in their interests and views. In fact, core labour standards are the matter of debate between the developed and developing countries for their implementation under the umbrella leadership of the WTO.

Thus, this section of this article focuses on the north-south debate with a view to find out a workable and acceptable solution to the parties concerned.

There are many controversies about the linkage of the labour standards and trade. The issue is also a matter discussion among the academicians. Hoe (1995) stresses the need to protect workers rights but considers that trade-related international labour standards may constitutes hidden trade barriers. According to Griesgraber and Gunter (1997) the reduction of tariff barriers on the world scale opens the weaker economics to the power of the transnational corporation, and often leads to greater impoverishment of already poor countries and people. Maskus (1997) considers the potential economic impact of international labour standards, especially for economic competitive advantage, and concludes that they could be counterproductive.

The issue of linking labour standard and trade came to existence also because of the working procedure of ILO and WTO in respect to protect labour Rights. The ILO is the norm-setting agency for international labour standards. ILO conventions are voluntary in nature and there are no penal sanctions to the member nation for breaching the requirements of conventions other than to put moral pressure on the member countries by the adverse publicity for not fulfilling voluntary obligations. It is because of the lack of legal remedies of ILO for the enforcement of its conventions. In this regard, the OECD (2000:5) remarks, "The approach of ILO work best where the parties have a will to conform... or where they are sensitive to public concerns when issues of non-conformity are raised". In such a situation, it is a true sense to design such a framework where the labour standards are respected with or without 'name and shame'. It will be possible only when there is a strong mechanism of implementing the agreements.

In this regard, therefore, WTO will be the right choice for it, because, unlike ILO, WTO has assumed a special mechanism called Dispute Settlement Mechanism (DSM) to enforce the rules and agreements of WTO. The Dispute Settlement Body (DSB) created under this mechanism has the power to sanction and dispute settlement in case of failure of the implementation of the rules and recommendations. The Dispute Settlement Body (DSB) of the WTO not only monitors the implementations of rulings and recommendations but also can exercise power to authorize retaliation when a country does not comply with a ruling (NRB, 2002: 26). Thus, WTO may ensure the implementation of rules and agreements agreed upon the WTO regime including labour standards. However, there should be a closer cooperation between the WTO and ILO to deal with labour standards and labour rights (Sharma, 2001: 16).

As the ILO and WTO are two different international organisations, there is a debate of supremacy over the question of labour standards. The issue of labour standards came prominently in the controversy when the CLS have been tried to insert into the WTO regime, especially after the Fourth Ministerial Conference held on 9-14 November 2001 at Doha, Quatar. The Doha Ministerial discussion is an important attempt to link international labour standards to international trade. It has challenged to ILO especially to link labour with trade, and the effective implementation of core labour standards in the WTO member countries. However, the matter of inserting the issue of CLS in the WTO regime is still in controversy and undecided among the member nations.

As per the agreement in WTO, social agenda covering labour standards requires the establishment of national standards regulations in a systematised and transparent system. The labour-trade linkage is being opposed by the developing countries of the South (poor countries) saying that this is the tactical movement of the industrialised countries of the North (rich counties) to undermine the comparative advantage of the low-waged trading partners in the South because labour is the most powerful means of developing countries like Nepal to build their comparative advantage over developed world in exportable products. Thus they say labour standards is the 'game of a trade politics' played by developed countries in order to minimise the comparative advantage of developing countries and maintain their domination in trade. At the same time developed countries are criticized for not fulfilling their obligations towards the WTO agreements. Governments from developing countries saw ILO standards as reducing their competitive edge (Chaudhri,2000:44) and discourage their export in the name of labour rights.

Another base of opposition from developing countries regarding the linkage of labour standard to trade is that they believe workplace conditions will improve through economic growth and development and it would be held up if developed counties apply trade sanctions to their exports for reasons relating to labour standards. Application of such sanctions, further they say, would perpetuate poverty and delay developmental efforts including those aimed at improving conditions in the workplace (www.ilo.org.labour standard/ Doha Ministerial 2001: Briefing Notes).

Since the voice from developed countries is strong because of unity among the labour, employers, NGOs and the government regarding for higher labour standards and they have already quite high labour standards to pointing a finger at the developing countries, the must common arguments in favour of the higher labour standards are that trade must be "fair" in addition to being "free". The implication is that countries with low labour standards enjoy an unfair competitive advantage (Verma and Gunderson, 1991:367).

The argument from the developed countries in favour of this issue is to discourage unfair and inhuman practices at work place and to preserve the higher labour standards and better human rights all over the world including developing counties like Nepal. Similarly, industrialized countries want developing countries to liberalise sectors such as banking, finance and insurance whereas developing countries have demanded greater labour mobility in rich nations (Shrestha, 2006).

As a matter of fact, developed countries have cheap capital, whereas labour is economical in the developing countries. However, the flow of the products from developed countries to developing countries became easy by the tariff reduction provisions of WTO but movement of products from developing countries is in constraints because of the issue of the use of acceptable 'core labour standards (CLS)' for the production of the goods and services.

Another fear from the side of developing countries is that the core labour standards embodied as the part of 'social clause' in the WTO could be a tool of unfair competition in the hands of the developed countries and thereby causing severe international trade losses and deteriorating developmental opportunities of the poor countries.

But in fact, inclusion of social clause embodying core labour standards in the framework of WTO should not be suspected by the developing countries like Nepal, because it would be an effective measure for obstructing liberalisation, economic competition and deregulation, which are the essential elements of globalisation. The finding of the study of OECD (2000) also reveals that strengthened core labour standards can increase economic growth and efficiency by raising the skill levels in the work force and encouraging innovation and higher productivity. Thus, this study concludes that countries with low core labour standards do not enjoy better export performance than high labour standard countries. Similarly, the study of the World Bank (2002) also concludes that the core labour standards help to establish sound industrial relations leading to a stable economy and prevention of disruption to national life.

WTO–ILO and Nepal: Opportunities and Challenges

Out of 149 members after the 11 years of its establishment to the end of February 2006, Nepal is 147th member of the WTO, which is expecting substantial gain in her trade with international community through access to world trade network. Nepal's membership in the WTO is the product of the long-term efforts taking almost fifteen years. Following a trade dispute with India, Nepal had formally applied for GATT on May 1989, which was lasted for 15 months. After various formalities, it was in December 1995 that Nepal obtained a status of the observer member in the WTO. Then after, Nepal had fulfilled various procedures for the accession to the WTO. In 1997, the application for membership in GATT transferred to the membership in WTO. According to the procedure for the accession to the membership of the WTO, Nepal had submitted a 'Memorandum of Foreign Trade Regime' in July 1998 and it was circulated among member nation for comments and quarries, if any, in August 1998. After the reply of HMG/Nepal on the quarries in 1999 and 2000 and the meeting of different rounds in WTO and discussion with stakeholder up to the end of 2002, the fifth Ministerial Conference of WTO held on 10-14 September, 2003 at Cancun, Mexico decided membership of Nepal in WTO and declared as a full member on 23 April 2004 (NRB, 2002 and www.ilo.org).

Nepal is one of the first countries of the least developed group, which has obtained the membership of WTO through agreement. At present, joining to WTO as a full member, Nepal has both challenges to face and prospects to gain in the international trade by linking various trade related issues including the issues of labour standards.

In the light of the membership, it is the responsibility of Nepal to respect the norms, standards and agreement passed therein WTO and ILO. In this regard, the following section of this paper is concentrated to highlight on the ILO standards ratified by the country. The challenges to be faced and prospects Nepal can gain from the insertion of CLS in the WTO regime are also the subject matter of discussion in the following part of the this paper.

ILO Conventions Ratified by Nepal

Since its membership from 1966, Nepal has shown a strong commitment towards the International Labour Standards passed by ILO. Regarding the core labour conventions of ILO, Nepal has ratified seven Core Labour Standard out of eight such standards and incorporated them in the respective Acts and Policies. A list of conventions ratified by Nepal till March 30,2006 has been given in the Table 1.

In case of the non-ratified convention, i.e. the freedom of association and right to form unions (convention No. 87), Nepal has declared freedom of association and unionism by covering the issue in the Constitution of the Kingdom of Nepal 1990, Trade Union Act 1992, Labour Act 1992 and the Labour and Employment Policy 2006. Similarly, many more other ILO Conventions, even if they have not been formally ratified, are also covered in laws and policies of the country to regulate the issue in concern. So that, by this, it is clear that Nepal is one step forward in the implementation and enforcement of the ILO Conventions.

Table 1
List of ILO Conventions Ratified by Nepal

Con. No.	*Years*	*Conventions*	*Date*
14	1921	Weekly rest (industry)	10:12:1986
29	1930	Forced Labour	03:01:2002
98	1949	Rights to organize and Collective Barging	11:11:1996
100	1951	Equal Remuneration	10:06:1976
111	1958	Discrimination (Employment and Occupation)	19:09:1974
131	1970	Minimum Wage Fixing	19:09:1974
138	1973	Minimum Age of Employment	30:05:1997
144	1976	Tripartite Consultation (International Labour Std.)	21:03:1995
182	1999	Worst Forms of Child Labour	03:01:2002

Source: www.ilo.org/ilolex (as of 30 March, 2006).

In Nepal, Labour Act 1992 and Trade Union Act 1992 are enacted to preserve the rights of the workers. Children's Act 1993 and Child Labour (Prohibition and Regulation) Act 2000 are the special types of Acts which are focused to abolish child labour and protect the rights of children and prevent them form hazardous labour.

Similarly, for the elimination of forced labours Kamaiya Labour (Prohibition) Act 2002 has been enacted in 2002. The Act is intended to prohibit and abolish bounded/Kamaiya labour (a form of forced labour) system from the country. The Trafficking and Selling in Persons Activity (Prohibition) Act, 1986 is another Act that prohibits the trafficking and selling of persons including prostitution of women through force, coercion, false promises or deception. The labour and

Employment Policy 2006 issued recently on 22 February 2006 by replacing the previous Labour Policy 1999 is the next progressive step towards the protection of worker's rights in the country. As compared to previous one, the present policy is more comprehensive and forward looking in order to protect labour's rights. They are aimed at effecting improvements in the working and living conditions of workers and to improve industrial relations.

Although the existing labour laws and the policy are required to improve according to the context of WTO and the demands of trade unions and employers, these laws are only the cornerstone to deal with core labour standards in the country.

Conventions Incorporated in the Labour Act and Labour Regulations

According to the norms, Nepal has shown its strong commitment towards the International Labour Standards (ILS) by incorporating them in the concerned legislations of the country. The provisions of the ratified conventions in the legislations are given in the Table 2.

For the implementation of all these above mentioned Acts, except of the Acts related with forced labour, requires the existence of a formal employer-employee relationship - which is possible in the formal organised sector in the country. Thus, all the provisions of these legislations are explicit in protecting rights and interests of the workers, with the active participation of the employer, in such sectors where the employer has control and supervision over the workers.

Most of the workers who have been working in the unorganized sectors like farms, streets, homes, construction and other informal sectors and the self-employed, with the requirement of existence of a formal employer-employees relationship, have been left out of the purview of these legislations. These laws have covered only formally designated workplaces such as factories, tea plantation, hotels, trekking, construction, and transportation.

Table 2
Provisions of the Ratified Convention in the Legislations

ILO Convention	*Concerned Legislations*	*Provisions*
C. 14 Weekly Rest eight (industry)	Labor Act, Chapter 3, section 16.	No worker or employee shall be deployed in work for more than hours per day or forty eight hours per week and they shall be provided one day as weekly holiday for every week.
C. 29 Forced Labour	Kamaiya Labour (Prohibition) Act 2002, Section 2 (4) and Trafficking and Selling in Persons Activity (Prohibition) Act, 1986,section 4(1-4)	The Kamaiya Labour (Prohibition) Act 2002 prohibits labour or services provided by a person to his creditor without any wages or at low rates of wages to repay loans (Kamaiya labour). The Trafficking and Selling in Persons Activity (Prohibition) Act, 1986 restricts the trafficking and selling of persons through force, coercion, false promises or deception.
C. 98 Right to Organise and Collective Bargaining	Trade Union Act, 1992 and Trade Union Rules, 1993	Detail rules and regulations regarding the formation and operation of recognized and registered trade unions have been given the Trade Union Act and its rules.
C. 100 Equal Remuneration	Labour Regulations, chapter 3, section 11.	Equal remuneration shall have to be provided without making discrimination to male or female worker or employee for engaging them in the works of the same nature of functions enterprise.
C. 111 Discrimination (Employment and Occupation)	Labour Regulations, chapter 3, section 11.	As under equal remuneration convention.
C. 131 Minimum Wage Fixing	Labour Act, Chapter 4, section 21(1 – 7).	Nepal government shall fix the minimum remuneration of workers or employees of enterprises on the recommendation of Minimum Remuneration Fixation Committee and the notice shall be published in the Nepal Gazette.

Contd....

ILO Convention	*Concerned Legislations*	*Provisions*
C. 138 Minimum Age Convention	Labour Act 1992, chapter 2, section 5 (1); Children's Act 1993, Section 17 and Child Labour (Prohibition and Regulation) Act 2000, Chapter 2, section 3 (1).	No child shall be engaged in work in any enterprise. "Child" means a person who has not attained the age of fourteen (Labour Act 1992, chapter 1, section 2.h). The Labour Act 1992, Children's Act 1993 and Child Labour (Prohibition and Regulation) 2000 protect the child rights including the abolition of child labour and worst form of child labour.
C.144 Tripartite Consultation	Different chapters, section and sub-sections of the labour Act	At different places in the Labour Act and Labour Regulation it is mentioned that matters will be decided, "having equal representation of worker or employee, Proprietor and Nepal Government". There is a National Tripartite Labour Advisory Committee, which is supposed to discuss all labour issues and policies in a tripartite way.
C. 182 Worst Forms of Child Labour	Child Labour (Prohibition and Regulation) Act 2000, Chapter 2, section 3 (2).	Child Labour (Prohibition and Regulation) protect the child from worst form of child labour, e.g. trekking tourism related occupations, laboratories, construction & public transportation, industries related with chemical production, mines, energy, cigarettes, carpet, biogas etc.

Source: Extracted from the concerned laws

Labour and Employment Policy 2006

The Labour and Employment Policy 2006 has tried to integrate the labour and employment together with a view to meet international labour standards and thereby obtain the opportunities of WTO. The long-term objectives of the policy are to provide productive, non-discriminating, decent, safe and healthy employment opportunities to the citizens at working age group by creating the investment-friendly environment, and to develop and manage labour market for building national economics capable to compete with international standard (MOLTM, 2006). In this regard, the labour policy has adapted various relevant strategies and action plans, and thus, it is necessary, on the other hand, to enact fresh laws, amendment of existing laws and issuance of different policies related to labour and employment to meet the spirit of the policy. However, in the present context, the Labour Act 1992 and Trade Union 1992 and associated regulations are only such laws in Nepal which have tried to cover and regularize most of the essential labour standards.

Whatsoever, such a legislative arrangement is a clear indication of strong commitment of Nepal towards the requirement of WTO/ILO. In this juncture, therefore, Nepal has to obtain comparative advantages over developed countries by exporting of the labour intensive goods and services like carpet, garments, handicrafts, ornaments, herbs, agricultural products etc. in the framework of WTO, with the care and caution over the core labour standards. The provision of social clause in the framework of WTO has loaded the cheap labour force and it would discourage the production of such goods in which Nepalese economy has comparative advantage, especially the production of carpet and garment, which currently constitute almost 75 per cent of exports (Jha, 2005:135). Thus, Nepal is to be careful in this aspect.

Suggestions/Implication

Considering the labour standards as a challenge, Nepal Government has undertaken different program and policies to improve labour standards according to the concerned ILO conventions and the issues raised in WTO Conferences. Despite the efforts in the Constitution of the Kingdom of Nepal and concerned labour laws and policies, multiple laws and policies for the protection of labour rights has yet to be tackled effectively to get fullest benefits from the arrangement of WTO by assuring trading partners that Nepal has fair labour practices and pays due respect to the CLS and human rights for the production of the goods and services. For this, the following suggestions are devised to:

- Not agreeing to enforcement of labour standards for trade sanctions or without bothering for inclusion of labour standards in WTO, Nepal needs to improve productivity and efficiency of manufacturing and service sectors.
- With the increase in global job mobility, Nepal needs to focus skill development program at national level and organisations to enhance quality of work life and to attract and retain skilled manpower.
- Nepal has to create international lobbies to prove that the exportable goods and services are produced according to the ratified conventions for the core labour standards and stakeholders are satisfied from the provisions. For this, visiting programs of the international communities at the workplaces should be organised.
- Nepal should be careful to maintain labour standards because the clause of labour standard may any time create evil effects to the volume of export trade and thereby economy.
- The trading partner should not be worry if the stakeholders are satisfied with the provisions of labour standards in the country, in general and in the production units, in specific.
- It is better to establish the practices of process labour standards rather than substantive labour standards because in process labour standards the standards are worked out by mutual agreement (process standards), which may be flexible and, thus would be permanent and acceptable to the parties concerned. Nevertheless, if they were designed

through substantive ways, they would be less flexible to the environmental change, resisted by the stakeholders, and difficult to govern at work place and to convince international community.

- Since most of the workers are uneducated, trade unions must be vigilance and conscious of their responsibility for enhancing the knowledge of their members about which ILO Conventions have been ratified by their nation in order to identify which rights they can claim for.
- In cases of the hesitation of the employers and government to implement the ILO conventions even after the ratification, trade unions, as a stakeholder, should monitor and report the same to ILO and WTO to put pressure from the international body for the enforcement of the labor standards and to ensure that the fundamental rights of workmen are well protected.
- As of other developing countries, cheap labour in production is one of the major competitive advantages of Nepal in international trade, Nepal should always be alert to maintain labour standards for its production to put aside of the blame of violating labour standards and thereby to increase the share of comparative advantage in some of the exportable products in the international market.
- If necessary, Nepal has to change the existing structure, policies, rules and regulations according to the requirement of the rules and norms of WTO to get full benefits from it.
- It is also necessary to assure international community that the goods and services in Nepal are produced without unfair labour practices by publishing and disseminating the information about the labour standards based on the research conducted with the participation of representatives of trade unions, employers, government and international agencies like WTO/ ILO.
- It is also necessary to solve the problems of unemployment, domestic labour, child labour, bonded labour, labourers in the informal sectors, health and security problems of the

workers by devising a comprehensive, integrative, and an effective master plan, programs and policies to address all issues together with.

- As the jobs available in the country are limited, government has to manage and explore foreign labour market by snatching the opportunities of WTO. For this, government has to search out the foreign employment in the countries like America, European countries, Arabian countries, Malaysia, S. Korea, Japan and other countries where the demand for Nepalese workers is high through the diplomatic machineries, and has to make an agreement with them for increasing employment quotas.

Conclusion

Although the purpose of the WTO is to establish rule governing world trade and to develop it as a platform to discuss about trade issues among the member nations and liberalise trade by reducing trade barriers of different kinds, the scope of the WTO has been extended beyond the trade in goods. Presently, concentration of the WTO has been extended in many more issues like services, intellectual property rights, environment, international labour standards, competition, regulations etc. In spite of compromise on the fact that ILO was the competent body to determine and promote worldwide core labour standard, WTO seems to be committed to the observance of the effective and rule-based implementation of these standards in its member nation with a view to protect fundamental rights at work.

While ILO has not succeeded in effective implementation of labour standards despite ratification a number of countries, WTO may be the right choice of workers for its enforceable labour clause.

The issue of core labour standards is discussed much but not accepted yet in the mainstream of WTO regime. Despite the failure of the efforts of developed countries to include labour standards in the WTO regime because of the refusal from the developing countries, the core labour standards have been brought into discussion in different rounds of WTO conferences, extensively from the Doha Ministerial Conference. The international trade negotiations, which are reached in international trade rounds, have been widely criticized by developing countries for being dominated by the economically powerful countries in the North and intransparent in nature. Being feared from the same notion and the fear of encroachment of developed countries in their competitive advantage of cheap labour, in the name of labour standards, the developing countries have been continuously denying for including labour standards in the WTO regime.

Developing countries believe that the labour standards is 'the game of a trade politics' played by developed countries in order to minimise the comparative advantage of developing countries and maintain their domination in trade. The confrontation between developed and developing countries came apparently from the Ministerial Conference in Cancun, Mexico, in 2003, which concluded without any concrete decision. The issue is still undecided. Nevertheless, because of the structural pattern of WTO, lack of enforcement power of ILO, incessant effort from developed countries and power-pray nature of the member nation, the issues of labour standards are certain to be included, in this or that forms and ways in the future multinational trade negotiations under the WTO regime. In other side, the future of international labour standards is in crisis because of the rift between developed and developing countries, relative supremacy of the ILO and the WTO and the diverse pressures from the stakeholders about the linkage between labour standards and deregulated labour market.

In such a situation, the dispute settlement mechanism specified in the WTO bound member nations to comply with WTO rules otherwise to face trade sanctions, which may have multiple and adverse impact on their developmental efforts. Therefore, there is no option to the developing countries like Nepal other than to change the existing structure, policies, rules and regulations according to the requirement of the rules and norms of WTO to get full benefits from it. Consequently, Nepal has also been changing different laws, policies and structures including labour related issues to assure the third world trading partners that the goods and services are produced with full respect of the labour standards. At the same time, Nepal should always be alert to maintain high labour standards for its production to put aside of the blame of violating labour standards from developed countries in order to minimise comparative advantage in some of our exportable products like carpet, garments, ornaments, herbs, agricultural products etc.

REFERENCES

Agrawal, Mita (1995), "International Trade, Labour Standards, and Labour Market Conditions: An Evaluation of the Linkage", *Working Paper No. 95-06*, Office of Economics, USITC, USA.

Burtless, Gary (2001), "Workers' Rights: Labour Standards and Global Trade", *The Brookings Review*, Vol. 19, No. 4, pp. 10-13.

Chadha, G.K. (2001), *WTO and The Indian Economy*, Deep and Deep Publications Pvt. Ltd, New Delhi.

Chakraborthy, D. (2001), "WTO and Its Impact on Indian Agriculture and Industry", in Chadha, G.K. (ed), *WTO and The Indian Economy*, Deep and Deep Publications Pvt. Ltd., New Delhi, pp. 159.

Charnovitz, Steve (1986), " The *Influence* of International Labour Standards on the World Trading Regime: A Historical Review", *International Labour Review*, Vol. 126, pp. 565-84.

Chaudhari, D.P. (2000), "Basic Human Rights, Core Labour Standards and Relative Educational Deprivation of *Youth* in India", *The Indian Journal of Labour Economics*, 43 (1), pp. 35-57.

Commonwealth of Australia (1991), *The World at Work: Australia and International Labour Organisation*, AGPC, Australia.

Dev Raj (2005), "Impact of World Trade Organisation on India's Foreign Trade: Trends and Prospects", *Indian Economic Association, Conference Volume*, pp. 22-42.

Elliott, K.A. and R.B. Freeman (2003), *Can Labour Standards Improve under Globalisation?* Institution for *International* Economics, Washington D.C.

Fields, Gary (1995), *Trade and Labour Standards: A Review of Issues.* Organisation for Economic Co-operation and Development (OECD), Paris.

Griesgraber, J.M. and B.C. Gunter (1997), *World Trade: Towards Fair and Free Trade in the 21st Century*, Plato Press, London.

Hoe, L.A.(1995), *Human Rights, International Labour Standards and Trade in a Globalised Economy: An Assessment of the Economic, Moral and Political Dimensions,* Dissertation submitted to the university of Birmingham, Birmingham.

ILO (1999), "Decent Work: Report of the Director-General", *International Labour Conference,* International Labour Office, Geneva.

Jha, Pramod Kumar (2005), *Nepal and the World Trade Organisation: A Challenging Path,* Mishra Trading Corporation, Varanasi.

Kayser, Folke (2004), *Defending Social Justice and Workers' Rights in a Globalised World: A Manual of Globalisation and Labour Standards,* Friedrich Ebert Stiftung, Jakarta Selatan, Indonesia.

Maskus, K.E. (1997), *Should Core Labour Standards be Imposed through International Trade Policy?* World Bank (International Trade Division), Washington, D.C.

MOLTM (2006), *Labour and Employment Policy 2006,* Ministry of Labour and Transport Management, HMG/N, Kathmandu.

NRB (2002), *WTO and Nepal,* Nepal Rastra Bank, Research Department, Kathmandu.

OECD (1996), *Trade, Employment and Labour Standard: A Study of Core Workers' Rights and International Trades,* Organisation for Economic Co-operation and Development (OECD), Paris.

OECD (2000), *International Trade and Core Labour Standards,* Organisation for Economic Co-operation and Development (OECD), Paris.

Palley, T.A. (2003, "After Cancun: Possibilities for a New North-South Grand Bargain on Trade", *Policy Discussion Paper,* Open Society Institute, Washington D.C.

Panchmukhi, V.R.(2001), "World Trade Organisation and India's Export Response", in Chadha, G.K. (ed), *WTO and The Indian Economy,* Deep and Deep Publications Pvt. Ltd., New Delhi, pp. 3-21.

Sharma, Gunanidhi (2001), "WTO, Globalisation and Social Security Systems: The Emerging Contradictions in Alternative Development Paradigms", In Shrestha, Ananda (2001).

Shrestha, Ananda (2001), *WTO, Globalisation and Nepal,* Nepal Foundation for Advanced Studies (NEFAS) and United States Embassy, Kathmandu.

Shrestha, Shyamal (2006). "Can Service Revive Doha". *The Kathmandu Post*, March 29, 2006 Vol. XIV, No. 39, p. 4.

Singh, Ajit and Zamit Ann (2004), "***Labour*** Standards and the 'Race to the Bottom': Rethinking Globalisation and Workers Rights from Developmental and Solidaristic Perspective", *Working Paper No. 279*, ESRC Centre for Business Research, University of Cambridge, Cambridge.

Stern, Robert N. (2003), "Labour Standards and Trade Agreements", *Discussion Paper No. 496*, Submitted in the Research Seminar in International Economics, Gerald R. Ford School of Public Policy, The University of Michigan, Michigan.

Turnell Sean(2001), "Core Labour Standards and the WTO", *Macquavie Economics Research Paper, No 31, Australia.*

Venkata Ratam, C.S.(1998)," International Labour Standards and India", *The Indian Journal of Labour Economics*, Vol. 41, No. 4. pp. 993-1003.

Verma, Anil and Gunderson, Morley (2001), "Labouring for Advantage: Worker Stakes in a Globalising Economy", *The Indian Journal of Labour Economics*, 44 (3), 363-74.

Williams, Frances (1996), "Singapore Deals Give a Boost to WTO", *The Financial Times*, December 16, In Stern (2003), p. 13.

World Bank (2002), *Union and Collective Bargaining: Economic Effects in a Global Environment*, World Bank, Washington D.C.

www. wto.org/engilsh/thewto_e/minist_/min96_e

www.ilo.org

www.ilo.org//ilolex/conventions

www.ilo.org/English/ ilostandards/Doha Ministerial 2001: Briefing Notes.

PROTECTION OF PLANT VARITIES IN INDIA

*Sreenivasulu N.S.**

Introduction

Protection of plant varieties was a long-standing and deeply felt demand. India being dependent on the agriculture sector, there were moves to accelerate the development in the sector in order to foster the development of the economy. In this context it is very much essential to protect the endeavors in the agriculture sector. A plant variety a result of endeavours in the sector attracts special attention here. Traditionally farmers and breeders involved in evolving new varieties of plants capable of meeting the needs of the society. Farmers and breeders played significant role in the conservation and improvement of plant genetic resources and use of such resources for the development of new varieties.

Research in the agriculture field mainly focuses on evolving new plant varieties capable of catering the modern day needs. Research in this field involves huge investment and laborious efforts which deserve protection. At the same time farmers and other groups contributed to the conservation of plant genetic resources and in making them available for use in evolving new varieties deserves recognition through rewards. Protection of such endeavors encourages further research in the field resulting in the growth of the industry and in turn the development of the economy. Therefore there is a need to encourage research in the agriculture sector by offering protection to the new plant verities.

Plant Variety

Before going for discussing the intricacies involved in the protection of plant verities it is pertinent to know what does a

* Guest Faculty, Department of Law, University of Mysore, Mysore-570006.

plant variety mean? The protection of plant varieties and farmers rights Act 2001 defines Plant variety to mean; "a plant grouping except microorganism within a single botanical taxon of the lowest known rank" which is distinct, stable, uniform and novel compared to the existing varieties. It includes propagating material of such variety, extant variety, transgenic variety, farmer's variety and essentially derived variety[1]. Propagating material means any plant or its component or part thereof including seeds capable of regenerating into a plant.[2] Extant variety means a variety, which is a part of public domain or common knowledge of farmer's variety available in India.[3] Farmers variety is given a meaning as a variety which has been traditionally cultivated and evolved by the farmers in their fields or a wild relative or land race of a variety about which the farmers possess the common knowledge.[4] Essentially derived variety in the sense a variety essentially derived from an initial variety or derived from a variety that is predominantly derived from such initial variety retaining the expression of the essential characteristics that result from the genotype or combination of genotypes of such initial variety but clearly distinguishable from the initial variety.[5] Transgenic variety is a variety possessing foreign genes incorporated unnaturally. It is variety, which is a result of genetic engineering. A variety defined under the Act means and includes a plant variety which may a extant variety or farmers variety or essentially derived variety or transgenic variety its parts, its propagating material and its seeds.

Who is a Breeder of Plant Varieties?

The Protection of plant varieties and farmers rights Act defines the term breeder. Breeder is a person or group of persons or farmer or group of farmers or any institution, which has bred, evolved or developed any variety[6]. Breeders includes farmer within its meaning. However farmer[7] is defined to mean any person who cultivates crops by cultivating the land himself or though any other person or conserves and preserves, severally or jointly with any person any wild species or traditional varieties or adds value to such wild species or traditional varieties through selection and identification of their useful properties. Breeders or farmers who endeavor in evolving a plant variety may seek protection for their variety provided their variety possess such required characteristic features as prescribed under the Act. Not all varieties are offered protection through registration; only such varieties possessing such specified characteristics are offered protection.

Characteristics of Plant Varieties

A plant variety must posses such prescribed characteristics in order to be protected. Only such varieties possessing such characteristic features are given protection. A variety must possess following characteristic features:

1. Novel
2. Stable
3. Uniform
4. Distinct

A variety must be novel in the sense; it must be a variety newly evolved, which is hitherto unknown or not available in the public domain or not a part of the common knowledge. Second characteristic feature is stability. A variety must be stable in expressing its characteristics; in the sense such variety must be stable in possessing and expressing its characteristics after its propagation. Third characteristic feature that a variety must possess is uniformity. A variety must possess common features through out its generations. In the sense it must transform same and uniform characteristics to its next generation. Its uniform characteristic features must be transferred from generation to generation. The last characteristic feature of a variety is distinctiveness. A variety must be clearly distinguishable from other varieties. Any variety possessing all the above characteristic features is eligible[8] for protection and deserves protection.

Protection of Plant Varieties

Plant varieties are offered protection through registration. A registered plant variety is protected from exploitation except by the breeder who has registered it after having worked on it. In the sense protection is not available to an unregistered plant variety. A farmer or breeder intending to get protection for their newly evolved variety shall apply for registration under the Act. The Central Government is empowered to establish an authority called Protection of Plant Varieties and Farmers Rights Authority.[9] The authority is a body corporate[10]; it consists of a chairman and fifteen other members representing different interests appointed by the Central Government. The objective behind the establishment of the authority is to encourage and promote the development of new plant varieties by offering protection. The above objective is served by providing for registration of new plant varieties. The authority intends to provide for the registration and documentation[11] of new plant varieties. For all the above practical purposes the authority is vested with the powers of Civil Court[12]. For the purpose of registration of new plant varieties there established a Registry known as the Plant Varieties Registry[13]. Registration is done through the branches of the Registry established at different locations through out the country. Registry maintains a register called The National Register[14]of plant varieties, which is kept at the head office of the registry. The details of the registered plant varieties such as; its silent features, its denomination, seeds, propagating material, along with the name and addresses of the breeder, their rights shall be entered in the National Register.

Registration of Plant Varieties

Any person intending to get his variety protected shall apply for registration before the registry. It is only the breeder of the variety or his successor, assignee or any farmer group or any University or publicly funded agricultural institution or any person authorized who are eligible to apply for the registration of a new variety.[15] Applications could be made either individually or jointly. There excluded few varieties from registration, such varieties could not be claimed in the application.

Varieties Excluded from Registration

In the public interest few varieties have been excluded or prohibited from registration. Varieties exploitation of which is against public order or morality or prejudicial to human, animal and plant life and health or to the environment are excluded from registration.[17] The Act specifically excludes a variety, which involves the use of any technology, which is injurious to human, animal, plant life or health from registration.[18] In particular use of technologies such as terminator technology in evolving a variety leaves the variety incapable of reproduction. Varieties evolution, which involves use of the above technology, are totally excluded from registration. Terminator technology involves using of gene technology to incorporate a gene into a plant, which terminates the plants capacity to reproduce. Besides a variety is not registrable if it is not identifiable[19] or is not different from other existing varieties. On the same lines if a variety is likely to deceive or confuse the public or hurt religious sentiments of any class of citizens of India is not registrable. Further a variety is not registrable it its denominated name or emblem is prohibited from use.[20] Dishonest denomination of a geographical name also leaves a variety unregistrable.

Varieties Registable

A variety, which is not prohibited and which confirms to the requirements under the Act, is registrable. A variety is registable if it is novel, distinct, uniform and stable. Considering the knowledge in the public domain novelty of a variety is determined. If the knowledge in the public domain does not possess the variety than the variety is said to be novel. A variety is distinct if its characteristic features are distinguishable from the existing varieties. A variety is uniform if it transfers its common characteristics to its next generation after propagation. A variety is stable if its essential characteristics are equally expressed in its next generation.

Process of Registration

Every application for registration shall be with respect to a variety that is registrable. Application shall be made in a prescribed form along with prescribed fee as specified in the Act and the regulations made there under. The application shall provide complete information about the variety. The application shall give information with regard to the varieties parental lines, its geographical location and acknowledgement of contribution of farmers or community group or tribal or rural families if any in evolving the variety.[21] The application shall contain a declaration that the genetic material or parental material used for evolving, developing and breeding of the variety has been lawfully acquired. There shall also be an affidavit sworn by the applicant that such variety does not contain any gene or gene sequence involving terminator technology.[22] However for a registration of a farmer's variety the above requirements does not apply.[23] The application shall be accompanied by a deposit of seeds of a variety to conduct tests with regard to its evolution and also to test its conformity with the standards underlined under the Act.[24]

An application made in the above manner and which is in conformity with the provisions of the Act and rules made there under shall be accepted and processed for further needful action. Registrar shall reject the application, which does not comply with the requirements. However the applicant shall be given an opportunity to present his case before proceeding to reject the application.[25] If the application is accepted it shall be advertised[26] to invite oppositions if any. Any interested person can file his opposition within three months from the date of the advertisement. Opposition may be on the following grounds, that;

1. The person opposing the application is entitled to the breeders right as against the applicant; or
2. The variety is not registrable under the Act; or
3. The grant of certificate of registration may not be in the public interest; or
4. The variety may have adverse effect on the environment.

On filing of opposition the registrar shall serve a copy of the notice of opposition on the applicant who shall within two months from the date of the receipt of such copy send a counter statement to the registrar, otherwise it shall be deemed that the applicant has abandoned his application.[27] Counter statement by the applicant shall be served on the opponent. Further the registrar shall give an opportunity of being heard to both the parties before making any decision. While presenting their case parties may submit evidence in support of their claim. The registrar may decide the case on the facts after considering the grounds of opposition and evidence submitted by the parties.

Certificate of Registration

If the application is in conformity with the requirements under the Act and if no opposition is made or if opposition is made but the same is rejected, the registrar shall register the variety claimed in the application. On registration, the applicant shall be issued a certificate with the seal of the registry. A copy of the certificate shall be sent to the authority for the purpose of determination of benefit sharing if any. The certificate shall be valid for nine years in the case of trees and vines and six years in the case of other crops. The certificate may be reviewed and renewed on payment of prescribed fee. However the maximum period of protection after renewal shall not exceed eighteen years in the case of trees and vines in other cases fifteen years.[28] From time to time the authority publishes the names and details of registered varieties and such other information relating to registered varieties.[29]

Benefit Sharing and Community Rights

Once certificate is issued it shall be published by the authority. The purpose behind publishing a certificate is to invite claims of benefit sharing if any with respect to the respective registered plant variety. Any citizen of India or group of citizen of India or a firm governmental or non-governmental organization formed and established in India may submit a claim of benefit sharing. If such a claim is made a copy the same shall be served on the breeder of the respective plant variety to invite his oppositions to benefit sharing.[30] The authority shall give an opportunity of being heard to both the parties before making any decision. The authority after considering factors such as; the commercial utility of the variety, demand of the variety, the extant and nature of the use of genetic material of the person claiming benefit sharing in the development of the variety shall determine the amount of benefit sharing. The breeder of such variety shall deposit[31] the determined amount of benefit sharing to a variety in the National Gene Fund constituted under the Act. The respective breeder is also required to deposit a quantity of seeds or propagating material of his registered variety.[32]Further, the annual fee payable to the authority by way of royalty, compensation payable to "any local community, any national and international organization and other sources for their contribution in the evolution of the registered variety", by the breeder shall also be deposited with the National Gene Fund.

Any village or local community in India may file any claim attributable to the contribution of the people of that village or local community in the evolution of any variety registered under the Act. If the authority is satisfied that such village or local community has significantly contributed in the evolution of a plant variety registered it may grant such sum of compensation to be paid to such village or local community.[33]

Rights Conferred to a Breeder on Registration

On registration of a variety the breeder or his successor shall be conferred with rights to produce, sell, market, distribute, import or export the variety. Breeder can assign or license his rights to any interested person provided the same is registered with the registrar. The terms and conditions of assignment or license shall also be registered with the registrar On the same lines breeder may authorize an agent to deal with his registered variety subject to conditions if any, provided the same is registered with the registrar.[34]

The rights conferred on the breeder on registration are subject to revocation by the authority on some specific grounds. [35]The authority shall revoke the registration only after giving the breeder of the respective variety an opportunity of being heard. The breeder himself may surrender his certificate of registration[36]at any time by giving notice to the registrar. In such situation registrar may accept the surrender of the certificate after giving an opportunity of being heard to the interested parties, including any person/persons who oppose surrender.

Enforcement of Rights Conferred on Registration

On registration certain rights are guaranteed to the breeder of the variety. Such rights shall be enjoyable only by the breeder or his successor or an authorized agent or an assignee or a licensee of the registered variety. If any other person exploits the registered variety without the authorization or consent of the breeder it amounts to violation of the rights of the breeder of the registered variety. Infact applying of the denomination of a registered variety[37] on any other variety does constitute infringement of a registered variety. In such cases the breeder can sue[38] the infringer against such unauthorized exploitation[39] of his variety. Relief may be given in infringement suit by way of injunction against the infringer to stop using of denomination of the registered variety on other varieties or attachment of his property to recover damages suffered by the breeder. Further offering varieties for sale that are falsely denominated does constitute an offence under the Act. There lies penalty for false application of denomination[40] and selling varieties to which false denomination is applied.[41]

Meanwhile persons who are aggrieved of their rights under the Act may prefer an appeal to the Appellate Tribunal. It is a tribunal constituted for the purpose of adjudication of grievances concerning the protection of plant varieties. Any person who is aggrieved by the order of the authority or decision of the registrar with regard to the registration of a variety may prefer an appeal to the Appellate Tribunal.[42] Further appeal may also lie to the tribunal from any aggrieved party with regard to the registration or benefit sharing or payment of compensation or grant of compulsory license of a variety.[43]The tribunal shall give parties an opportunity of being heard before passing such order that it deems fit.[44]

Compulsory Licensing of a Registered Plant Variety

The breeder of a registered plant variety shall exploit the variety. He shall see that the variety is available in the market for sale at affordable prices. Seeds and propagating material of the registered variety shall also be made available to the public at reasonable prices. If the breeder of a registered variety does not endeavor for the above any interested person may make an application to the authority under the Act for the grant of compulsory license to work on the registered variety. If reasonable requirements of the public[45] for seeds and other propagating material have not been satisfied it does constitute a valid ground to apply for compulsory license.[46]

However application for compulsory license shall not be made until the expiry of a period of three years from the date of issue of the certificate of registration of a variety. Compulsory license shall be issued to undertake production, distribution and sale of the seeds or other propagating material of such registered variety. The authority shall issue an appropriate order only after hearing both the parties i.e., the applicant for compulsory license and the breeder of a registered variety to work on which application for compulsory license is made. The authority may grant compulsory license if the application is made on valid grounds. The grant of compulsory license shall be in the public interest. The authority may subject the compulsory license to any conditions that it deems necessary.[47] The duration of a compulsory license is not fixed and it depends on each and every case. However the duration shall not exceed the total remaining period of the protection of the respective variety.

The objective behind offering protection to novel plant varieties is to encourage the breeder or such authorized persons to work on it. When a variety is exploited it could be made available to the public to satisfy their requirements. When a registered variety to which protection is guaranteed is not exploited in such a way to satisfy the needs of general public than there may be granted a compulsory license to exploit it. In one or the other way exploitation of the registered variety most be stimulated. The ultimate objective behind the screens is the benefit of the society. The protection of plant varieties system tries to exploit a novel variety in such possible ways by guaranteeing its protection. At the same time when protection is offered and guaranteed to novel varieties, it stimulates further research and investment in the field. This may lead to further innovations in the field, ultimately benefiting the society.

Conclusion

Protection offered to plant varieties is a leap forward in recognizing the efforts of farmers and breeders in the agriculture field. The rights are guaranteed to the actual farmer who endeavored for the evolution of a variety. It is only a farmer or farmer groups or governmental or non-governmental organizations or village communities or tribal communities or a university or a publicly funded institution that can seek protection for plant varieties. Multinational companies, which are grabbing the inventions through the grant of patent monopoly, cannot claim for plant variety protection. This arrangement is made deliberately in order to keep plant varieties, the endeavors of farmers and village communities out of the reach of multinational companies. At the same time any person or group contributed to the conservation of plant genetic resources, which are used in evolving a variety are recognized and rewarded through this system. Further the village or tribal communities endeavors are rewarded while offering protection to plant varieties. The Protection of plant varieties and Farmers Rights Act is a significant advancement in recognizing the efforts of farmers or farmers groups or the endeavors of tribal or village communities.

In contrast to the patent system the plant variety protection mechanism tries to identify, recognize and reward the people who are actually involved in the evolution of a particular plant variety. The system of benefit sharing and community rights guaranteed under the system is worth appreciating. Compared to patent system, which offers protection for a period of twenty years, the plant variety protection system offers protection only for six years. (Nine years in the case of trees and vines) Hence the variety falls into the public domain quickly and general public may use it. The period of monopoly is very less and even during the period also there is a possibility of compulsory licensing of the registered variety in the public interest. The interests of the public or the society could be best served under the plant variety protection system. The system of protection of plant varieties is really a manifestation of the desires of farmers who deserve their efforts to be recognized. The system is quite adequately equipped to secure the farmer community of their rights. The efficiency of the system depends on its proper implementation. Hence proper implementation and enforcement of the system shall be guaranteed in order to best serve its purposes. Than only the objective behind the system flourishes towards the prosperity of the farmers community.

NOTES

1. See: Sec: 2 ® of the Protection of plant varieties and farmers rights Act 2001.
2. See: Sec: 21(Za) for definition of the term 'variety'.
3. See: Sec: 2(j) of the Act. Sec: 5 of The Seeds Act 1966 also speak about an extant variety.
4. See: Sec: 2(l) of the Act, 'Farmers Variety'.
5. See; Sec: 2(i) 'Essentially derived variety'.
6. See: Sec: 2© 'breeder'.
7. See: Sec: 2(k) 'farmer'.
8. See; Sec: 15: Registrable varieties.
9. See: Sec: 3: Establishment of Authority.
10. The Authority possess all the characteristics of a body corporate such as perpetual succession, common seal, power to acquire and dispose property, capacity to sue and be sued etc, See: Sec: 3 of the Act
11. See: Sec: 8 general functions of authority.
12. Authority is vested with powers of civil court such as power to receive evidence, administering oaths, enforcing the attendance of witness, compelling the discovery and production of documents and issuing commissions for the examination of witness.

13. See: Sec: 12 Registry and offices thereof.
14. See: Sec: 13 National Register of Plant Varieties.
15. See: Sec: 16 Persons who may make application.
16. See: Sec: 29 Exclusion of certain varieties.
17. See: Sec: 29 Exclusion of certain varieties.
18. See: Ibid.
19. See: Sec: 15 Registrable varieties.
20. See: Sec: 3 of The Emblem and Names (Protection from improper use) Act, 1950.
21. See: Sec: 40 Certain information to be given in application for registration.
22. Variety which involves terminator technology is excluded from registration, See: Sec: 29 Exclusion of certain varieties.
23. See: Sec: 18 Form of application, See also sec: 39 Farmers right.
24. See: Sec: 19 Tests to be conducted.
25. See: Sec: 20 Acceptance of application or amendment thereof.
26. See: Sec: 21 Advertisement of application.
27. See: Ibid.
28. See: See: 24 Issue of certificate of registration.
29. See: Sec: 25 Publication of list of varieties.
30. See; Sec: 26 Determination of benefit sharing by authority.
31. Ibid.
32. See; Sec: 27 Breeder to deposit seeds or propagating material.
33. See; Sec: 41 Rights of communities.
34. See; Sec: 28 Registration to confer right.
35. See: Sec; 34 Revocation of protection on certain grounds.
36. See: Sec: 33 Surrender of certificate of registration.
37. See: Sec: 68 Prohibition to apply the denomination of a registered variety.
38. See: Sec: 64 Infringement.
39. Ibid.
40. See: Sec; 69 Meaning of falsely applying the denomination of a registered variety.
41. See: Sec; 70 Penalty for applying false denomination, See also sec: 71 Penalty for selling varieties to which false denomination is applied.

42. See; Sec: 54 of the Act empowering the central Government to establish a tribunal called Plant Varieties Protection Appellate Tribunal.
43. See: Sec: 56 Appeals to the tribunal.
44. See; Sec; Orders of the tribunal.
45. See: Sec: 48 when requirements of public deemed to have not satisfied.
46. See: Sec: 47 Power of authority to make order for compulsory license in certain circumstances.
47. See; Sec; 51 Authority to settle terms and conditions of license.

INTELLECTUAL PROPERTY RIGHTS AND INDIA–ISSUES AND IMPERATIVES

*V. Basil Hans**

Introduction

The importance of intellectual property is well established at all levels–statutory, administrative and judicial–in India.[1] The agreement on trade related aspects of Intellectual Property Rights (hereinafter, IPRs) came into force on January 1, 1995, the same day as the starting of WTO. The purpose of this Agreement was to lay down certain minimum standards for protecting and enforcing the IPRs in WTO-member countries with a view to reducing distortions and impediments to international trade. The member countries may provide for higher standards of protection as deemed fit by them, but the Agreement on Trade Related Aspects of Intellectual Rights lays down the minimum standards to be adopted by the member countries for the protection of IPRs.

IPRs which include patents designs, confidential information and know-how plays a crucial role in the development of industry, commerce and trade. In the saga of scientific development the birth of IPRs is the result of human endeavour to protect and sustain his creative effort in the sphere of industry, business, technology and culture. In short it is a step at protecting knowledge itself. Changing scale and dimensions of knowledge business-such as that denoted by the concept of Information Technology–have made IPRs essential and important. In fact the phenomenal growth of commerce, industry and trade is largely due the knowledge component –

* Head, Arts Department St Aloysius Evening College, Mangalore-575 003, D.K. District, Karnataka, India.

the K-factor (ala Ektha 'K'apoor?) Knowledge is universal but its use is unique. Today its possession also has become unique and has acquired all the features of commercial property, mainly due to the rights over it, viz., IPRs. With the birth of WTO and the creation of Trade Related Intellectual Property Rights (TRIPs), IPRs have become all the more important. Hence we need to know more about IPRS.

India being a developing country had a transition period of five years (i.e., till January 1, 2000) to apply for the provisions of the Agreement plus five years for extending product patenting to areas of technology, hitherto unprotected, such as pharmaceuticals. India already had its Patent Act 1970. Need for its revision was felt. A bill to amend the same was placed in the Parliament on December 20, 1999. It was notified on June 15, 2002 to make the TRIPs compatible. With this began India's efforts at modernization of IPR administration (inclusive of patents, trademarks, designs and geographical indications). Today the IPRs cover broad range of areas, ranging from the internet to health care to nearly all aspects of science and technology and literature arts etc. Many areas are still emerging and converging. Therefore, understanding the concept and role of intellectual property in these areas often requires significant new research and study. Education and awareness in this dynamic field will promote intellectual and informed discussion. Industrialists, inventors, innovators, legal experts, and all touched upon by IPRs need to have a thorough-going knowledge of IPRs, and its implications for India.

Importance of IPRs for India

Today it is not enough for India to possess land, labour, capital and technology, in order to succeed in the competitive, knowledge-based and innovation driven global economy. It needs to adopt and adapt creativity, innovation and promotion– in the domain of intellectual capital–as the main drivers of techno-economic change. In this regard, the policies that it initiates and implements time to time will determine the well-being of its people too. A systematic approach to building the country's intellectual property system, vis-à-vis rest of the world, is essential. From a holistic perspective, an effective IPR system will serve as a dynamic tool for wealth creation through domestic enterprises, foreign trade and investment and sustainable resource management. India, therefore, has to take appropriate measures on two counts: *one* to do on its own what best it can to strengthen its IPR system; and *two*, how effectively it can play its role in the multilateral system of exchange and property rights management, globally. One has to be cautious while selecting a good brand name, which is to the extent possible free from potential litigation in future. Good brand names must not only be easy to remember, but easy to see, pronounce, spell and read, and most importantly they must be distinctive. Legal apparatus will have to be strengthened to avoid disputes with employees. It is essential to get skilled advice before entering into any agreement with the employees. Here, documentation and maintenance of secrecy is considered as prime issues.

Another way by which Indian Companies can benefit monetarily to a large extent is by IP licensing.[2]

Areas of Concern

In India we need to cover the following areas in a meaningful discussion of IPRs.

- Conceptualization: not just product patenting, but trade secrets, plant varieties, geographical indicators, performance rights and so on.
- Need–is it for opportunities (e.g. revenue, innovation)? or threats (e.g. loss of oral knowledge, exploitation by outsiders) or both?
- How would IPRs protect from piracy of ideas?
- What are the existing mechanisms of protection? How do they function? How strong are they?
- What are the efforts at rights management? What are the steps taken to educate about rights management (both owners and adopters)?
- What are the provisions–civil and criminal - regarding infringements of Rights?

- Are legal proceedings themselves a threat?
- Emerging issues of IPRs: Open Source vs. Restricted Access, the role of internet and digitization, art and IPRs, the economics of IPRs: affordability, marketability and factors.
- Laws and negotiations: WIPO Internet Treaties since 1996. In this respect the practical issues are the following.

1. Knowledge (knowledge as infrastructure) vs. Entertainment.
2. Manufacturing vs. Marketing (today marketing has changed from seeing to sensing).
3. Infrastructure Development.
4. IPRs as private rights–what is privatized are they publicly available?
5. Low levels of domestic IP creation.
6. Co-operation between producers/possessors and users (Social Reciprocity).
7. International Standard- rules under WTO–the way they affect countries especially LDCs-they may lose on account of inconsistency and poor coordination.
8. Bulk access in education (e.g. e-books controversy).
9. Coordinating the changes in factors (e.g. technological changes) with IPR changes.
10. A synthesis of aspects: economic, social, legal and cultural included.

Implications of IPRs for India

Since India is a signatory to TRIPs, the laws governing the IPRs apply to it and this has an enormous impact on Indian business and trade partnerships. Accordingly, India has complied its obligations by amending the Indian Patents Act 1970 more than three times. In the last few years, India has enacted fully TRIPs compliant Trademarks Act, Copyright Act, Designs Registration Act etc. However, though most acts have been TRIPs compliant, in the Patents Acts there are areas where substantive or procedural amendments could be considered for complying with the TRIPs. So changes maybe required, specially keeping in view the Indian companies, by giving protection under the Patents Acts to business methods qualifying as technology, which at present is not patentable. For example, business methods/models or computer programmes comprising only of mathematical or scientific principles are not presently patentable. However, in certain sectors the need is being felt for getting a patent protection for certain software in addition to copyright. India, a computer (industry) giant must, therefore, do its home work properly before further demands and amendments are made.

Similarly it is interesting to see how Indian companies can avoid falling into trap over misuse of trademarks and patents i.e., protection of IPR. The strategy of licensing IP is perhaps the best way for all Indian companies to walk the middle road between services and products, specially software. Intellectual property protection is the key factor for economic growth and advancement in the high technology sector. The developed world has come to an accommodation with them over a long period. Even if their disadvantages sometimes outweigh their advantages, by and large the developed world has the national economic strength and established legal mechanisms to overcome the problems so caused. Insofar as their benefits outweigh their disadvantages, the developed world has the wealth and infrastructure to take advantage of the opportunities provided. It is likely that neither of these holds true for developing countries like India.

Globalization and the rapid proliferation of technology have elevated the importance of intellectual property protection for small and medium sized enterprises (SMEs).This is another area of concern for India The intangible nature of intellectual property and the worldwide inconsistency of standard practices create challenges for those businesses wishing to protect their inventions, brands, and business methods in foreign markets.

The three most common vehicles for protecting intellectual property are patents, trademarks, and copyrights. The Biotechnology Industry Organization advocates a strong and effective intellectual property system. Strong intellectual property protection is essential to the success and in some instances to the survival, of the biotechnology companies in this country. The implications of IPRs on India's health sector should be viewed in the same context.

Thus, the crux of the intellectual property rights is to give credit where, and when, it is due. With the emergence of the knowledge society and virtual products, the issue of safeguarding the investment in the information-based products has certainly gained high importance. We, as consumers or producers in the information chain, cannot afford to be ignorant about the intellectual property rights. India being one among the developing countries-has miles to go, as she has a vulnerable collection of traditional, oral, folklore, customary, agricultural, traditional medicinal like Ayurveda etc. But at the same time, not having much wealth and infrastructure, lack of awareness of IPRs among all strata of people is a major set back to India.

Under the terms of the WTO, India was required to implement WTO-standard IPR protection laws by 2005. It must be acknowledged that there has been remarkable progress in IPR protection in some fields such as software and cinema products. India's general argument was that it does acknowledge in principle the case for strict IPR protection, but this can be done only in phases suited by its own ground reality.[3]

Trademark protection is another area full of vital issues. Enforcement of trademark owner rights had been weak in the past, and is so even now. This has 'special' adverse effects on international pharmaceutical trade. India's patent act prohibits product patents for any invention intended for use or capable of being used as a food, medicine, or drug or relating to substances prepared or produced by chemical processes. Consequently, many drugs invented by foreign companies are widely reproduced. Processes for making drugs are patentable, but the patent term is limited to the shorter of five years from the grant of patent or seven years from the filing date of the patent application. As a signatory to the Uruguay Round of GATT, including its provisions TRIPs, India has had to introduce a comprehensive system of product patents no later than 2005.

The Indian government formed an advisory committee to recommend changes in the 1970 Indian Patents Act. In July 1996, the U.S. initiated WTO dispute settlement procedures over India's failure to implement its TRIPs obligations. The final panel report on this case was issued in August 1997, and ruled that India had failed to meet its obligations under the TRIPs agreement. India pledged to introduce another bill in parliament which will put India in compliance with its TRIPs obligations. In 1999 came India's new Patent Act that provides for the granting of Exclusive Marketing Rights (EMRs) in lieu of the government securing the company's patent legislation. The EMR is almost like a product patent.

The bottom-line is that India considers itself a responsible member of the WTO which suggests that international class IPR protection should be in place by 2005. It is to be noted that Bill Gates, the chief executive officer of Microsoft Corporation, has distinguished India as a most promising base for software development. If such an IPR-conscious business leader like Gates is of this opinion, one can only conclude that India's IPR scene is no deterrent to foreign companies. One should view this in the light of the fact that IP as a business asset is growing in significance for India.

IP as a Business Asset for India

It is worth noting that intellectual capital has become critical to the industry and its growth in India as elsewhere in the globalization era. Successful MNCs undisputedly give tremendous value to their intellectual property In the Information Technology Sector, IBM and Verizon are estimated to have intangible capital of USD 134 Billion and USD 105 Billion respectively. This demonstrates the immense value and critical nature of intangible assets for effective participation in the evolving 'knowledge economy'. Many Indian companies have placed importance on the protection of IPRs and taken initiatives to promote awareness and protection within the companies with IP as a policy. It is widely believed, that stronger IPRs in India will encourage greater product development industries such as in the software industry.[4]

There has been significant increase in the appreciation of intellectual property and the awareness level has also increased tremendously. This is evident from the increase in the number of patent applications filed in the Indian Patent office. According to the recent WIPO Report on PCT filing, India ranks among the top Asian countries in terms of PCT filing. The trademark filings have also increased from 38,109 in 1995-96 to 60,985 in 1999-2000. To keep up with the international pace, however, we need to steadily build up our IP investment and in view of the advancement in technology and innovation re-look at our existing legislations and consider the new emerging issues.

Emerging Issues

Some of the emerging issues in the filed of IPRs for India are:

- Internet piracy and circumvention of technological measures[5]
- Protecting the innovations of indigenous and local farming communities
- Protecting geographical indications, handicrafts etc
- Establishing a mechanism for disclosure of the source of information as in the case of biological material used in an invention - this is an implementation issue.

Thus, in India while the substantive provisions of copyright law viewed in isolation are laudable, there emerge drawbacks in practice, implementation and enforcement of the Copyright Act. Therefore, the importance of IPRs for the protection and promotion of industrial innovations, products and for the growth and development of the industry as a whole cannot be understated. Creating awareness of importance of creative thinking and innovation among people and getting about a mind shift in the way people think about creativity and intellectual property is therefore, crucial. A modified education and curriculum is therefore called for. It is heartening to see that already some B-Schools have done it. Similarly India requires industry entrepreneurship coupled with an enabling legal and policy framework. This will go a long way in developing the much needed global competitiveness for India. India should be ready to proactively seize the opportunities that creation of intellectual property affords and gain again and again as it moves up the value chain. Notwithstanding the economic gain it should also strive for achieving a true and sustainable increase in social and cultural well-being.

Conclusion

The imperatives of IPRs in India clearly show that there is nothing but an implementation crisis today. This is not insurmountable. First of all what is required is that there be a synthesis of various policies geared to increasing each country's national capacity, enhancing its knowledge resources and helping it to use intellectual property as a tool to enable these resources to be transformed into value. Today it can be affirmatively stated that IPR plays a great role in furthering the growth of Indian manufacturing sector industry and thereby increasing investment that will further benefit the nation at large. Secondly, an awakening of the corporate players in the market may well be in order - an awakening to the importance of intellectual property and its role in the future of any corporate entity. Thirdly, India must do everything that she can for modernization of patent offices incorporating (i) HRD; (ii) Infrastructure Support; (iii) Computerization and Modernization; and (iv) Elimination of backlog of Patent Applications.

Finally, India, along with the like-minded developing countries, should continue to press for redressal of her concerns of "implementation of TRIPs Agreement".

To conclude India needs to....

- demystify IPRs in the interests of innovators and adopters,
- adopt holistic approach taking cognizance of all players (civil society, parliaments, citizens, educationists, scientists and researchers, entrepreneurs etc), and all factors;
- make economic and social analysis of impacts;
- allow greater openness but with transparency too;

- create favourable economic/geographical domain: e.g. Free Trade Areas (FTAs).

All these measures will help India became a strong IPR country and stand firm with confidence in the field of competition and run the race of economic development with ease and pace required. Its reforms will then have a potential meaning and practical message to all.

NOTES

1. The concept of 'property' has evolved and changed-from elements to land and tools of farming and to non-physical objects, all with the growth of civilization and economies. The latest addition to the concept of property is that of 'intellectual property'.
2. Licensing is the sharing or the renting of IP through a legally binding contract that specifies certain conditions with another company in exchange for the payment of royalties or may involve a sharing of IP by cross licensing in which both parties have IP and exchange it without financial exchange between the parties.
3. The reality is that absence of international IPR protection for some decades has spawned employment for millions, so an overnight clampdown on IPR violators would-unnecessarily-drum up social unrest.
4. At present the Indian software industry employs over 500,000 software engineers, and software services in India have gained a worldwide reputation. Strong levels of protection for intellectual properties have encouraged foreign investment in India, with many companies choosing to either set up their own facilities in India or to outsource a large part of their business to India.
5. For India it is estimated by the IDC-BSA study that a 10% reduction in India's piracy rate will create 50,000 new high tech jobs and will add an additional USD 92 million in tax revenues. In addition, such reduction would ensure that the projected rate of growth of the IT industry moves from 148% to 163% by 2006.

REFERENCES

Ahmed Tabrez (2006), "R & D and Intellectual Property Rights in Information and Communication Technology in India", available at http://www.ficci.com/ficci/general/it-spam/back.pdf, accessed on March 28.

Gandhi, P. Jegadish (ed.) (2003), *Globalised Indian Economy–Contemporary Issues and Perspectives,* Deep & Deep Publications (P.) Ltd., New Delhi.

Hans, V.B. (2002), *Money, Banking and Public Finance,* Mangala Publications, Mangalore.

Link Exchange (2006), "Intellectual property rights in India", available at http://leader.linkexcgange.com/33/X1089042/clickle, accessed on March 18.

Mathur Vibha (2002), *Indian Economy and the WTO–New Challenges and Strategies"* New Century Publications, Delhi.

Ramanna, Anitha (2002), "Policy Implications of India's Patent Reforms: Patent Applications in the post–1995 Era, Economic & Political Weekly, May 25, pp. 2065.

Dadibhavi, R.V. and S.T. Bagalkoti (ed.) (2003), *World Trade Organisation-Implications for India,* Department of Economics, Karnataka University, Dharwad.

Vaidya Vandana (2006), "Intellectual Property Rights-A Boon To Indian Companies", Available at Legal Service India.com, accessed on March 18.

WTO AND TEXTILE EXPORTS: EMERGING ISSUES

Bipasha Choudhary[*]
and Swati Jain[**]

Throughout modern history, trade has been regarded either as an international public good from which everyone benefits or a battleground in which there are winners and losers. The earlier period of 20th Century was marked with distrust and conflict between various nations of Europe, Latin America, Asia and Africa. The resultant effect was a decline in the levels of International trade. Following World War II, the world again experienced an era of trade and liberalisation and expansion, largely as a consequence of successive rounds of trade negotiations carried out under the auspices of GATT. International trade grew even more rapidly than did national economies. Consequently International trade integrated national economies more closely with one another.[1] GATT, a Bretton Woods Institution was based on the principle of Most Favored Nation, which meant:

(a) Non-discrimination between countries for the source of the good.

(b) National treatment for the goods after they have entered in the geographical territory of a country.

GATT was acceptable to all member countries, as it did not affect the country's domestic policies at all. Moreover countries also used certain non-tariff barriers to protect the sensitive areas such as agriculture and textiles, even though

* Research Scholar, Department of Economics, University of Allahabad, Allahabad- 211002.

** Junior Research Fellow, Department of Economics, University of Allahabad, Allahabad- 211002. Email: chitralekha_jain@rediffmail.com they were against the principle of MFA. It must be remembered that agriculture and textile sector have great importance for all countries whether developed or developing countries, as:

(a) They contribute for more than 50 per cent to the national income.

(b) These sectors provide employment to a large population especially so in developing countries.

Thus, Agriculture and textiles were the two most protected areas of every country with regards to international trade even after 50 years of GATT. Even after the formal ratification of GATT agreement during the fifth decade of 20th Century, US was seriously concerned about textile and agriculture imports from the developing countries especially from Japan and other Asian countries. Around 1940s and 1950s Japan became a major producer and exporter of textiles. It started capturing U.S market so much so that in 1936 US and Japan entered into "Gentlemen's Agreement"[2] restricting Japan's textile exports to USA. Japan applied for the membership of GATT in 1955 and almost every textile importing country was worried and wanted to create safeguards through escape clause or "Gentleman's Agreement" as was done by U.S. VER agreement of U.S. was of great significance as textile exports to U.S. fell to 28% in 1960 from 63% in 1958. US were still not satisfied and were negotiating textile trade in GAIT through what may be called the concept of "Trade disruption"[3].

In November 1960 under the supervision of GATT the concept of market disruption was formally accepted and techniques of its avoidance were discussed on US pressure and an agreement was reached, which was known as Short term Arrangement (STA). STA was campaigned to avoid market disruption, which authorized US government to implement one-year restrictions for 64 categories of cotton textiles. In February 1962, 19 major textile importers entered into a long-term arrangement. With exporters on bilateral basis regarding import of cotton textiles. These arrangements were renewed in 1967 and continued till 1973. In this way short term arrangement turned into long-term arrangement and then to MFA (Multi-fiber Agreement) in 1973.

MFA (I) - The arrangement regarding international trade in textiles known as Multifibre Arrangement, which came into force on January 1, 1974, MFA provided legitimacy for extension of textile control on bilateral basis. In these arrangements every importing country fixed a quantitative ceiling for each importing country which' was negotiated bilaterally. At the same time to avoid the problems of exporting countries6 per cent annual growth of quotas was assured to them.(through U.S. agreed to increase only 5%).Various provisions like "Swing-provisions', "Carryover", "Carryforward" etc were also used to make quotas more flexible and friendly to promote textile exporters.

MFA (II)-MFA was renewed in 1977. In fact more tight protection regime was forced through MFA (II) by US as well as EU. Although USA was the main proponent of MFA I but Europe took a tougher stance and opted for greater protection in textile through MFA (II) because of excessive domestic pressure. EC become more aggressive in restriction than US. The "reasonable departure" clause of them MFA (I) agreement helped in this regard. The EC bilateral agreement of 1977 divided Textile five groups and144 categories. The "Basket extractor", (II) mechanism gave more freedom to EC. The US bilateral agreement under MFA II also extended in the coverage of textile agreement from cotton to man made fibres.

MFA (III)-Negotiations in 1981 for the second renewal of MFA began. MFA became more comprehensive in coverage and scope. By the early eighties there were 43 signatories to MFA, representing 54 countries. The United States had bilateral agreements with 34 countries under MFA and around 80% of US textiles and appeared imports from Developing Countries are under these agreement. Eight major countries US, Canada, Japan, EC, Austria, Finland, Sweden, Switzerland were members of the agreement. The principle objective of EC in the MFA included outright cutbacks in quota of dominant suppliers (Primarily Hong-Kong, Taiwan and Korea) and of quota growth- for other countries to well below 6% annually on grounds that domestic demand was stagnant or growing much more slowly. MFA was a more comprehensive agreement Two countries Japan and Switzerland despite their membership did not maintain their quotas under bilateral agreement. China accepted membership of MFA in 1984.

MFA (IV)-On July 31, 1986 the day MFA III expired, the members agreed to extend the agreement for another five years. 54 countries agreed to renewal of the MFA. MFA (IV) included all textiles made of vegetable fibres, blends of vegetable fibres and blends containing silk, and thus, it covered all kinds of textiles under restrictive trading. In sum the renewal was in the direction of tightening of the agreement. The representatives of the Developing Countries criticized the renewal. China and India in particular opposed its expansion of coverage and charged that this renewal was against the spirit of GATT agreement and should be abandoned.

Despite the objections of various countries MFA arrangement continued till the formation of WTO, which was a result of various rounds of multilateral trade negotiations. In the last round of GATT (Uruguay round) Developed Countries pressurized the developing countries to negotiate entire new aspects such as TRIPS GATS and TRIMS. Developing countries were not in favour of including these sectors and asked developed countries that if they wish to include such items then MFA and Agriculture protectionism is also be negotiated After long negotiations Developed and Developing Countries came to an understanding that paved the way for the establishment of W.T.O. on January 1, 1995.

Major steps were taken towards further trade liberalisation with successful competition of Uruguay round of negotiations (1993) created the World Trade Organisation. WT.O is an agreement of agreements. There are sixteen agreements, which can be classified under three sub groups-Annex 1A, 1B, and 1C. 1A is related to commodities and known as GATT (1994). It includes Agreement on Agriculture (AOA), Textiles, Subsidies, automobiles, Sanitary and Phytosanitary measure etc. 1B is related to trade of services. Annex 1C is related to intellectual property, which includes-Patent, Copyright, Geographical indication, Trademark, Industrial design etc.

At the opening of 21st century, the free trade regime is threatened by intellectual, economic and political development. The shift from comparative advantage to competitive advantage as the basis of trade, the implications of the new strategic trade theory, & other developments has undermined the theoretical or intellectual arguments for trade liberalisation. It has been analyzed that trade liberalization will stimulate production of labour intensive sectors particularly in India and like countries. (Kapila 2002). Productive resources would then get allocated more efficiently as compared to the liberalization situation these countries would specialize in the sectors where it has comparative advantage. There may of course be transitional costs due to inter-sectoral movement of factors of production. Beyond such welfare gains, trade liberalization is also expected to have a "pro-competitive" effect on domestic firms, resulting in additional gains from the realization of economies of large-scale production. When firms get protection from foreign competition through tariff and non-tariff barriers, they may take advantage of their market power by raising their prices and reducing their domestic sales. The result is that the protected firms may produce below their minimum cost-efficient plant size. Trade liberalization should then bring about competitive pressures on the formerly protected firms and induce them to raise production and productivity and also to achieve more efficient plant size and lower per unit costs. (Nayyar 1997). Thus, gains in economic welfare are expected to come from improved allocation of resources, lower prices to consumers and business firms, and availability of more varieties to consumers and firms. The realization of economies of scale in manufacturing also reinforces the welfare enhancing effect.

A highly competitive environment is rapidly emerging, driven by rising economic and social aspirations on the one hand and external conditions predominantly W.T.O related market prices on the other. Global integration of markets is also challenging the conventional concept of comparative advantage based on the narrow static interpretation of relative factor endowment s of nations. Comparative advantage is today the sum total of technology, entrepreneurial & managerial capabilities of the constituent firms of a country. It has been estimated that Developing Countries could realize over US$ 700 billion in the form of export earnings if industrialized countries end the protection of labour intensive products. (ICFAI, 2004). Potential export earnings of Developing Countries in textiles, clothing and other labour intensive products alone are estimated to exceed $ 500 billion if advanced industrial countries open up their markets.(UNCTAD 2002). Anderson and others (2000) estimated an annual gain of US $ 9 billion to Developing Countries from unrestricted access to the Developed Countries markets in textiles and clothing. It was also estimated that potential annual gains comes out to be lower than agriculture& food, other manufactures. Global trade in textiles and clothing is expected to increase from US $385 billion in 2003 to US $ 600 by 2010. India's share in he global textile trade is forecasted to grow the fastest of all countries, post M.F.A, as it's quota allocation in Developed Countries during the M.F.A was among the lowest. However, the growth of the Indian textile industry right from the 1970's has been adversely affected by the quota régime, lack of industry-friendly government policies and technological obsolesce. (CII, 2005). Vision 2010,a plan which was the result of interaction between the government and the industry, has envisaged growth in textile industry from US$ 36 billion in 2003-04 to US$ 85 billion by 2010 giving an annual growth target of 11-12%. Vision 2010 also proposes the creation of an additional 12 million jobs.

Agreement on Textile and Clothing under W.T.O.

The Agreement on Textile and clothing is an integral part of WTO agreement, thus applicable to all WTO members. The agreement on textile and clothing (ATC) was a ten-year transitional agreement with a programme to gradually reduce trade restrictions in textile and clothing products so that by 2004 all the protections are finally abolished. The main objective of the agreement is to integrate the regulation of international trade in textiles and clothing into general W.T.O. framework.

The main features of ATC are as follows:

1. The product coverage, which comprises an extensive list of yarns, fabrics, made-ups, textile products and clothing.
2. Four-stage integration process by increasing quota after every three years and finally integrating the textile trade by completely integrating the quotas by 2005.
3. A transitional safeguard mechanism to deal with cases of serious damage or actual threat of serious damage to domestic industries, which may arise during the transition period.
4. The Textile Monitoring Body (TMB)- the TMB is the primary forum within the W.T.O. structure entrusted with that task of supervising the implementation of ATC.
5. The liberalization process is end loading in the sense that the quotas would be increased by 16% in 1st three year, 17% in the next three years, 18% in the next phase and 49% in the final phase. A liberalized process which automatically increases the existing quota levels, inherited from the MFA to completely integrated system of textile trade without any discrimination.

Table 1 explains the phasing out schedule with the following underlying assumptions:

1. The schedule for freeing textile and garment products from import quota (and returning to GATT rules) and the scheme pertaining to it.
2. The example is based on the commonly used 6% annual expansion rate of the old Multifibre arrangement. In practice the rates used under the MFA varied from product to product and country-to-country.

Stage 1 of this agreement (from the date of entry into force of WTO Agreement to the 36th month that it is in effect inclusive) shows that the level of each restriction under MFA bilateral agreement is in force for the 12 month period and has been increased annually by not less than the growth rate established for restriction, increase by 16%. It means that the quotas are now growing by 6.96% in the place of 6%. During

Table 1
Phasing Out Schedule of MFA

Step *up*	*Percentage of product to be brought under GATT* *(including removal of any quotas)*	*How fast remaining quotas should open* *it 1994 rate was 6%*
Step 1 : 1stJan. 1995 (to 31 Dec. 1997).	16% (Minimum taking 1990 imports as base	6.96% per year
Step 2: 1st Jan. 1998 (to 31stDec 2001)	17%	8.7% per year
Step 3 : 1stJan. 2002 (To 31stDec. 2004	18%	11.05% per year
Step 4: 1stJan. 2005 to full integration into GATT (and final elimination of quotas) Agreement as textiles and clothing terminates	49%	No quotas left.

the second phase starting from 1st January 1998,the rate of growth of quotas was 25% of 6.69% (*Le.* at a rate of 8.7 per cent.) The third phase starting from 1stJanuary 2002 the growth rate of quotas was 27% of 8.7 per cent (*Le.* at a rate of 11.05 per cent).

The gradual phasing out of quotas is called as "end-loading" system. The phasing out of quotas had sufficient time (10 year transitional period), so that both Developed and Developing Countries can prepare themselves for the liberalized trade regime. The liberalized trade regime has increased the opportunities for Indian textile industry. According to a study by CRISIL (commissioned by ICMF) the Indian textile and apparel industry can achieve a potential size of US $ 85 billion by 2010 of which the domestic market potential would be US $ 45 billon. Nearly 60% of exports would comprise of garment exports. This would create 12 million job opportunities, 5 million jobs in textile industry and 7 million jobs in allied sectors. Top textile importing countries like USA and EU are looking at India for meeting their import requirements.

Impact of ATC on Indian Textile Exports

The textile sector occupies a position of prime national importance accounting for over one third of India's total merchandise export. This industry accounts for 4% of the GDP, about 14% of national industrial production and about 35% of total export earning. This is the largest net foreign exchange earner for the country. Textile trade over last two decades has contributed a substantial and rising share of India's total exports, bringing in about US $ 12 billion per annum and capturing 3.4% share of the world textile market. Indian textile exports have grown at an average of 11% per annum in this period. India ranked 8th in 2003-04 among the textile exporting countries of the world. Indian textiles known for it's captivating designs and colours are exported all over the world. This sector is highly diverse and covers the entire supply chain from fibre production through spinning, weaving, knitting, dyeing and finishing to production of finished goods such as apparel and home textile. The industry comprises of three sectors:

1. HandloomSector
2. Power loom Sector
3. Mill Sector

Handloom Sector plays the most important role in the economy. It provides direct employments to 65 lakh persons engaged in weaving and allied activities. The Handloom industry employing over four million looms is engaged in the production of natural fibre fabrics like cotton, silk, woolen and in man made fibre fabrics. The industry is an integral part of India's Socio-Economic; life. This sector is unique in its flexibility, versatility, experiments and encouraging innovations. The Powerloom sector is more recent vintage and has shown enormous growth since 1970's. Today this sector plays a very important role in meeting the clothing needs of the country and accounts for a share of around 59%of total fabric production The mill sector consists of spinning and composite units. In the year 2002 there were 1859 mills in India consisting of 1578 spinning mills and 281 composite mills. India's major textile exports on the basis of fibre can be broadly classified as follows:

1. Cotton (yarn, fabric, made-up)
2. Silk (yarn, fabric, made-up)
3. Wool (yarn, fabric, made-up)
4. Manmade (yarn, fabric, made-up)
5. Readymade garments (yarn, fabric, made-up)
6. Miscellaneous (i.e. Jute, Fur, Leather etc.)

India is one of the largest cotton producers (After USA and China), The Indian textile industry is predominantly cotton based with 70% of raw material consumed being cotton. After 1996-97 the growth of cotton sector has slowed down. Silk is another important area of textile products. The percentage of silk exports in total textile exports was 3% in the year 2000-01. Due to the steep decline in silk production in Japan and South Korea, China and India gained a greater share in the market and are now leading silk producers in the world. In the export basket of India wool is of less importance. The percentage of woolen textile exports in total textiles exports is around 2 per cent. The most important industry among textile products is man made fibre and yarn industry. Over 39% of raw material consumed in manufactured textiles is from the man- made fibre and yarn industry. Exports of man made fibre textiles has recorded constantly high rates of growth in nineties. Last but not the least comes readymade garment, which enjoys the status of being the largest net foreign exchange earner for the country. Five products dominate the Indian garment industry they are - Women's skirts, blouses, dresses, men's shirts and knitted garment. The miscellaneous group of textile consists of jute, coir, fur, and leather as potential textile exports. The main destination for Indian textile based items have been traditionally USA, UK, Germany, UAE, Italy, Hong-Kong, South Africa, Bangladesh, Japan, Belgium, France, Mauritius, Span, Canada and Australia. The trend in textile exports of India during 1996-97 to 2002-03 (See Table 4) reveals that the readymade garment of cotton and cotton yarn, fabric and made-ups dominate textile exports, whereas the percentage of silk exports in India's textile export basket is marginal. After the steep decline in the silk production of Japan and South Korea, India and China had a lot of opportunities to take advantage of the expanding markets of liberalized regime. Therefore India has to work out its strategies to increase the production of silk. The history of Indian silk exports is centuries old. In the decade of the fifties silk waste dominated in the silk exports of India. Indian silk exports can be divided in two parts:

- Mulberry
- Non-Mulberry

Traditionally there were a lot of varieties in the Indian silk like Tussar, Eri, Muga, etc. At present India needs to revive its tradition of silk products. The overseas markets for Indian silk is divided into two categories:

1. Traditional markets like South Asian countries, Middle-East and African countries
2. Non-traditional markets like West European countries, U.S.A. etc.

India is capable of increasing the production of silk, the producers can take advantage of available large export market, in the form of Indian diasporas who have a greater preference for traditional Indian silk markets like- dupion, matkasilk, noil varieties, embroidered Garments etc. Indian textile producers and exporters should take advantage of trend, fashion to substantially make their presence felt in India's textile exports. Indian textile producers and exporters should take advantage of the emphasize that India's must make all out effort to increase its share in world exports by concentrating on all kinds of textile.

After the phasing out of MFA Indian textile industry is supposed to get a great boost. It is expected that Indian textile exports could fetch around 50 b $ per annum by 2015. To realize this export objective a co-ordinated effort is required from government including state Government, export promotion councils and textile manufactures. In fact the phasing out does not only provides a great opportunity for Indian exporters but also greater challenge as India, (is no longer assured of fixed quotas allotted by USA and EU for last so many years. Although, it is too early to assess the impact of removal of quantitative restricts on textile exports, an indication towards the need of more concrete steps ahead is providedd by the Table 2 presented below which shows the trends of export in various items during the Post-MFA phase (April-Sep 2006).

Table 2

ITEMS	*EU 25*	*USA*	*Others*
RMG	6338 (32.37%)	4269 (9.58%)	3128 (-24.09%)
Cotton Textiles	1895 (-1.47%)	1398 (8.54%)	4156 (-6.66%)
Man-made Textiles	706 (-12.78%)	298 (-11.4%)	2707 (-19.83%)
Silk	532 (17.13%)	376 (-4.67%)	421 (-2.45%)
Wool & Woolen Textiles	336 (20.15%)	274 (-21.7%)	316 (-19.62%)
Jute	143 (-10.93%)	134 (8.52%)	343 (19.24%)
Coir& Coir Manufactures	102 (11.97%)	106 (20.13%)	47 (29.77%)

The trends presented in the above table exhibits the J–curve effect of post M.F.A regime on various items of textiles .In most of the items we have lost our traditional markets of CIS and other countries (excluding E.U and USA) in terms of man–made textiles, wool and woolen textiles and readymade garments.

Thus we can say, that Indian exporters have to compete in open market where a large number of manufacturing counties like China along with new entrants from Latin America are ready to fight for a share in $ 300 billion market of textiles. Indian textile industry has a great export potential provided it gear up to compete with the best in the world and the government also supports this industry whole heartedly. To make this industry price and quality competitive, certain aspects, which need to be focussed, are analyzed below. These areas can be classified as follows:

1. Supply side constraints.
2. Competitiveness.
3. Marketing and information management.
4. Arbitrary and discriminative restrictions by EU and other importing countries.

Supply side constraints—India is a labour abundant country, so it is generally taken for granted that it will result in lower cost of production against the popular belief that Indian labour costs are very low. *According to the study made by Werner International*-The hourly labour cost in case of India in textile manufacture was US $ 0.55 during 1991 and India ranked 45th in the descending order among a *vey* of 52 countries. It means that there are seven countries that have labour costs less than India. The low labour costs do not necessarily lead to lower cost of production because labour costs are only one component of total production. Cost of production also includes the price of raw material, cost of credit, cost of energy and transportation etc. In India most of these are very costly so the advantage of low *es* in Indian, textile industry is neutralized. The high pre-shipment and post-shipment export credit rate and high interest rates in general are also making the things more difficult. The Indian tax regime is also on the higher side than most of its competitors. Beside the price competitiveness there are some non-price factors which also plague Indian textile exports. There are complaints about quality and reliability of Indian textiles. For example- the strength and count variability of Indian yarns is far below international standards. Such quality complaints also occur for fabrics. In garment and problems of shrinkage, running of colours, stitching defects, poor finishing are also recorded. Another problem of Indian textile exports is delivery schedules, which are not adhered to. This is mainly because of administrative and procedure bottlenecks. In the following pages an analysis regarding the supply side problems of major textile products are presented.

Cotton—India has a comparative advantage in cotton since ancient period. At present it has 25% of world cotton acreage yet it provides 13% of the world cotton output. It means per hectare productivity of cotton in India is low that itself speaks of cost of cotton yarn production. This is a matter of great concern. To remain competitive in International market India has to pay sufficient attention to cotton production and its productivity. The farmers should be given sufficient incentives to raise their productivity. India should develop its own high yielding variety seeds, as huge royalty is to be paid for using foreign patented seeds. Till Indian researchers come out with some domestic variety the farmers may use imported seeds and there is no need to make a hue and cry for imported seeds as is being done presently.

Synthetic Products—The cost of manufacturing yarn and fabrics is similar in case of cotton and synthetics, but the higher excise and custom duties on synthetic products compared to cotton products seems the prime reason for India's low share of synthetic products. In the liberalized regime the excise and custom duties on synthetic products must be rationalized which can result in an increased share of synthetic products in international market.

Garment—Readymade garment sector is the largest net foreign exchange earner for the country. India is competitive at various stages of production such as spinning, weaving and stitching of garment, however the cost of dyeing and finishing are quite high. India should try to replace these costly dye and finishing so that the cost in totality can be reduced, besides this, garment exports has some additional costs involved such as- freight, insurance, custom duties, agency fees, inventory carrying cost etc. which must be rationalized .A comparison of India's pre-post shipment with other countries makes the picture clear in Table 3.

Table 3
Retailer cost in USA of Shirts Produced in Various Countries (1994) (US $.1)

	Usa	*Mexico*	*India*	*Thailand*
Total FOB Cost/ Shirt	8.55	5.44	4.91	5.36
Import costs	0.00	1.22	2.18	2.21
Cost of Retailer	8.55	6.66	7.09	7.57

Source: Werner International Inc. Management consultants various issues Brussels, Belgium.

India lacks the infrastructure facilities (lack of ports, roads and energy), which increases the additional costs. At least a few ports in India need to be developed to international standards with sufficient berthing facilities for mother vessels. Road transportation is also a serious problem. There is some positive development in this sector like the Golden Quadrilateral project.

Competitiveness—In liberalized regime of textile trade India has to complete with countries like-China, Korea, Taiwan, Japan, Vietnam, Pakistan, Bangladesh, Indonesia, and Malaysia etc. Competition with China is a major threat for India. China has the cheapest labour and one of the strongest textile industries in the world. India is concerned that her products will not be able to complete in the global market if China exports without limit. Even with quotas, Chinese textiles have ballooned on the US market taking 30-40% of the market share in areas like brassieres and dressing gowns, but there is a hope for India and other textile exporting countries that US and other Developed Nations will take advantage of an exception in ATC that allows for 'Safe guard' tariff to be placed on Chinese textile goods until 2008 as a mitigating measure for market disruption. So that India will get three year to take advantage of quota free trading environment and win precious market share in the US and EU before China is able to fully compete.

Information Management & Marketing strategy—The most important factor in promoting exports is the foreign demand. If we want to increase the textile exports then we must concentrate on the tastes, preferences and demand of the consumer and the counties where we want to export. This can be done through R & D. On marketing side market surveys for specific product categories, access to buyers database should be done. India should participate in International trade fairs, buyers seller meets etc. India has a large number of small and medium producers of textiles. So cluster management can also be promoted. The existing schemes of government such as setting up Apparel park and SEZ's planned for large textile manufactures should integrate grassroots producers too. For India aggressive marketing strategy is a must for greater share in the world market.

Arbitrary and Discriminative Restrictions by EC and other Importing Countries

Today it is a matter of great concern and challenge for India and other developing textile exporting countries to solve the health hazard, child labour, environment related issues imposed by powerful contractors. They are often arbitrary, selective and unpredictable. They seriously damage business and export of the Developing Countries. Government has also taken a number of steps from time to time to strengthen the industry so that it can meet the emerging global competition. Some important steps taken by government are:

1. Technology up gradation fund (TUFS) has been established to modernize and upgrade the sector.
2. Technology mission on cotton (TMC) has been launched to improve the productivity and quality of cotton. The mission has four mini missions with specific objectives of:

   MM I -Research.

   MM 11- Dissemination of technology to farmers.

   MMIII-Improvement in marketing infrastructure.

   MMIV-Modernizing of ginning and processing factories.
3. The government has launched centrally sponsored scheme titled "Apparel park for export scheme" for imparting focused thrust for setting up of apparel manufacturing units of international standards at potential growth centers.
4. Textile center Infrastructure development scheme (TCIDS) has been launched for upgrading infrastructure facilities etc.

Government has also taken the following measures like-elimination of limits on FDI, reduction of customs duties on imported textile machines, permitting imports of used machines and acceleration of depreciation schedules on new machinery etc.

In this changing scenario of textile trade, textile sector of India needs to be given a serious thought. In the modern world marketing strategy, which includes advertisement, Brand Name and sales costs are very important. So India has to work out strategy in such a way that it could turn its advantages in terms of cost, price and variety into dominant share in textile exports. For this the following steps should be taken:

- In order to capture larger share in world markets it is necessary to concentrate on both quality and cost competitiveness. To regain the past glory of cotton textiles India must develop high yield variety seeds in the place of using foreign-patented seeds.
- Technological up gradation is very important for this sector to compete in the world market.
- India lacks the infrastructure facilities (lack of ports, roads and energy), which increases the additional costs. Proper infrastructure should be developed for this sector. All state electricity boards are making huge losses, so, captive power generation needs to be freely allowed.
- Indian Textile Industry has relatively low wage rates in comparison to other textile exporting countries, which affects the work efficiency. Government should take some steps in this regard.

Conclusion

In this way in the liberalized regime of world trade, to make India globally competitive a multi-pronged strategy is required by the planners, policy makers, industrialists and the exporters. A final point to note concerns the treatment of non-tariff barriers into tariff equivalents that rise and fall with changing supplies and demand of trade. The tariff equivalents generate quota rents that accrue to whatever group is granted the rights to trade under restriction, which is the case of the MFA in the textile and apparel exporting countries. Liberalisation of these non-tariff barriers reduces or eliminates these quota rents and this can be costly to those who possessed them disproportionately beforehand. Therefore, it is not the case that exporting countries necessarily benefit from the relaxation of these barriers. Since their loss of Quota rents can more than overweight their gains from increased exports. Indeed, their exports can actually decline, along with their national welfare, if increased exports from other countries displace them in world markets.

NOTES

1. see Gilpin, R (2004) for further discussions.
2. This agreement paved the way for a commercial instrument what is known as VER (Voluntary export restraint).
3. When the import of a particular commodity rising by more than 10% in anyone year from one source, which may have adverse effect on domestic producers (Sharp import increase) not attributable to dumping.

REFERENCES

Kapila (2003), Economic Reforms: Strategy for Next Decade, Academic Foundation, New Delhi.

Nayyar, D. (1997), Trade & Liberalisation Oxford University Press, New Delhi.

ICFAI (2004), Indian Textile Exports: Post MFA Scenario on Website.

UNCTAD (2000), Trade & Development Report.

CII (2005), Post MFA Indian Textile Exports. A Study on website.

Table 4
Textiles Exports from 1996-97 to 2002-03

No.	Item	1996-97	1997-98	1998-99	1999-00	2000-01	2001-02	2002-03
1.	Cotton Raw Incl. Waste	443.52	221.15	49.18	17.83	48.39	8.95	9.74
2.	Cotton Yarn, Fabrics & Madeups	3121.73	3264.28	2771.76	3096.79	3460.69	3072.91	3271.27
3.	Natural Silk Yarn, Fabrics & Madeups	128.79	176.43	178.18	238.26	306.88	278.24	299.84
4.	Manmade Yarn, Fabrics & Madeups	702.66	804.87	699.99	813.24	1058.49	1064.95	1315.51
5.	Woollen Yarn, Fabrics & Madeups	103.65	109.75	74.61	50.10	62.42	52.21	50.27
6.	RMG of Cotton including Accessories	2940.60	2874.55	3147.29	3330.04	3927.10	3700.02	4183.53
7.	RMG Silk	77.51	94.37	59.37	124.52	185.24	151.04	125.88
8.	RMG Wool	86.78	89.72	84.95	177.08	297.05	236.89	216.12
9.	RMG Manmade Fibre	529.86	691.04	923.50	1010.12	975.01	774.56	697.03
10.	RMG of other Textile Material	118.53	126.50	149.63	134.37	184.93	144.13	150.98
	(P) Provisional							

Source: Foreign Trade Statistics of India (Principal Commodities & Countries) DGCIS, Kolkata.